UNCTAD/ECDC/PA/4/Rev 1.

UNITED NATIONS CONFERENCE ON TRADE AND DEVELOPMENT

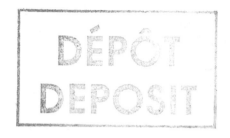

GLOBALIZATION AND LIBERALIZATION:
EFFECTS OF INTERNATIONAL ECONOMIC RELATIONS ON POVERTY

INTER-AGENCY THEMATIC CONTRIBUTION TO THE
INTERNATIONAL YEAR FOR THE ERADICATION OF POVERTY

New York and Geneva, 1996

NOTE

DB # 1397541

• The opinions expressed in this book are those of the authors and do not necessarily reflect the views of the UNCTAD Secretariat or of the organizations and institutions with which the authors are connected.

• The designations and terminology employed and the presentation of material in this publication do not imply any expression whatsoever on the part of the United Nations concerning the legal status of any country, territory, city or area, or of its authorities, or of its frontiers or boundaries.

• Application for permission to reproduce or translate all or part of this publication should be made to the UNCTAD Secretariat.

UN2
TD/UNCTAD/ECDC/PA/4/Rev. 1

UNCTAD/ECDC/PA/4/Rev.1

Contents

Part II: Regional and national experiences: lessons from diversity

Asia

Latin America

Sub-Saharan Africa

Annexes

Abbreviations

ACP	Africa, Caribbean and Pacific
APEC	Asia Pacific Economic Cooperation
ASEAN	Association of South East Asian Nations
D/PI	direct and portfolio investment
DESIPA	United Nations Department for Economic and Social Information and Policy Anaysis
EPZs	export processing zones
ESAF	Enhanced Structural Adjustment Facility
EU	European Union
FDI	foreign direct investment
G/L	globalization/liberalization
GATS	General Agreement on Trade in Services
GATT	General Agreement on Tariffs and Trade
GDP	gross domestic product
GNP	gross national product
GSP	Generalized System of Preferences
IDA	International Development Association
IFC	International Finance Corporation
ILO	International Labour Organization
IMF	International Monetary Fund
LDC	least developed country
LIBOR	London Interbank Offer Rate
LICs	low-income countries
LRIEs	larger, richer and more industrialized economies
MERCOSUR	Southern Cone Common Market
MFA	Multifibre Arrangement
MFN	Most Favoured Nation
MTNs	multilateral trade negotiations
NAFTA	North American Free Trade Agreement
NGO	non-governmental organization
NIEs	newly industrialized economies
NPV	net present value
ODA	official development assistance
PPP	purchasing power parity

QRs	quantitative restrictions
RTAs	regional trade agreements
SIMICs	severely-indebted middle-income countries
SMEs	small and medium-sized enterprises
SOEs	state-owned enterprises
SPCEs	smaller, poorer and more commodity-dependent economies
TNC	transnational corporation
TRIMs	Trade-Related Investment Measures
TRIPs	Trade-Related Intellectual Property Rights
UNCHS	United Nations Centre for Human Settlements (Habitat)
UNCTAD	United Nations Conference on Trade and Development
UNDP	United Nations Development Programme
UNEP	United Nations Environment Programme
UNESCO	United Nations Educational, Scientific and Cultural Organization
UNFPA	United Nations Population Fund
UNICEF	United Nations Children's Fund
UNIDO	United Nations Industrial Organization
UNRISD	United Nations Research Institute for Social Development
UNU	United Nations University
VERs	Voluntary Export Restraints
WDI	World Development Report (World Bank)
WHO	World Health Organization
WPO	World Food Programme
WTO	World Trade Organization

Preface

This compendium is the product of an inter-agency seminar on *Globalization and Liberalization: Effects of International Economic Relations on Poverty* that was held in Geneva, Switzerland, from 15 to 17 April 1996. The seminar was organized by the secretariat of the United Nations Conference on Trade and Development (UNCTAD) as an inter-agency contribution of the United Nations system to the 1996 International Year for the Eradication of Poverty. As indicated in the List of Participants at the end of the book, 28 representatives of 17 agencies and departments of the United Nations system participated in the seminar. In addition, eight independent experts were invited to participate in their individual capacity.

The 14 papers that comprise the present compendium were prepared by the 8 independent experts and by 6 agency participants possessing specialized knowledge on the subjects on which they wrote. These papers were presented during the panel discussions part of the inter-agency seminar. The immediate purpose of the panel discussions was to foster an exchange of views and information that would assist the agency participants formulate their conclusions and recommendations on the issues of the seminar. The other primary purpose for organizing the panel discussions was to elicit the preparation of papers that comprise the present compendium. Brief annotations on the papers and conclusions and recommendations contained in this compendium are presented in the introduction of the book.

The topic of the effects of globalization and liberalization on poverty is both timely and important. The rapid growth and liberalization of international trade, foreign direct investment and global financial flows are transforming international economic relations in ways that, *inter alia*, may significantly reduce absolute poverty in the world. For example, it is estimated that over 20 million additional manufacturing jobs have been created in the developing countries due to increased trade with the developed countries alone.

In conformity with the theory of comparative advantage, most of the exports of developing countries to developed countries have been in low-skill, low-wage products. With the continuing expansion of international trade and investment, it is hoped that this job-creating, poverty-reducing phenomenon will grow in importance in future years. It should be recognized, however, that not all developing countries will benefit alike. Indeed, the globalization process could reinforce the marginalization of least developed countries (LDCs) in the world, as well as of certain economically vulnerable population groups within the developing countries themselves.

The origins of the present compendium date back to July 1995. UNCTAD was then asked by Mr. Nitin Desai, the United Nations Under-Secretary-General for Policy Coordination and Sustainable Development who is responsible for coordinating all United Nations system contributions to the International Year for the Eradication of Poverty, to be the lead agency in organizing an inter-agency seminar on the effects of international economic relations on poverty. The conclusions and recommendations of the seminar were consequently presented to the International Year through the coordination segment of the United Nations Economic and Social Council's substantive session, which in 1996 had as its theme the coordination of activities of the United Nations system for the eradication of poverty. The seminar proper was organized and chaired by Mr. Anthony Woodfield, of the UNCTAD secretariat, who also edited the present book. Mr. Woodfield was assisted in these tasks by Mr. Matti Vainio, Mr. Martin Mandl, Ms. Micheline Massabni and Ms. Janet Bullett of the UNCTAD secretariat.

In closing, I would like to thank the Government of Switzerland for funding both the printing of the present book and the participation of the eight independent experts at the seminar.

Rubens Ricupero
Secretary-General
United Nations Conference on Trade and Development
Geneva, September 1996

1

Introduction

Globalization as a term refers to the growing interaction of countries in world trade, foreign direct investment and capital markets. The globalization process has been abetted by technological advances in transport and communications, and by a rapid liberalization and deregulation of trade and capital flows, both at the national and international levels. A growing number of developing countries are benefitting from this increased dispersion of economic activity, while countries with initial conditions that make them less suited to take advantage of the opportunities presented by globalization are at risk of becoming further marginalized.

The implications of globalization for poverty reduction are conjectural and, hence, a matter of dispute. While the estimated creation of 20 million jobs in the developing countries as a result of exports to the developed countries is far from negligible, this sum nevertheless amounts to an addition of only between 1 and 2 percentage points to the share of manufacturing in total employment in the developing countries. However, the effects of globalization on poverty do not end with the number of jobs created and their multiplier effects on the economy. The related adoption of liberalization policies could have long-term social as well as economic effects that might considerably surpass the direct impact of trade, foreign direct investment and portfolio investment. Opinions differ, however, as to whether liberalization policies are beneficial for poverty reduction. The globalization process could also give rise to subtle cultural adaptations at the national and local levels that could have a significant social impact. For instance, the demonstration effect of export processing zones that mainly employ young women could in some localities induce more poor families to send their daughters, in addition to their sons, to school.

The present compendium captures and reflects the pluralism of views that exists on the benefits, risks and drawbacks of globalization and liberalization. In fact, symmetry is sought in this collection of papers through the juxaposition of "optimistic" and "pessimistic" papers on the main issues concerned. As with the agency participants whose task it was to formulate the conclusions and recommendations of the seminar, it is up to each reader to weigh the arguments of differing authors and reach his or her own final interpretation of the issues.

Given the variety of viewpoints and backgrounds of the inter-agency participants, it was rather remarkable that they were able to agree on the clear, consistent and unambivalent conclusions and recommendations that are listed in the next section of this volume. This set of conclusions and recommendations concentrated on the elements that constitute the globalization and liberalization process; the channels through which the effects of globalization and liberalization are transmitted to the poor; the different categories of positively and negatively affected poor; and measures that can be adopted to enhance the poverty-reducing benefits of the globalization process while mitigating the negative consequences for certain poverty groups. The agency participants who actively contributed to the formulation of the conclusions and recommendations represented the following agencies and departments of the United Nations system: United Nations Department for Economic and Social Information and Policy Analysis (DESIPA); International Labour Organization (ILO); International Monetary Fund (IMF); United Nations Development Programme (UNDP); United Nations Educational, Scientific and Cultural Organization (UNESCO); United Nations Children's Fund (UNICEF); United Nations Industrial Development Organization (UNIDO); United Nations Conference on Trade and Development (UNCTAD); United Nations University (UNU); World Bank (IBRD); World Food Programme (WFP); and World Health Organization (WHO). The views embodied in their conclusions and recommendations, however, are those of the agency participants and do not necessarily coincide with the positions of the agencies which they represented.

The papers in Part I of this volume are concerned primarily with the main issues and constituent elements of the globalization and liberalization process and their effects on poverty. This part of the book includes the main paper: *Globalization and liberalization: concepts and issues* by Mr. David Woodward. Whereas Part I is conceptually oriented, Part II of the book is more empirically oriented: it focuses on divergent and significant trends and experiences at the level of developing country regions and of specific, individual countries. Indeed, an underlying premise of Part II is that the effects of globalization and liberalization on poverty vary considerably from situation to situation – hence no generalization on the implications of globalization and liberalization for poverty fits all developing countries.

In Part I, the paper by Mr. David Woodward (independent expert) entitled *Globalization and liberalization: concepts and issues* is the main reference paper of this compendium. The size alone of his paper takes up about 40 per cent of the book. The paper provides an in-depth, comprehensive description and analysis of the components of the globalization process, their macroeconomic and development effects, and their implications for poverty. While generally of the view that the globalization process is important for reducing aggregate poverty in the world, Mr. Woodward is sceptical and sometimes pessimistic in his paper about various aspects of globalization and liberalization and their effects on poverty. In particular, the author distinguishes between the Asian countries that have most benefitted from globalization and the African and other least developed countries that he believes may be harmed by the globalization and liberalization process. Mr. Woodward also warns in his paper that a balance of payments crisis could be precipitated if foreign direct investment and portfolio flows are not sustained over the long term, in which case they would be increasingly offset by the corresponding outflows. He also makes the point that developing countries specializing in low-skill manufacturing production for export could become susceptible to the fallacy of composition problem that cocoa and coffee producing countries have already experienced. In terms of the social effects of the globalization and liberalization process, Mr. Woodward's paper focuses on government expenditure, urbanization, the environment and gender effects. He assesses the implications of this process for poverty in terms of its effects on real incomes, relative prices, primary health and education, and factors that lie outside the realm of individuals' consumption of goods and services.

The principal companion paper to Mr. Woodward's paper is the paper on *Globalization and liberalization: an opportunity to reduce poverty* by Mr. Ishrat Husain (World Bank). In this paper, Mr. Husain takes exception to aspects of Mr. Woodward's arguments where he feels Mr. Woodward is unduly negative and pessimistic about the likely effects of globalization and liberalization on growth and poverty. However, Mr. Husain's paper is much more than a critical comment on the Woodward paper. Mr. Husain articulates a clear, unambivalent and positive assessment of the likely effects of globalization and liberalization on poverty. He also identifies some of the transmission channels through which poverty may be reduced as a result of globalization and liberalization.

Like Mr. Husain's paper, the paper by Mr. Zdenek Drabek (World Trade Organization) on *Trade and the Uruguay Round: some misconceptions dispelled* challenges a number of the views and statements made by Mr. Woodward in his concepts and issues paper. For instance, Mr. Drabek refutes Mr. Woodward's assertion that the level of protectionism by developed countries against developing country exports is high. Mr. Drabek's rejoinder should be read in conjunction with the Uruguay Round and policy chapters of Mr. Woodward's paper.

Rather than taking issue with the Woodward paper, Mr. Peter Heller (International Monetary Fund), in his paper on *Global financial integration and related domestic liberalization policies*, has sought to deepen the analysis on this complex topic. While the globalization of trade and production has been facilitated by the globalization of finance, the latter is not simply a derivative of present trends in trade and production. Global financial integration, moreover, has been propelled by the progressive deregulation and liberalization of controls in financial movements, to the point that money is very ready to move around the world as investors see fit. The main focus of Mr. Heller's paper is on the implications of this process of global financial integration for macroeconomic managers in developing countries.

Another paper that focuses to a large extent on macroeconomic policy is the paper entitled *Implications of macroeconomic policies for equity and poverty* by Mr. Rolph van der Hoeven (International Labour Organization). In his paper, Mr. van der Hoeven reviews current research that indicates that macroeconomic stability contributes positively to long-term growth, except for its effects on fiscal and public expenditure policies and on interest rates. He also summarizes core findings of the so-called new growth theory that stress the importance of public investment in infrastructure and human capital. Mr. van der Hoeven accordingly recommends that macroeconomic policy not only retain those features that support long-term growth but that it also be made more equitable and pro-poor through changes in tax and expenditure policies that favour investment in infrastructure and especially human capital. The strengthening of human capital is also important, *inter alia*, for enabling low-income developing countries to compete more effectively in the global economy.

The paper by Mr. Santosh Mehrotra (United Nations Children's Fund) on *Domestic liberalization policies and public finance: the implications for poverty* reviews the trends in the 1980s and early 1990s with respect to government revenue and expenditure in Latin America and Sub-Saharan Africa. His conclusions are consonant with Mr. van der Hoeven's recommendations that government revenues from personal taxes should be increased and that more public expenditure ought to be channelled to basic education and health care.

The paper on *Safety nets and compensatory measures* by Ms. Carol Graham (independent expert) examines ways in which government expenditure can mitigate the negative impact of globalization and liberalization on certain categories of the population, in particular adversely-affected individuals living below the poverty line. These measures are analyzed from a political economy perspective in terms of their actual and potential efficiency and effectiveness.

As already noted, Part II of the present compendium focuses on regional and national experiences having to do with globalization and liberalization. The first paper in this part of the volume is by Mr. Rajah Rasiah (independent expert), and is on the subject of *Globalization and liberalization in East and South East Asia: implications for growth, inequality and poverty*. The paper describes and analyzes the experiences of 5 Asian economies: Republic of Korea, Taiwan Province of China, Indonesia, Malaysia and Thailand. As is well-known, these economies have benefitted in a substantial way from the globalization process, although their conversion to liberalization policies has generally only been quite recent. The paper attributes rapid poverty reduction in these economies not only to sustained high levels of economic growth but, in some cases, also to human capital formation and equitable policies in areas such as agrarian reform. While income inequality has generally not been very extreme, Mr. Rasiah's paper points to evidence that the income distribution may be becoming more skewed as liberalization policies begin to take hold.

Much of the globalization-related decline in absolute poverty that has taken place to date in the world can be attributed to China. As explained in the paper by Ms. Padma Mallampally (United Nations Conference on Trade and Development) on *The importance of foreign direct investment for exports, economic growth and poverty reduction in China*, that country has been extremely successful in attracting foreign investment and participating in international trade, which in turn have helped China significantly reduce its incidence of poverty.

The country more than any other that holds the key to any future massive reduction of absolute poverty through globalization and liberalization, however, is India. The paper by Mr. Sumit Roy (independent expert) entitled *What potential does India have of benefitting from globalization?* discusses the prospects of India reducing its poverty levels in the future if it is successful in becoming more integrated in the world economy.

Generally speaking, Latin American governments have taken swifter and more radical steps to liberalize their economies than Asian governments. However, although promising, their performance in the global economy, like their recovery from the debt crisis of the 1980s, has been more fragile and vulnerable to negative shocks than in the case of the East and South East Asia. The paper by Mr. André Urani (independent expert) entitled *Globalization and Liberalization in Latin America: implications for growth, inequality and poverty* focuses in particular on Argentina, Brazil and Chile. Mr. Urani points out that poverty has declined (compared with the mid-1980s) as a result of the economic recovery and taming of inflation that have been achieved in the 1990s. He notes, however, that if Argentina and Brazil are to benefit fully and sustainably from the globalization process, they must emphasize deficit-spending containment more than exchange rate overvaluation as a means of keeping inflation under control. Mr. Urani's paper also makes some mention of Mexico, and should be read in conjunction with the paper by Ms. Eugenia Correa that follows.

Mexico has been the most dramatic example to date of how fragile economic recovery can turn out to be in Latin America, as well as how risky a developing country's insertion in the globalization process can prove to be. Ms. Eugenia Correa (independent expert) analyzes the Mexican debacle in her paper on *Mexico's financial crisis and its effects on income distribution and poverty.* An important lesson to be learned is that external financial liberalization policies and import liberalization policies should be carefully phased and sequenced. Mexico's experience is a warning to other Latin American countries such as Argentina and Brazil, and even South East Asian countries such as Malaysia and Thailand, regarding the potential dangers posed by short-term speculative flows. A companion paper that should be read in conjunction with Ms. Correa's paper is Mr. Heller's paper on portfolio flows in Part I of this volume.

Whereas the rapidly industrializing economies of East and South East Asia are an inspiration to other developing countries in terms of the gains to be obtained from globalization, and Latin America countries have shown promise, albeit fragile, in this direction, Sub-Saharan Africa remains the region that has failed to date to reap rewards from the globalization process. The paper by Mr. Paul Mosley (independent expert) entitled *Globalization and liberalization in Sub-Saharan Africa: implications for growth and poverty* points out that the principal agent of globalization in the region continues to be official development assistance (ODA). His conclusions and recommendations focus on ways in which the effectiveness of aid can be enhanced in terms of transforming the economic prospects of Sub-Saharan Africa and raising the level of its human capital, with the twin aims of reducing poverty and enabling the countries to diversify their export base.

The last paper of Part II is by Mr. Fantu Cheru (independent expert), who seeks to answer the question *Is the Asian NIEs approach relevant for Sub-Saharan Africa?*. Mr. Cheru believes that there are practical limits to the effectiveness of trade liberalization and export promotion drives under conditions of static comparative advantage. He concludes that African governments can learn more from countries such as Indonesia and Malaysia that have augmented their exports of both primary and low-skill manufactured products, rather than countries such as the Republic of Korea that have limited endowments in natural resources but possess a highly educated labour force.

The book contains two annexes: the background paper for the inter-agency seminar and the list of participants who attended the seminar. The background paper is a short primer prepared by Mr. Anthony Woodfield (United Nations Conference on Trade and Development) to inform and stimulate thinking on the part of agency participants and the independent experts regarding the range and nature of the issues to be addressed at the inter-agency seminar.

As a final point, it is important to reiterate that the views expressed in the papers of this book are those of the authors and do not necessarily reflect the views of the United Nations system or its constituent parts.

2

Conclusions and recommendations

1 Conclusions

1. In terms of its implications for trade, productive investment and finance, globalization is an increasingly important dimension of international economic relations. Spurred by reduced transport costs and advances in communications and other technologies, globalization has fostered greater interdependence and cross-border linkages between the countries of the world. Countries that seek to delink, and opt instead for isolationism, risk paying a high price in future economic growth. In response to the trade and foreign investment opportunities resulting from globalization, a large and growing number of developing countries have embarked on the liberalization of their trade and foreign investment regimes, as well as the adaptation of their domestic economic structures and strengthening of their export capacity.

2. Although there will be short-term transitional costs for many developing countries as they adopt more outward-oriented liberalization policies, globalization provides hope of significant poverty reduction over the long term through its contribution to economic growth, productivity and consumption benefits. The significance of globalization to economic growth and poverty, however, can be expected to vary for different categories of developing countries. While most developing countries will gain from the globalization process, some will benefit more than others, and a number of countries with initial conditions that make them less suited to take advantage of globalization will lose out and become more marginalized in relation to other countries. However, it is expected that total benefits for the developing countries as a whole will be greater than

total costs, and that absolute poverty will as a result decline in global terms.

3.   East Asia has gained the most to date from globalization, while the situation of much of Latin America, though still fragile, appears promising. Sub-Saharan Africa, on the other hand, shows little sign of being able to benefit at this time. In view of their share of absolute poverty in the world and their capacity to benefit from globalization, most of the absolute poverty reduction associated with globalization is likely to occur in East, South and South East Asia, where close to 70 per cent of the world's absolute poverty is concentrated.

4.   One of the main benefits of globalization is its role in promoting trade in the world. Since the mid-1980s, there has been a 10 per cent annual expansion of trade of the developing countries with the industrialized countries, and a 12 per cent increase in intra-developing-countries trade. The Uruguay Round agreement and regional trade arrangements will facilitate continued trade growth through their effects on the extent and security of access to international markets. On the consumption side, import liberalization should make more affordable the purchase of manufactured goods which, reflecting world prices, are likely to be less expensive than under economic regimes that shelter domestic production from competition. The expansion of international trade is important for poverty reduction, as fuller utilization is made of low-cost labour that is the main comparative advantage of developing countries.

5.   As illustrated by China's displacement of Brazil as the world's leading footwear exporter, the entry of more developing countries into export markets has led to increased price-based competition for global market share in goods for which demand elasticity is low. Such competition, of course, creates hardships and uncertainty for workers in the declining industries of higher-cost, usually middle-income developing countries. However, to the extent that lower labour costs play a significant role in this competition between countries, there will be a net reduction worldwide in absolute poverty as a result of the shift in competitive advantage to countries where absolute poverty is greater.

6.   A country's comparative advantage, however, need not be static. As the experience of East Asia in particular suggests, countries can move up the trade hierarchy and export more sophisticated products. Incomes go up in the process and the competitive advantages of those countries' exporting firms in labour-intensive manufacturing may be eroded. In such cases, countries lower down the ladder replace those that have graduated from labour-intensive export production. In this manner, absolute poverty is substantially reduced in the countries that have reached the higher rungs and begins falling in countries having footholds on the lower rungs.

7.   Another pillar of globalization is foreign direct investment (FDI). FDI has financed productive investments, created instant export markets, increased overall productivity and competitiveness, and enabled developing countries to capture economies of scale through international production systems. FDI during the past 15 years has grown rapidly in terms of absolute dollar volume and as a share of GDP in all developing regions except the Middle East and Africa. Although FDI is concentrated on a relatively small number of developing countries, China and, to a lesser extent, Indonesia are significant recipients of FDI and, between them, account for a large share of the world's absolute poverty. A shortcoming of most FDI, however, is that its backward and forward linkages to the local economy are often weak, which means that the economic growth and employment generated through multiplier effects can be relatively low. While there are outflows as well as inflows associated with FDI, unlike debt financing, profit repatriation only takes place if the investment generates positive returns, and it should be noted that those remittances are net of tax payments and profit reinvestment. In terms of net job creation that helps reduce poverty, FDI that is directed at labour-intensive export sectors has been preferable to FDI that competes with domestic enterprises for local market share.

8.   Greater openness of the financial sector has encouraged increased portfolio investment flows into a number of middle-income countries, which has helped ease their foreign exchange constraint, augmented the marginal efficiency of capital in the countries concerned, and encouraged economic discipline while punishing policy failure. By contributing to

the appreciation of the real exchange rate, such inflows have also helped dampen inflation. However, except when offset by other measures such as a reduction of export taxes, this appreciation has been detrimental to export-promotion strategies and, if the inflows are not dampened, may necessitate high interest rates having fiscal tightening implications that negatively affect economic growth and poverty reduction objectives in the short term. Domestic macroeconomic management has also been made more difficult by the procyclical nature and contagion effects of these flows, as well as by fluctuations in world interest rates.

9. It is not just the pace of economic growth that matters for poverty alleviation, but also the kind of growth. Certain East Asian economies, for instance, proved successful in achieving a rapid expansion of output and employment in labour-intensive industries geared to exports, with consequent rises in real wages spread across a large section of the labour force. Governments helped make possible these accomplishments through the adoption of trade and industrial policies that boosted exports, disciplined investors and curtailed domestic consumption. This success in industrial policies, however, was not matched by other developing regions. Import substitution practices in many developing countries instead emphasized capital- and technology-intensive investment rather than investment making fuller utilization of low-cost labour. Moreover, due to weak institutional and implementational capacity, a large number of developing countries allowed industrial policies to benefit rent-seeking interests disproportionately. Furthermore, some policies toward the private sector have been counter-productive in terms of their direct effects on poverty. Government regulatory harassment of the urban informal sector, for instance, has constrained the growth of micro-entrepreneurship in many developing countries.

10. Reaping the benefits and mitigating the transitional costs of global-ization and liberalization presuppose good governance at the level of the state and civil society. Good governance is associated with the rule of law, equity, democracy, participation, and the provision of basic services. In its absence, undesirable by-products of globalization and liberalization can take hold, including widespread non-compliance, corruption and organized crime and drug trafficking. Good governance has grown

mainly from within each society and has corresponded to firm policy commitments on the part of society. International organizations have played only a secondary, complementary role in facilitating exchanges of experience, policy concertation, goal setting and, in some cases, conditionalities in connection with the observance of good governance.

11. The growth effects of globalization and liberalization affect both absolute poverty, through poverty reduction, and relative poverty, through changes in a country's income distribution. If economic growth is initially slow and, at the same time, inequality grows, absolute poverty may not decline and conjunctural poverty could increase. Without structural change, moreover, existing elites are likely to be better positioned to benefit from externally oriented liberalization policies. This is particularly true of persons holding scarce and internationally tradeable assets. On the other hand, globalization has helped supplement, through corporate savings and investment, the role of household savings in fueling investment. In such circumstances, poverty has declined as a result of the jobs created. In fact, to the extent that the globalization process has encouraged the reinvestment rather than the consumption of profits, a worsening of functional income distribution has not necessarily aggravated household income inequality.

12. A critical question is how the aggregate gains of globalization are translated into net benefits for the poorer segments of the population in the gaining countries. While economic growth is the main transmission channel, there are many other factors to take into account which makes the analysis especially complicated. In general, international trade and investment-related liberalization policies, through financial and exchange rate policies, affect the incomes and consumption of the poor in terms of employment, output growth, curb lending rates and, in general, shifts in relative prices. However, the effects also depend, among other things, on the size of the countries concerned, their degree of economic openness, their per capita income, the composition of their output growth and trade, and the efficiency and equity of their policy and institutional environment. There are also intertemporal effects to consider in which the secondary and indirect effects often offset or reverse the first order effects.

13. Whereas globalization is largely exogenous and inexorable, developing countries have a certain degree of discretion and control over the liberalization policies that they adopt. Such policies are seldom neutral in their effects on different income groups and, in fact, may involve transitory effects that are directly detrimental to some groups of the population, ranging from vocal and well organized middle-income groups to certain categories of the excluded, powerless poor. While the economic policies responsible for these effects may be short-term in nature, the poor whose health and well-being are affected may become incapacited or destitute and thus unable to recover when economic conditions eventually improve. Such negative effects may occur when countries implement sweeping liberalization policies before macro-economic stability is assured. Damaging results can also occur when liberalization policies are not properly phased and sequenced, as when externally oriented financial and import liberalization policies are pursued simultaneously. The simultaneous combination of improperly sequenced liberalization measures and macroeconomic imbalance poses the greatest risk of policy failure and massive social hardship.

14. With the benefits of globalization unevenly spread between as well as within developing countries, global income distribution is likely to become more skewed, even as the aggregate incidence of poverty in the world gradually declines. With respect to the variety of poverty groups that are better or worse off as a consequence of globalization and liberalization, distinctions can be made, among others, between poor persons engaged in agriculture and manufacturing production, and between the conjuncturally and chronically poor.

15. As concerns those poor whose incomes place them around the poverty line and who depend on agriculture directly or indirectly for their livelihood, the net effects of globalization and liberalization could be favourable in the long term throughout much of Sub-Saharan Africa and in some parts of Asia where land tenure is not concentrated and agricultural production is labour-intensive. This is because relative prices for farm output can be expected to rise as a result not only of the removal of exchange rate distortions and price controls on farm products, but also of the effect of the Uruguay Round agreement on world prices

in the cases of food-importing countries. On the other hand, food-deficit, extremely poor rural households can be expected to be worse off, although for some a rise in food prices will be offset by higher incomes from increased farm labour opportunities. Lower prices for manufactured goods – a likely outcome of import-liberalization policies – should help redress the terms-of-trade imbalance between rural and urban areas, as well as make incentive goods available to rural households. As for the urban areas, in certain Asian countries the creation of new export-oriented jobs should help reduce urban poverty. Higher food prices, however, will negatively affect the poorest of urban households, unless food aid of some sort is provided. As concerns Latin America where land ownership is more concentrated and farming has become increasingly mechanized in response to growing export markets, rural poverty could increase and lead to further rural outmigration. However, in the rural areas of many of the countries of the region, most working-age poor households have already migrated to the cities. As for the urban areas, because of the evolution of subregional trade arrangements, export-oriented jobs are being created that are helping absorb some of the urban labour surplus in a number of Latin American cities.

16. There will be people who, though not initially poor in an absolute sense, may be severely affected by the transition process resulting from globalization and liberalization. These include in particular retrenched workers in the public and parastatal sector, privatized firms, and import-competing enterprises. In middle-income developing countries that are enjoying positive per capita growth rates, many of these people – given their educational background – should be able to find work in other formal-sector enterprises, including firms set up in conjunction with foreign capital. In low-income developing countries in particular, however, the absorption of redundant workers is likely to be more difficult, particularly in countries where there is little or no economic growth over the short and medium term. Many retrenched formal sector workers who are unable to find other comparably paying work will join the ranks of the "new poor" that started in much of Africa and Latin America with the debt crisis of the 1980s.

17. The majority of the absolute poor, many of whom are functionally

illiterate, or are from different ethnic or language groups than the dominant class, or live in remote backward areas, are likely to be little affected by globalization and liberalization since they are already marginalized. However, in cases where the insertion of the country in the globalization process brings about long-term economic growth, these groups should also eventually be able to benefit from the spread effects of growth. Such effects are likely to be felt both in terms of income gains and, due to the increased fiscal resources made possible for social expenditure, in principle in terms of basic needs consumption as well.

18. Public revenue and expenditure in most of Africa and Latin America have declined since the 1980s. Per capita real expenditure on basic education and health has likewise fallen. With respect to government revenue, the effects of globalization-related liberalization policies have been indeterminate. The tariffication process has tended to raise the import trade tax share in total taxes, while the reduction of tariffs and export taxes has had an offsetting effect. Investment inflows associated with privatization schemes have provided one-off sources of revenue that have helped certain countries partly reduce their external debt. Sizeable financial inflows in the cases of some countries have been a factor in driving up interest payments, but have also helped ease the liquidity constraint created by the debt crisis of the 1980s. In general, servicing payments on foreign and domestic debt is the primary reason for reduced public expenditure in other sectors. Increased reliance has been placed on regressive consumption taxes to generate the necessary revenue. Given the difficult circumstances, commendable efforts have been made by many developing countries to protect the share of social expenditure for primary education and health care. The World Bank has played an important role in this respect by increasing its volume of lending to primary education and health care, and by making the protection of those sectors a conditionality in structural adjustment lending. However, user charges which some international organizations have advocated for primary health clinics, for instance, have provided only limited cost recovery while deterring the poorest of the poor, in particular women and children, from availing themselves of necessary care.

19. Globalization and liberalization are but one possible approach to reducing

poverty in the world. The impact of this approach on poverty is likely to differ between countries and could be insignificant in countries where trade and foreign investment are not sizeable. Moreover, since rural households who benefit directly from globalization and liberalization generally own land, and since workers in export industries typically have at least a primary education, the immediate benefits of globalization and outward liberalization are more likely to accrue to people close to the poverty line than to people in extreme poverty. Well targeted social programmes have proved essential for reaching and benefiting the latter group. In this connection, the World Summit for Social Development made clear that sustainable development, and in particular a successful attack on poverty, must be multisectoral and holistic, emphasizing social and cultural as well as economic approaches to reducing poverty.

20. The economies in transition of Central and Eastern Europe and of the former Soviet Union are also confronted with the challenges and opportunities associated with globalization and liberalization. Starting with a more egalitarian structure than most developing countries, these countries have experienced growing income inequality and conjunctural poverty, even as liberalization policies foster private entrepreneurship and bolster the prospects of structural change leading to sustained economic growth. According to World Bank estimates, the number of absolute poor in the economies in transition of Eastern Europe and Central Asia grew from 2.2 million in 1987 to 14.5 million, or 3.5 per cent of the population, in 1993. This increase has been due to the erosion in real wages and entitlements in recent years. The capacity of these countries to adjust to globalizing forces has been hindered by the fact that a substantial part of their productive capacity remains tied up in what is, or recently used to be, a state sector that is often inefficient and overdependent on subsidy support but which remains important as a producer of basic goods as well as a significant employer of the labour force. In countries where state enterprises have been privatized on a massive scale, their change in ownership status has not yet led to significant changes in the ways that they function, which can be partly attributed to the weak market enviroment in which they operate. On the other hand, the economies in transition generally compare favourably with developing countries in terms of human capital and physical infrastructure. Because of these

endowments and their geographical proximity and historical ties to Western Europe, some have received substantial inflows of foreign direct investment which have helped increase their share of international trade and competitiveness in world markets.

2 Recommendations

1. It is essential that Governments achieve macroeconomic stability and attach importance to institution-building if they are to develop a sustainable approach to globalization. Externally oriented liberalization policies must likewise be carefully planned and monitored as to any possible undesired effects or outcomes. Certain basic principles can be suggested. For one, a sweeping liberalization of import regimes should not precede but should go together with enhanced export capacity and performance. Also, exchange rates should be maintained at realistic levels. An over-appreciation of the exchange rate will reduce the competitiveness of export industries and therefore should be avoided through prudent and credible macroeconomic policies. Liberalization of the capital account may need to be sequenced in line with a strengthening of the capacity for prudential supervision in the financial sector.

2. A more effective international institutional framework for oversight, regulation and compensation is necessary to deal with shocks emanating from the volatility of short-term international financial flows.

3. Further official debt reduction is necessary to reduce the debt servicing obligations of the least developed countries. Such reductions would free up budgetary resources which, in principle, could be directed, among other areas, to basic education, health and nutrition. There is, moreover, usually substantial scope for developing countries to augment resources to primary education and health through intersectoral and intrasectoral re-allocation. In terms of revenue sources, overreliance on regressive consumption taxes should be replaced by a renewed commitment to increasing direct taxes and making their collection more effective.

4. Not only must cuts in basic social services be avoided, but resources to

those sectors should be restored at the very least to their earlier levels per head. The 20-20 initiative (a mutually-agreed commitment between interested developed and developing partners to allocate, on average, 20 per cent of ODA and 20 per cent of the national budget to basic social programmes) that grew out of the World Summit for Social Development could serve as a benchmark for donor and recipient Governments with respect to pro-poor social expenditure. Besides increasing the allocation of expenditures to the basic needs requirements of the poor, Governments should also redouble their efforts to make sure that the poor are adequately reached and served. This means increasing the efficiency and quality of public expenditure, and targeting it more effectively to the poorer segments of the population.

5.   The practice of applying user charges as a vehicle for cost recovery should be re-examined, with a distinction made between those public services that are used disproportionately by the non-poor, such as public universities, those that are used by both the poor and the non-poor, such as urban primary schools and primary health facilties, and those that are used largely by the poor, such as rural primary schools and health clinics. It is the appropriateness of user charges in the latter instances that particularly needs to be reviewed. For instance, with respect to rural health clinics, provision could be made for the fees of the poorest users to be cross-subsidized by the less poor, and each clinic could be allowed to retain its collected revenue for the purchase of inputs essential to serve the community on a continuous and sustainable basis.

6.   As unchecked liberalization may lead to increased income inequality, equity-oriented policies should be included in economic decisions related to globalization and liberalization. In fact, evidence based on time series data shows that there need be no contradiction between equity concerns and rapid growth. It is also important that an appropriate investment strategy be adopted from the start. Experience has shown that if the fruits of growth go mainly to one set of factors of production, such as capital-intensive investment, the consequences will be more difficult to undo later on. In this respect, consultations between the main social partners on the appropriate course for economic development to take can contribute to more equitable development.

7. Augmenting the human capital of the poor is essential if they are to contribute to globalization-related national goals and not be further marginalized in an increasingly competitive world. Improved education is also necessary to facilitate the adjustment of the conjunctural poor to liberalization policies by improving labour mobility. The kinds and levels of education needed will depend on many factors, not least of which are the stage of development and degree of insertion in the global economy of the countries in question. As a minimum, a completed primary education is a prerequisite for employment as an unskilled labourer in export-oriented production. In many cases additional technical training will prove necessary for the poor as well as the non-poor. Further research is recommended into the changing requirements of labour markets with respect to education in a globalizing economy.

8. Because globalization and, in particular, liberalization imply a redistribution of benefits and opportunities, compensatory and safety-net measures will be important for certain population groups. Since trade-affected redundant workers in the formal sector are likely, because of their education, to find other work in the economy, primary emphasis should ideally be given to safety nets that are targeted at the poorest and most vulnerable of the affected poor. "Self-selection" emergency public works schemes can help satisfy the minimum income requirements of the conjunctural poor, while food distribution in peri-urban settlements or vouchers and other forms of subsidies on "inferior" food staples that are primarily consumed by the poor can help them attain their minimum calorie requirements. There are also "cost-free" measures that Governments can adopt, such as facilitating the access of the poor to legal titles on their urban land plots and rural land. Such measures help create gainful work in housing upgrading and, through the incentives they create for smallholders, to increase agricultural output.

9. Governments can also foster the creation of jobs available to the poor by providing support to micro- and small-scale enterprises, including those that are linked to the export sector. Such enterprises are normally more low-skill and labour-intensive than large firms and therefore helpful at directly reducing poverty. Moreover, through the flexibility that they provide in absorbing fluctuations and shifts in demand, micro- and small-

scale enterprises augment the competitiveness of large exporting firms by lowering their fixed costs. At the same time, through extended subcontracting chains, such enterprises can also function as a bridge to help integrate the informal sector with the formal sector – assuming official regulatory harassment of the informal sector is relaxed or eliminated – thereby enhancing the poverty-reducing role and economic potential of the informal sector in the economy. A critical concern is the question of Sub-Saharan Africa's insertion into the globalization process. As opposed to private investment flows, the principal global flows that the region receives continue to be in the form of official development assistance (ODA). This assistance should be partly re-directed to facilitate Sub-Saharan Africa's incorporation into the globalization process. Besides building up the human and physical capital needed for investment and trade, ODA should focus on institution-building, such as strengthening accounting structures and the legal system, in order to make the recipient countries more robust with respect to the requirements of globalization. For their part, African Governments should emphasize good governance and, as concerns local private investment and foreign capital, be consistent over time in their policy approaches so that investors can be confident of what to expect. Under such conditions, more domestic and foreign investment is likely to be made available to help those countries diversify beyond their existing static comparative advantage.

10. Current understanding is limited regarding the nature and relative strengths of the transmission channels and linkages that determine the effects of globalization and outward-oriented liberalization on poverty. The task is made more complicated by the need to consider the immense diversity of local circumstances, the variations of the globalization and liberalization processes and their economic and social effects over time. It is therefore recommended that further research be carried out on this subject, utilizing a sample of countries that represent a typology of differing initial conditions, in order that pro-poor policies related to the globalization and liberalization process can be more precisely identified and applied.

Part I

Poverty-related elements of globalization and liberalization

3

Effects of globalization and liberalization on poverty: concepts and issues

David Woodward[*]

Contents

[*] Independent consultant, London.

Introduction

Globalization consists of the integration of free markets, investment flows, trade and information. The reduction of natural barriers, such as transport and communication costs, and artificial barriers, such as tariffs, quotas and exchange controls, have contributed to the growth of trade and foreign direct investment in the world. As a result of the greater dispersal of economic activity, the division of labour has become increasingly internationalized.

In response to the trade and foreign direct investment opportunities resulting from globalization, a large and growing number of developing countries have voluntarily embarked on policies to liberalize their trade and foreign investment regimes, and have sought in particular to strengthen their export capacity. Deregulation and liberalization policies with respect to globalization in many cases grew out of the stabilization and adjustment measures that were adopted, often following arm-twisting by external creditors, in the aftermath of the debt crisis of the 1980s. Because outward-oriented liberalization policies particularly distinguish the present globalization process – and indeed are virtually inseparable from this process – from past globalization tendencies, the present paper treats globalization and liberalization as two elements of a single phenomenon.

Because of its positive effects on trade and investment, the globalization process has been widely interpreted as offering the best prospects for economic growth in both developed and developing countries, and thereby for the reduction of poverty over the long term. However, scepticism remains in some quarters; and there is widespread concern about potential adverse effects on some developing countries, most notably in Sub-Saharan Africa (SSA).

This paper seeks to investigate the linkages between the processes of globalization and liberalization (G/L) on the one hand, and development, growth and the sustainable reduction of poverty on the other. It should be emphasized that this is intended as a discussion of the nature of the processes which may be involved, and not a rigorous attempt at quantification or empirical investigation.

The present paper focuses primarily on three key elements of G/L:
- the Uruguay Round of the GATT;
- the *de facto* shift towards foreign direct and portfolio investment as a source of finance for developing countries; and
- liberalization policies at the national level embodied in structural

adjustment programmes, particularly those supported by the IMF and the World Bank.

The linkages between G/L and development and poverty inevitably depend on the precise nature of the G/L process. They will also vary markedly between countries, and between the short term and the long term. Accordingly, this paper considers which countries can be expected to gain and to lose in economic terms, in the short term and the long term, and the nature of their gains and losses; and how the expected economic effects of G/L are translated into effects on the poor. In doing so, it seeks to identify possible knock-on and spill-over effects at the global, national and sub-national levels, which may be overlooked in discussions of the issue which focus at a single level. The paper concludes by considering the implications for policies in international institutions and developed and developing countries.

3.1 Trade in goods and services: the Uruguay Round

The Uruguay Round is of importance to developing countries primarily through its effect on the trade policies of the developed countries. The trade policies of the developing countries themselves have been, and will in all likelihood continue to be, determined primarily by their own autonomous or World Bank supported efforts at liberalization[1]. In Sub-Saharan Africa, in particular, the level of bound tariff commitments under the Uruguay Round agreement is far above the current level in most cases, so that the Uruguay Round commitments will not represent a binding constraint on policy (Harrold 1995). Accordingly, trade liberalization by the developing countries is discussed in the later section on liberalization.

Historically, the impediment to development imposed by developed countries' trade barriers has been a rare area of agreement between orthodox commentators (e.g. Finger and Messerlin 1989 and World Bank 1992a) and more critical voices (e.g. Barratt Brown and Tiffen 1992 and Coote 1992). The orthodox view also presents protectionist trade policies in developing countries as an important obstacle to their own economic efficiency and growth (e.g. World Bank 1992b). In consequence, the global trade liberalization implied by the Uruguay Round agreement might be expected to provide unmitigated benefits for developing countries. However, there are some important caveats to this view, as discussed below.

3.1.1 Factors limiting benefits to developing countries

Clearly, the Uruguay Round represents an important step towards freer trade, at least in goods. However, the actual improvement in the trading environment facing developing countries is substantially more limited than it might at first appear.

(a) The pattern of developed countries' tariff reductions on industrial goods is skewed towards imports from other developed countries, and away from the primary-based and labour-intensive manufactures on which developing countries are primarily dependent. As a result, the average reduction on imports from most developing regions is about half of that on developed country exports (20-25 per cent, as against 45 per cent); for Asia, the reduction is about one-quarter less than for developed countries (World Bank 1995d: Figure 2-1a)[2].

(b) Even after full implementation of the Uruguay Round, the average tariffs applied by the US, the European Union (EU), Japan and Canada on imports from developing countries will remain higher than their respective averages for imports from all sources (though low in absolute terms), even allowing for General System of Preferences (GSP). This general pattern also prevails within most sectors and sub-sectors (UNCTAD 1994: 141).

(c) While tariff peaks are reduced, they remain important in a number of critical industries, such as textiles and leather and rubber goods; and while tariff escalation has been reduced somewhat, it is by no means eliminated. According to Page and Davenport (1994), the Uruguay Round will clearly reduce tariff escalation for five of eleven products considered. It will be reduced on balance for three more. In only one case (zinc) is tariff escalation clearly increased; and in two others (lead and tobacco) the effect is, by implication, increased on balance.

(d) The phasing out of the Multifiber Arrangement (MFA) is likely to be substantially slower than it might at first appear, limiting the immediate benefits.

  • The phasing is heavily end-loaded, 49 per cent of the Quantitative Restrictions (QRs) being lifted only at the end of the implementation period.

  • Each importing country has almost complete discretion over the products to be included in each round of liberalization, and can be expected to liberalize the products for which the markets are least restricted first.

- Importers can invoke safeguard provisions more easily than before, and thus limit the extent of liberalization in the sectors affected.

Hertel et al (1995) found that the net benefits to developing countries as a whole of eliminating the MFA will be minimal, net benefits to China, Association of South East Asian Countries (ASEAN) and South Asia being off-set by welfare losses in the Newly Industrialized Economies (NIEs), Latin America and Sub-Saharan Africa.

(e) The effects of tariffication and tariff reduction on agricultural goods will in practice be relatively limited.

- The base period used (1986-8) represents the peak period for agricultural protection by developed countries in recent years, so that the actual reduction in tariffs will be substantially less than the headline figure. It has been estimated that equivalent reductions from *current* levels of protection would provide double the welfare gain of the actual Uruguay Round terms (Goldin and van der Mensbrugghe 1995).

- Ingco (1995), found evidence of "dirty tariffication" – use of a baseline substantially higher than the actual level of protection during the base period – for six out of seven major agricultural products in the EU, and five out of seven in the US. In the EU, even the final level of tariffs remained above the actual 1986-8 rate of protection in four cases.

- The use of an unweighted average for the overall (36 per cent) reduction requirement renders it almost meaningless. The actual extent of tariff reduction is likely to be closer to the minimum level of 15 per cent.

- The safeguard clause permits the levying of additional duties if import volumes exceed, or import prices fall below, specified trigger levels.

- Minimum access commitments have been based on aggregated categories of commodities rather than individual tariff lines, and existing special arrangements (e.g. the Lomé Convention) are included, despite their non-Most Favoured Nation (MFN) basis. As a result, "With a few notable exceptions, the minimum access commitments will provide relatively little additional access and even less additional trade" (Ingco and Hathaway 1995: 16).

Overall, "Apart from Japan the highly protected markets in OECD countries were liberalized little if at all", and liberalization is most limited for those commodities which are most protected: "border protection for sugar and dairy products was maintained or even increased" (Ingco and Hathaway 1995: 8 and 15).

(f) Similarly, the starting point for export subsidy reductions on agricultural goods is the higher of the average in 1986-90 and in 1991-2, again increasing the level of subsidized exports initially allowed. Also, food aid (implicitly including non-emergency food aid) is excluded from the definition of subsidized exports, so that programmes such as the US PL480 programme will continue. Other Uruguay Round signatories (e.g. the EU) could in principle develop similar mechanisms to dispose of agricultural surpluses in excess of the GATT limits.

(g) The effect of the domestic support provisions for agriculture is limited by the exclusion of subsidies ostensibly "decoupled" from output levels, and by the inclusion of cuts in import tariffs and export subsidies in the measurement of subsidy reduction. The US and the EU "agreed to exempt [their own] major support policies...even though neither met the strict criteria for belonging in the 'green box' or non-distorting category". As a result "the hoped for cut-backs in subsidized output are unlikely to be realized" (Ingco and Hathaway 1995: 21). In addition, the domestic support provision applies only to the agricultural sector *as a whole*, so there is no assurance of any reduction in particular sub-sectors. In the EU, for example, the switch to compensatory payments based on historical regional yields in the 1992 cereals reform was more than enough to meet the entire domestic support requirement, so that other sub-sectors will not be affected (Gardner 1993).

(h) To the extent that market conditions for developing country exports are improved by the Uruguay Round, the actual benefits (especially to low-income countries) will be limited by the existence of preferential arrangements such as the Lomé Convention and the GSP. The terms of such arrangements will not be improved; and the margins of preference enjoyed by the beneficiaries will be significantly eroded. The benefits to eligible countries of higher world prices for agricultural produce (a major element of the expected benefits of the Agreement on Agriculture) will also be limited, as prices under preferential arrangements are often insulated from changes in the world market and may be reduced by the changes in importing countries' policies required under the Uruguay Round. In some cases, such exports represent a very large proportion of the total[3]. These factors will tend to skew the benefits of the Uruguay Round towards middle-income countries. However, this effect will be damped by the relatively limited success of most low-income countries in exploiting preferential arrangements outside the agricultural sector, due to poor supply response and strict country-specific rules-of-origin criteria.

In addition to its potential effects on access to developed country markets, the Uruguay Round is expected to benefit some developing countries by increasing the world prices of certain agricultural exports – primarily those produced by the developed countries (notably cereals and beef) or which compete with their products (e.g. cane sugar). However, there are relatively few developing countries which produce temperate agricultural products for export, for geographical reasons; and most developing country sugar exporters depend at least partly on preferential export arrangements with developed countries (e.g. the EU's sugar protocol, and the US import quota system), which will be adversely affected by the Agreement on Agriculture (Woodward 1994b). At the same time, net importers of temperate produce stand to lose as a result of higher prices – and almost all low-income countries are net importers of cereals. In the long term, however, higher prices may stimulate increased domestic production.

In consequence, the prospective benefits of the price effects of the Agreement on Agriculture are heavily concentrated in a handful of middle-income countries – notably Argentina, Brazil, Uruguay, Cuba, Thailand and the Philippines. Low-income Sahelian beef exporters (e.g. Mali, Niger and Burkina Faso) would benefit if EU dumping in neighbouring countries were reduced (Madden 1993); but this is by no means assured. More generally, low-income countries are likely to be adversely affected by increased prices for imports, particularly of cereals, and less favourable terms under preferential arrangements (Pryke and Woodward 1994). It should be noted, however, that all of these effects will be dampened by the limitations in the terms of the Agreement on Agriculture, as noted above.

Perhaps of greater importance than the *extent* of market-opening required of industrial countries is the greater *security* of market access (assuming full implementation), which could significantly increase the incentives for investment in export sectors.

• Tariff bindings have been extended to cover 99 per cent of industrial

country imports.
- No new voluntary export restraints can be negotiated.
- Dispute settlement procedures have been greatly strengthened, providing more effective control over ostensibly retaliatory measures; and some legitimate subsidies (e.g. targeted regional subsidies and support for research and development) have been exempted from the application of countervailing duties.
- Various technical issues have been clarified, to prevent their abuse as protective instruments (e.g. sanitary and phytosanitary regulations, technical standards, etc.).

Here too, however, there are some limitations. Some temporary import quotas are possible under safeguard provisions, and there is some concern that this procedure may in practice be open to abuse (UNCTAD 1994); little has been done to restrain the use of anti-dumping measures; and the threat of Voluntary Export Restraint (VERs) does not appear to have been eliminated (e.g. for Mexican exports of tomatoes to the US[4]). The Agreement on Agriculture also substantially increases uncertainty regarding the extent and terms of access under preferential arrangements such as the EU's Sugar Protocol (Woodward 1994b).

3.1.2 Estimates of the impact on developing countries

A number of simulations of the effects of the Uruguay Round (e.g. Harrison et al 1995, Francois et al 1995, Goldin and van der Mensbrugghe 1995) have nonetheless found substantial benefits to developing countries.
- In the simplest simulations, considering static effects in a world of perfect competition, with constant returns and full employment, global gains are estimated to be in order of about $50bn ($4-16bn accruing to developing countries).
- Taking account of increasing returns and imperfect competition increases the estimated benefits to between $50bn and $115bn, depending on the elasticities assumed. Almost all of this variation arise in the benefits to developing countries, which range from $5bn to $63bn.
- The investment induced by increased efficiency and higher rates of return is estimated to generate additional income of around $190-250bn in the long term, $62-137bn of this in developing countries.

However, considerable caution is needed in interpreting these results. Firstly, the scale of the benefits is more limited than the absolute numbers might appear to suggest. Even the last of these approaches implies benefits of only about 1-3 per cent of 1993 GDP. Three more detailed points are also important: the distribution of the estimated benefits between developing countries; the nature of the assumptions about trade liberalization under the Uruguay Round; and the way in which the benefits are estimated.

The distribution of benefits to developing countries is extremely unequal. While Harrison et al's simulation suggests that most regions will gain, Sub-Saharan Africa is projected to lose $1.2bn[5]. It is also likely that the aggregate results for other country groupings conceal losses for individual countries. The loss for Sub-Saharan Africa also suggests that the losses may be concentrated in (or the benefits most limited for) countries with similar characteristics to those typical of this region – that is, relatively small low-income countries, with low levels of industrialization and heavy dependence on exports of primary commodities.

Goldin and van der Mensbrugghe's (1995) static full-employment analysis finds much more widespread losses, amounting to 0.1-0.4 per cent of GNP in 2002 for China and every non-Asian country or country grouping except Brazil (+0.4 per cent) and the Gulf (neutral)[6]. Nonetheless, the strength of the gains, especially in high-income Asia (1.3 per cent), India (0.5 per cent) and Brazil (0.4 per cent) produces a favourable overall result for developing countries as a whole. Allowing for unemployment (and assuming input subsidy reductions which are not included in the Uruguay Round agreement) substantially increases the overall benefit, and provides more widespread gains. However, it eliminates the gains to India and Brazil, and magnifies the losses of Sub-Saharan Africa, the Maghreb, China and Mexico.

Second, there is a serious risk of over-simplifying the substance and implementation of the Uruguay Round Agreement. In practice, the relationship between the terms of the Uruguay Round Agreement and the actual changes in trading conditions affecting developing countries which are likely to result from it is often indirect and highly complex, particularly where there is a substantial element of discretion in implementation and phasing, as in the agriculture and textiles sectors[7]. Moreover, the effects of the Uruguay Round in any individual country will depend on its particular circumstances, economic structures and productive potential; on its preferential trading arrangements with other countries; on the financial situation, efficiency and productive capacity of its major enterprises, etc.

Such complexities cannot be adequately captured by what is necessarily a very simplified, highly aggregated and mechanistic econometric model. The result is to exaggerate the degree of liberalization, and to misrepresent its pattern; and to ignore the limitations which may be imposed on some countries' ability to benefit by their particular economic circumstances.

This simplification is critically important to the distribution of benefits between developing countries, as well as their overall extent. Access to preferential arrangements is enjoyed disproportionately by smaller and poorer developing countries, not least those in Sub-Saharan Africa. Such countries will not merely fail to benefit from MFN tariff reductions, but will also be adversely affected by the erosion of their preference margins in relation to their competitors. This group of countries also broadly corresponds with those which face the greatest obstacles to responding to the changes in incentives resulting from G/L. Taking account of such considerations would tend to skew the benefits of the Uruguay Round still further away from these countries.

The importance of preferential arrangements is clearly demonstrated by Page and Davenport (1994), who estimate the potential effects of the Uruguay Round on exports and net exports at the country level, taking account of such arrangements. They estimate an overall positive effect on developing country exports of 1.3 per cent but a negative impact on Africa, Caribbean and the Pacific (ACP) countries, not merely at the aggregate level, but also for all but one (Fiji) of the individual countries in these categories for which separate estimates are made, and for some other low-income countries. In some cases, the negative impacts are considerable – between 8 per cent and 20 per cent for Bangladesh, Mauritius, Jamaica and Nepal; and 4-6 per cent for Ethiopia, Malawi, Mozambique and Guyana. India and China, however, gain substantially (+7.7 per cent and +3.9 per cent respectively), largely because they are less dependent on preferential arrangements.

A key problem in the estimation of benefits is that adjustment costs, such as the consumption forgone to finance higher levels of investment, are ignored: while the final simulations estimate the (comparative static) *benefits of being at* the new equilibrium position, they exclude the (dynamic) *costs of getting to* this position. These costs should be off-set against the benefits, and could, in principle, outweigh them (Harrison et al 1995, footnote 25). Conversely, for countries or regions which lose from the Uruguay Round, the estimated losses would presumably be moderated, as the lower investment levels implied by the projections would free additional resources for consumption in the medium term.

The *nature* of the benefits considered is also critically important in interpreting the results. Because a welfare measure is used in the static approaches, a major component of the benefit is the increase in consumer surplus which accrues from each country lowering its own trade barriers. The benefits accruing from other countries' liberalization are thus substantially less than the estimates recorded above. Since trade policy is within the control of each individual country – and trade reform in developing countries is motivated primarily by pressures for structural adjustment rather than by the Uruguay Round – this is arguably misleading[8]. The benefits of increasing consumer surpluses in terms of development and poverty-reduction are also likely to be more limited than those of improved access to export markets.

3.1.3 GATS, TRIPs and TRIMs

Little empirical work has been done on the implications of the General Agreement on Trade in Services (GATS), Trade-Related Intellectual Property Rights (TRIPs) and Trade-Related Investment Measures (TRIMs) elements of the Uruguay Round for developing countries. Any assessment of their effects must therefore be essentially speculative in nature.

The **GATS** agreement is very limited in scope, and is of greater significance as a basis for future liberalization than for the liberalization it actually entails. If and when it does occur, liberalization of services should be favourable overall for developing countries, allowing them to take greater advantage of the increased opportunities for service exports offered, in particular, by improvements in information and communications technology. The prime examples of distance services facilitated by these changes are data entry and remote data processing of various types. At a higher level of sophistication, computer programming has been contracted out on a substantial scale, most notably to Bangalore in India.

The World Bank (1995d) has estimated that the potential market for distance service provision by developing countries is in the order of $140bn (13 per cent of exports of goods and services, and 3 per cent of GDP, in 1993). However, the extent of the increase in developing countries' access to this market will depend on the actual extent of liberalization by the developed countries; and the $140bn estimate itself depends on the ambiguous impact of technological changes, which is likely to increase the feasibility of distance service provision, but to reduce the overall value of the market (by reducing prices). Other service sectors in which developing countries have a potential comparative advantage (e.g. construction) seem unlikely to be liberalized substantially in the near future.

The benefits of liberalization, particularly in the case of distance services, are likely to be more widely spread than in the case of trade in goods. The conditions for competitiveness in this sector relate primarily to basic educational standards, wage costs and the communications infrastructure; and while these requirements would largely exclude many low-income countries, some small low- and lower-middle income countries could hope to benefit substantially. Current exporters of distance services include, for example, Barbados, Jamaica and Kenya.

The net benefits of service exports may be limited, at least in the short term, by their means of delivery. At present, this tends to occur primarily by companies in developed countries establishing wholly-owned subsidiaries in developing countries to service their own data-processing requirements. This limits the scale of the operation, and is likely to lower the price paid for the service. In the longer term, however, experience with the provision of such services might provide the basis for the establishment of locally-owned companies providing services more widely on a commercial basis.

Developing countries also stand to benefit from liberalization of trade in production-supporting services, such as telecommunications and commercial transport, as greater market access should increase technology and competition, thus reducing costs and competitiveness in other sectors. While the GATS commitments undertaken by most developing countries outside the tourism sector have been limited (Page and Davenport 1994: Table 7.2), this does not preclude further liberalization either autonomously or under structural adjustment programmes. However, there may also be a financial downside, in terms of the profit remittances on the Foreign Direct Investment (FDI) embodied in such services (as discussed later).

The **TRIPs** agreement largely consolidates, universalizes and strengthens previous international agreements, and makes them legally enforceable through the WTO dispute settlement mechanisms. In doing so, it substantially increases the extent to which developing countries will be required to respect patents, copyrights, etc. held outside their territories.

The immediate benefits will accrue to the holders of intellectual property rights, which are overwhelmingly multinational companies based in the developed countries. For developing countries, the effects are ambiguous: their access to technology developed in other countries will be reduced, and its cost increased; but it is argued that this will encourage the transfer (and domestic development) of technology, increasing productivity, competitiveness and incomes. A second cost is that of enforcement: this will be particularly high in many low-income countries, where the resources available to the public sector are limited, and the capacity of administrative and judicial systems are already seriously over-stretched. Effective enforcement will also divert scarce technical manpower away from development of indigenous technology and intellectual property.

Some developing countries (e.g. India and Brazil) which have relatively high levels of technological capacity may benefit from the TRIPs agreement overall. In the vast majority of cases, however, the effect seems likely to be negative, at least in the short term. In the longer term, the absorption of high-level technical manpower in policing TRIPs obligations seems likely to weaken the potential for indigenous technology development, especially where such personnel are scarce; and this could be compounded by direct contracting of developing country nationals in technology-development occupations by multinational companies (cf. the software engineers of Bangalore). There is a danger, at least, that the TRIPs agreement, assisted by GATS, could perpetuate the concentration of the ownership of intellectual property in the developed countries.

The effects of the **TRIMs** agreement are more limited. This effectively prevents the application of trade-related criteria (e.g. local content and trade-balancing requirements) to foreign-owned enterprises. The potential importance of these measures lies in the limitations they impose on development strategies: such policies played a significant role in the FDI policies of some of the first-generation NIEs. Trebilcock and Howse (1995: 293) also argue that the absence of a list of GATT-consistent measures "means that no further protection is extended to Contracting Parties against unilateral retaliatory action by the United States [against "grey area" measures] on the basis of its market access approach". This could significantly tip the balance of advantage from host countries towards investors.

3.1.4 Conclusion

Overall, it seems likely that significant benefits will accrue to developing countries as a whole from the Uruguay Round agreement over the long term, through its effects on the extent and security of access to developed country markets and (to a lesser extent) on world market conditions for some primary commodities. However, these benefits are substantially smaller than they might at first appear, and are likely to be overstated in some of the simulation exercises that have been carried out to date, particularly in terms of long-term development. They are also strongly skewed towards larger, higher-income and more industrialised countries, and away from smaller, lower-income and more commodity-dependent countries. The benefits to countries in the latter group, which includes most of Sub-Saharan Africa, will be at best limited, and are likely to be substantially negative.

3.2 Foreign direct and portfolio investment

3.2.1 Recent trends in direct and portfolio investment

Since the late 1980s, there has been a very strong shift of international financial flows to developing countries towards portfolio investment (equity, bonds and financial instruments[9]) and foreign direct investment. For developing countries as a whole, public and private sector bond issues and equity investments amounted to 14 per cent of total non-official external financing in 1980[10]. By 1993, this had risen to 86 per cent. This partly reflects the growth of direct and portfolio investment (D/PI), which increased from just $7.9bn to $136.5bn; and partly the virtual disappearance of syndicated bank lending following the debt crisis.

The rapid growth in D/PI since the late 1980s has been driven in part by the increase in confidence in the major commercial debtors' economies following the Brady Initiative; and the progressive liberalization and opening of many developing countries' economies under the auspices of structural adjustment programmes. At the same time, the debt crisis of the 1980s has seriously weakened confidence in sovereign lending by commercial banks. Such confidence is unlikely to be restored over the medium term in the absence of substantial changes in the international financial system. At the same time, as discussed later, the debt crisis increased relative confidence in bonds as a mechanism for lending to developing countries.

The recent surge in portfolio investment in emerging markets has also been encouraged by the external economic environment – and particularly the relatively low real rates of return available on investments in the major developed economies. The marked reduction in portfolio investment in 1994, at least partly in response to a relatively small increase in real US interest rates, suggests that this has been a particularly important factor. Regulatory changes in developed countries – most notably the US – have also been significant in encouraging equity flows to developing countries.

However, while flows of D/PI to developing countries have increased dramatically in recent years, they remain heavily concentrated in a relatively small group of countries (Table 3.1). In 1993, inflows of equity financing were recorded for only 19 developing countries; and these were mainly the largest and richest developing economies. In terms of size, the group was

Table 3.1: Direct and Portfolio Investment Flows to Developing Countries, 1993 (per cent of GNP)

Countries with GDP greater than $40bn	Equity	Bonds (pub)	Bonds (pvt)	FDI	Total
Upper-middle-income countries:					
Argentina	1.4	1.5	1.3	2.5	6.8
Brazil	1.0	0.2	0.8	0.1	2.2
Chile	0.8	0*	0.7	2.0	3.5
Korea	1.8	0.9	0.5	0.2	3.4
Malaysia	6.0	1.5	0	7.0	14.6
Mexico	4.3	1.1	1.8	1.5	8.7
Venezuela	0.1	2.6	0.2	0.6	3.4
Lower-middle-income countries:					
Colombia	0.2	0.9	0	1.7	2.8
Indonesia	1.4	0	0.4	1.5	3.2
Peru	3.1	0	0	0.9	4.0
Philippines	2.0	1.4	0.4	1.4	5.1
Thailand	2.6	0.1	1.4	2.0	6.1
Iran	0	0	0	-0.0	-0.0
Low-income countries:					
China	0.6	0.7	0.1	6.6	7.9
India	0.7	0*	0.3	0.1	1.2
Pakistan	0.4	0	0	0.7	1.0
Countries with GDP less than $40bn					
Upper-middle-income countries:					
Mauritius	0.5	0	0	0.2	0.8
Trinidad & Tobago	0	3.5	0	4.3	7.8
Uruguay	0	2.1	0	0.6	2.7
others (6 countries)	0	0	0	2.1	2.1
Lower-middle-income (34) *countries*	0	0	0	1.3	1.3
Low-income countries:					
Liberia	20[e]	0	0	0	20[e]
Vietnam	0.5	0	0	0.2	0.7
others (47 countries)	0	0	0	0.8	0.8

Notes: Countries in Europe and the Former Soviet Union are excluded. Data on financial flows are from World Bank (1995f), while income groupings are based on World Bank (1995g). Figures for groups of countries are weighted averages. Entries marked [e] are estimated on the basis of GNP in an earlier year; * signifies that financial flows were zero in 1993, but non-zero in 1991-2.

40

made up mainly of 16 of the 17 developing countries with total GDP of more than \$40bn[11]. Only five (India, China, Pakistan, Vietnam and Liberia) were low-income countries.

Bond issues were concentrated in almost exactly the same group of countries: all but five equity-recipients issued bonds in 1993 (and two others in 1991-2), while only two other developing countries did so (Uruguay and Trinidad and Tobago). While much smaller, these are both upper-middle-income countries. The bond/equity countries also receive a disproportionate amount of FDI – about 1.9 per cent of GNP on average in 1993, compared with 0.6 per cent for other developing countries as a whole.

FDI flows are more widely spread than equity investment, but still favour middle-income countries. Within income per capita categories, the ratio to GNP is highest for very small economies (GNP less than \$500m), with a much lower peak at the upper end of the scale, reflecting the attractions of larger markets. The poorest performers are middle-sized low-income countries: of 19 low-income countries with GNP between \$4bn and \$25bn in 1993, only one (Sri Lanka) received more than 0.5 per cent of GNP in FDI. Among low-income countries, FDI flows tend to favour countries with particular advantages in terms of location or natural resources: "The few [Sub-Saharan] African countries that were successful [in attracting FDI in the second half of the 1980s] are all small and most of them had some out-of-the-ordinary characteristics, either natural resources-wise (Botswana, Gabon), or location-wise (Swaziland)" (Bachmann and Kwaku 1994: 1).

Even within the equity/bonds group, D/PI flows are heavily concentrated. Just seven countries (China, Korea, Malaysia, Thailand, Mexico, Argentina and Brazil) accounted for between 83 per cent and 90 per cent of each category of D/PI flows to the group as a whole. With the conspicuous exceptions of FDI to China and equity flows to Liberia[12], flows within each category also appear to increase broadly in line with income per capita, suggesting a still more regressive distribution.

As a result of these trends, low-income countries (with the notable exceptions of India and Pakistan[13]) have become still more dependent on official financing. The proportion of total net flows to the small and medium-sized low-income countries coming from non-official sources fell from 29.8 per cent to 7.0 per cent between 1980 and 1993, as the absolute amount declined from \$5.9bn to \$1.7bn. Coupled with the relatively slow growth of official flows (an average of 3.5 per cent per annum over this period, compared with average dollar inflation[14] of 3.0 per cent per annum), this led to a cumulative decline in real net financial flows to these countries in the order of 20 per cent between 1980 and 1993.

Among low-income countries, there is also a very strong negative correlation between net official financing as a percentage of GNP, and the overall size of the economy. For Los-Income Countries (LICs) with GNP less than \$500m in 1993, net official financing averaged 40 per cent of GNP; at the other extreme, net flows to India and China were 1.3 per cent and 0.9 per cent of GNP respectively. The result is to leave middle-sized and larger LICs (except China) with very limited – and increasingly insecure – access to net financial flows.

3.2.2 The stability and sustainability of direct and portfolio investment flows

As noted above, a significant factor underlying the rapid increase in D/PI flows to developing countries was the relatively low real rate of return available on investments in developed countries in the early 1990s. As well as increasing investors' willingness to look to alternative markets for their investments, this contributed to the improvement in the creditworthiness of developing countries with large debts at floating interest rates, making such investments more viable. However, the partial reversal of this trend in 1994, coupled with the impact of the Mexican crisis, reduced these flows substantially. The flow of portfolio investment to developing countries as a whole in 1995 is estimated to have been less than half of its 1993 level (though still 50 per cent above 1993), with a particularly sharp reduction in Latin America (World Bank 1996).

In addition to these time-specific factors there are a number of other reasons to expect the recent increase in **equity investment** to be at least partly temporary in nature. There are four key points.

- A significant part of the surge in foreign equity financing has in many cases been associated with privatization (notably in Argentina). This factor was particularly important in the Transition Economies (where privatization accounted for 43.4 per cent of total FDI in between 1988 and 1993) and Latin America (14.9 per cent), and to a lesser extent in Sub-Saharan Africa (6.4 per cent) (Sader 1995: Table 1). This source will become progressively less important as the process of privatization is completed.

- In some cases (e.g. Mexico and Chile), a second major source of equity flows has been the return of flight capital[15]. Again, this represents a finite source of capital which will ultimately be exhausted.
- When a new equity market is opened to foreign investors[16], this can be expected to prompt a stock adjustment in the portfolios of investing institutions. Once the country's share in such portfolios has reached its optimum level, inflows will be much more limited.
- It has been argued that the extent of equity investment in emerging markets is partly associated with the high level of pricing inefficiency in these markets (Claessens and Gooptu 1993). With increased foreign participation, such inefficiency might be expected to decline, thereby reducing the incentives for new investment.

The likely time horizons of these various factors are uncertain, and will vary considerably between countries. Privatization appears to have peaked (though perhaps temporarily) in terms of total sale value in 1992, and as a proportion of direct and portfolio investment in 1991 (at 15 per cent and 46 per cent respectively). The value of privatisation-related D/PI continued to rise in 1993, as the share of foreign participation increased; and this trend could continue, as foreign investment was still only 35 per cent of the total. However, the falling absolute value of privatization will ultimately predominate.

Particular uncertainty surrounds the return of capital flight, as it is difficult to measure, and the extent to which it is likely to return is unclear. Estimates of its value suggest that a considerable volume of capital remains. The World Bank's (1993a) estimate puts the total at $700bn, which would in principle be enough to sustain the current level of equity flows to developing countries for 17-18 years without any other sources of funding. However, the methodology used results in substantial over-estimation of the amount; and it is unrealistic to expect more than a small proportion of actual flight capital to return, as its owners can also be expected to maintain globally diversified portfolios. Also, capital flight includes resource transfers which have been accompanied or followed by owners as refugees or migrants. These may account for a substantial part of the total in some cases[17], and are less likely to return to their country of origin.

There is also considerable scope for stock adjustment. According to

International Finance Corporation (IFC) estimates, equities on emerging stock markets account for 12 per cent of the world total, but only 1 per cent of the assets of US pension funds (World Bank 1995f). This is probably an extreme case, as US fund managers are particularly inward-looking; but it does suggest the likelihood of a continued shift towards developing country assets in the portfolios of major institutional investors.

Pricing imperfections can be expected to decline over time, as markets become deeper and more open, but the pace of this process is very unclear. There is little sign of this occurring as yet (Claessens and Gooptu 1994).

Overall, it seems likely that the demand-side components of the current surge in equity investment (returning flight capital and stock adjustment) will continue to outstrip the supply-side component (privatisation). This can be expected to create artificially high rates of return over the medium term. In the longer term, however, these tendencies will be reversed: as the bulk of the privatization and stock adjustments are completed, the stock of flight capital is depleted, and price inefficiencies are eliminated, inflows will fall and rates of return will return to more normal (though still high) levels.

These tendencies may be compounded by a herd instinct on the part of investors. In the medium term, the perception of strong inflows and high rates of return can be expected to encourage additional investment. Once the turning-point is reached, however, there is a serious risk that the market will over-adjust, as rates of return are reduced and the herd instinct is reversed, causing a substantial outflow of capital. If this were to occur abruptly, this could have a lasting adverse effect on market perceptions. The likelihood of such a scenario is increased if the transition coincides with a deterioration in the external economic environment.

FDI is often seen as a more stable and durable source of external financing, reflecting the longer time-horizon of investors. There is some validity to this view, at least in the sense that net disinvestment is unusual. While net capital outflows are by no means unknown, and may persist for some time, either continuously or intermittently[18], they are generally limited. With one or two exceptions, the cumulative amount has been up to about up to about 3 per cent of GNP.

However, there is still a significant degree of variation in FDI flows over time; and the procyclical nature of such investment means that it tends to compound the impact of external shocks rather than off-set them. Thus FDI flows dipped sharply in the early 1980s, as most developing countries were facing sharp foreign exchange constraints and a consequent recession, and only returned to their long-term trend in the early 1990s, when the situation had improved. Even then, they largely by-passed those countries where the situation remained weakest.

In the case of **bonds**, a major factor underlying their recent growth is the experience of the debt crisis. Not only did this crisis create disillusionment with bank lending as a mechanism of financial flows to developing countries, it also significantly enhanced the reputation of bonds. Bank loans were subject to long delays in payments, protracted and expensive renegotiations, concerted new lending agreements effectively imposed on creditors, and latterly some (albeit limited and notionally voluntary) debt and debt-service reduction. Bonds escaped these processes, and maintained a relatively favourable record of debt-service payments: between 1983 and 1989, annual principal repayments on bonds by severely-indebted middle-income countries (SIMICs) averaged 9.1 per cent of the amount outstanding, compared with only 2.8 per cent on commercial bank debt[19]. As a result, bonds have come to be seen as a relatively safe form of lending.

However, a major reason for the continued servicing of bonds held by foreign creditors was that they represented a relatively small part of the debt (4.7 per cent for SIMICs, as defined in 1995, at the end of 1980). As this proportion rises, so the prospect of maintaining service payments on bonds at times of balance of payments pressure becomes more difficult. For middle-income countries as a whole, bonds had risen to 19.8 per cent of total public and publicly guaranteed debt by 1993[20]. This proportion can be expected to continue growing so long as bonds represent an important source of external financing. Multilateral debt, for which there is also no rescheduling mechanism at present, represents a further 16.2 per cent (compared with 9.4 per cent in 1980).

This has two implications. Firstly, it suggests that the scope for concerted financial action in response to future debt problems will be substantially more limited than in the 1980s, making the adjustment process more difficult. This may be further compounded by the different attitudes of bondholders as compared with commercial bank creditors. The former tend to seek longer-term relationships with major borrowers, and may be more subject to peer pressure, encouraging a (relatively) constructive and conciliatory response to payments problems. The latter tend to be a less cohesive group, and to be more single-minded in seeking a favourable rate of return on individual investments. Together with the absence of an effective mechanism for an orderly collective response to payments problems, this suggests that a debt or balance of payments crisis in a country whose debts are dominated by bonds would be much more difficult to deal with effectively than that of the 1980s.

Secondly, the increasing predominance of bonds (and of other non-reschedulable liabilities such as multilateral debt and D/PI) makes it much less likely that, in the event of debt problems, debt-service payments on bonds will be maintained to the same extent as in the 1980s. The realization of this potential problem could actually precipitate precisely such a problem, by reducing the supply of bond finance, much as the Mexican payments crisis of August 1982 precipitated a more general debt crisis in the 1980s by demonstrating the true risks of sovereign lending by banks.

3.2.3 The foreign exchange cost of direct and portfolio investment flows

The down-side of D/PI is their high cost. The average rate of return on **equity investments** in 1976-92 in 15 emerging markets which had attracted foreign equity inflows by 1993 was 29 per cent per annum[21]. In only two cases (Indonesia at -12 per cent and Malaysia at +14 per cent) was the rate of return less than 20 per cent; and in the former case the data covered a period of only three years (1990-92). In three cases (Argentina at 68 per cent, the Philippines at 45 per cent and Colombia at 43 per cent) it was above 40 per cent.

The balance of these rates of return between capital gains (which are implicitly reinvested) and dividends (which are likely to be expatriated) is not specified. However, data given by Glen et al (1995) suggest that the latter may be in the order of 1-2 per cent of the current value of shares[22]. The remainder of the rate of return will take the form of capital gains.

The outflows on equity investment (in the form of dividend payments) will vary broadly in proportion to the value of externally-held equity. In the early stages, the stock is relatively small; but growth will be very rapid, as new investment is large relative to the initial stock, and the value is increased further by rapidly rising equity prices. As the market matures, the rate of growth will slow, but is likely to remain strongly positive. Dividend payments will follow a similar pattern.

From a foreign exchange perspective, it is not the rate of return on an individual investment which matters, but rather the rate of return which could be realised in the event of a net outflow of resources. This is substantially lower, because a general exit of foreign investors from the market could be achieved only by selling their shares to domestic residents; and this would result in a substantial fall in the prices for which equity could be sold (particularly if the factors which prompted selling also applied to domestic investors). This would be further compounded if there were a significant impact on the exchange rate.

Nonetheless, the rate of return on equity investments in foreign exchange terms could still be very high. Hypothesising a capital gain of 25 per cent per annum (roughly in line with the above estimates), annual dividends of 1-2 per cent per annum, and a potential loss of value of 50 per cent in the event of a general exodus of foreign investors, the overall rate of return would still be positive on any investment held for more than three years. Thereafter, the rate would increase rapidly, to 6-7 per cent per annum after four years, 10-11 per cent per annum after five years, and 18-19 per cent per annum over 10 years.

The overall cost would be a weighted average of the rates of return on investments of different ages: in effect, the very high rates of return on older investments would be diluted (or off-set) by the lower (or negative) rates on newer investments. Nonetheless, the rates of return could remain very high. With a constant nominal level of investment, the rate of return would be negative for the first five years, rising to 6 per cent in year 7, 14 per cent in year 10 and 20 per cent in year 15.

Even in the absence of a general capital outflow, the foreign exchange cost of equity flows could in principle be high, if rapid price increases were sustained over a prolonged period[23]. With price rises of 25-30 per cent per annum, and dividend pay-outs of 1-2 per cent per annum, the rate of return would become positive after 9-13 years, rising rapidly thereafter to 10 per cent after 13-20 years and 20 per cent after 20-40 years.

The high rate of return on **direct investment** also represents a potentially important problem. However, this is a more complex issue than for portfolio equity investment. It is often argued, explicitly or implicitly, that profit remittances on FDI are relatively unimportant, because they can take place only to the extent that profits are made (unlike debt-creating flows). However, this is an over-simplification, as profits do not necessarily imply net foreign exchange benefits.

There are essentially two types of FDI flows: the purchase of equity stakes (exceeding 10 per cent) in existing productive capacity or enterprises; and the creation of new productive capacity in the host country. In the former case, there is no direct effect on net foreign exchange earnings, and the foreign exchange effect is essentially similar to that for smaller equity investments, as discussed above.

Where new productive capacity is created, however, the foreign exchange effects are not limited to the initial capital inflow and subsequent profit remittances. In addition, the initial investment will have some import content, reducing the net inflow; and future production is likely to have some import content, and may include exports and/or import-substitutes. In addition, part of the additional income generated within the economy will be spent on imports; and exports by other producers may be encouraged by catalysis or cost reduction, or displaced by competition.

While data are not available for an empirical analysis of the net impact, the balance between these factors is likely to vary considerably between sectors.

- In the case of a strongly export-oriented investment in a labour-intensive sector, using few imported inputs, the net foreign exchange effect should be substantially positive (although extractive industries may be an exception, if natural resources are under-priced, as discussed below).
- In the case of non-tradeable services which are important inputs to the production process (e.g. telecommunications), the direct effect is likely to be substantially negative, but more than off-set by the catalytic benefits to other producers.
- In the case of non-tradeable consumer goods and services the net foreign exchange effect may be negative even without taking account of profit remittances. Examples include investments in soft-drinks bottling plants using imported concentrates, which compete mainly with established local producers; and fast-food restaurants using imported inputs.

Other benefits of FDI may also have indirect effects on net foreign exchange flows; and these are generally positive, though of uncertain magnitude. Such benefits include access to technology and to export markets. The former may be of limited value in the case of production of tradeable goods and non-tradeable consumption goods and services. Here, if the technology remains with the producing firm, the investor will be in a position to retain (most of) the benefits in the form of higher profits. This limitation will be strengthened to the extent that the protection of technology is strengthened by the TRIPs agreement (although this may also increase the volume of technology-bearing investment in these sectors). There may, however, be some indirect benefit in terms of human capital, to the extent that local staff are engaged in positions which entail the learning of transferable skills or technologies.

The potential for wider benefits from FDI-related technology transfer arises mainly in the production of non-tradeable goods and services which are used (directly or indirectly) as inputs by other producers (e.g. telecommunications and banking services). Here, the effect should be to reduce costs and increase the quality of services, with potentially significant benefits in terms of productivity and competitiveness. In key sectors, the benefits could be substantial.

The access to international markets which can be provided by FDI is potentially significant, but is in some respects a mixed blessing. This most commonly takes the form of intra-firm trading with other subsidiaries of the parent firm, or network trading with other multinational companies, as part of a much broader commercial relationship. The former exposes the investment to the risk of transfer pricing, while the latter may involve the local subsidiary in transactions designed primarily for the benefit of the two parent companies. In either case, there may be a substantial price to be paid by the host economy in terms of the prices received for exports.

Country data for rates of return on FDI in developing countries are limited. However, they suggest a typical rate of return (including reinvested profits) in the order of 20 per cent per annum, varying inversely (and very strongly) with income per capita, at least among middle-income countries – from around 10 per cent in upper-middle-income countries to around 30 per cent in lower-middle-income countries[24].

Aggregate data, however, suggest a substantially lower rate of return, at least for the major recipient countries[25]. Comparing stock data from UNCTAD (1995: Table II.2) with profit remittance figures from World Bank (1996) suggests an average rate of return for developing countries as a whole of around 5 per cent per annum.

However, three important points should be noted in comparing these two estimates.

- Firstly, it is not clear that the two sources are directly comparable.
- Secondly, while the figures for profit remittances in World Bank (1996) in principle include reinvested profits, it is not clear that this is the case for all countries, so that profit figures (and thus the rate of return) may

be under-stated.

- Thirdly, the concentration of FDI flows in recent years (34 per cent of the end-1993 stock represents flows during 1991-3) will tend to bias the rate of return downwards if there is a time-lag before full profitability is achieved (as might be expected, particularly for investment in new productive capacity).
- Fourthly, the 5 per cent figure is effectively a weighted average. Given the concentration of FDI in higher-income countries (where the rate of return is lowest), an equivalent figure based on the 10-30 per cent range might be in the order of 15 per cent rather than 20 per cent. Unfortunately, the country groupings used in the two sources are not directly comparable, except for Latin America and the Caribbean (where the implied rate of return in 1994 is 5.9 per cent).

Nonetheless, the UNCTAD figures would appear to imply substantially lower rates of return for the major FDI recipients than suggested by the country data. For the smaller recipients, however, this is not necessarily the case, as the heavy geographical concentration of FDI means that their contribution to the weighted average is relatively limited. It also seems unlikely that the minimum expected rate of return on FDI, in dollar terms, will be significantly lower in the long term than the rates available on lower-risk alternative investments, e.g. US prime lending and corporate bond rates (currently around 8 per cent per annum).

It should also be noted that data on profit remittances (and hence the above estimates of rates of return) may substantially understate the true rate of return on FDI, due to practices such as transfer pricing[26]. By way of illustration, if one-third of total profits were transferred through pricing arrangements rather than formal profit remittances, this would have been sufficient to reverse the inward net transfer on FDI in 1987-90 for developing countries as a whole. It is possible that liberalization of FDI regimes may shift the balance of incentives from transfer pricing to formal profit remittances, but it is unclear how far (or whether) transfer pricing has been or is likely to be reduced as a result.

While the immediate foreign exchange cost of FDI is limited to profit *repatriation*, this represents a substantially greater proportion of the overall return to investors than in the case of equity investments. While there is a vast range of experience between countries, the available data for 1984-91 suggest a median of 70 per cent of profits are repatriated, with an inter-quartile range of about 50-90 per cent.[27] Moreover, reinvested profits add to the stock of foreign-owned investments, increasing the base for future profit remittances.

Clearly, there is both a great deal of uncertainty about the true rate of return (and thus the long-term foreign-exchange cost) of FDI in developing countries, and considerable variation between countries. It is, however, apparent that the cost to the least attractive locations (primarily the smaller low-income countries) is likely to be high, relative both to more favourable markets and to alternative sources of funding. If rates of return in low-income countries are indeed in excess of 20 per cent per annum, the net economic benefits are likely to be limited or even negative, except where the net trade effects are most strongly positive.

By definition, inward net transfers on FDI can be sustained only as long as new capital inflows remain greater than profit remittances; and this means that annual inflows must be greater than the rate of profit remittance times the existing stock, and grow at the overall rate of return or faster. This may be feasible in fast-growing upper-middle-income countries; but, given the high overall rates of return, it is unlikely that this could be sustained over a prolonged period in most low-income countries, particularly where the existing stock is already substantial and/or economic growth is relatively slow.

It should also be noted that the division of profits between reinvestment and remittance is again likely to be procyclical, off-setting any countercyclical tendency in the overall level of profits. In times of economic stress, profits are likely to be lower, but a greater proportion of the total is likely to be repatriated rather than reinvested.

The danger of outward net transfers on FDI is most clearly illustrated by Sub-Saharan Africa. Here, profit remittances have exceeded net inflows of FDI in every year since at least 1984, generating a cumulative outward net transfer over the last decade in the order of $20bn – equivalent to 8 per cent of GNP, or around 20 per cent of the increase in the region's external debt over this period. Figures for 1970 and 1980 (-$662m and -$3,923m) suggest that this trend may have continued for considerably longer, and that the cumulative amount may be considerably greater[28]. The considerable increase in the outward net transfer between 1987-9 and 1990-93 (from $1.3bn per annum to $2.8bn per annum) also suggests that the situation is deteriorating further (World Bank 1991 and 1995f).

3.2.4 The evolving nature of equity investment

Equity investment is not a uniform process, but involves different types of transactions and different investors and recipients. The nature of the process has significant implications for the effect on the economy as a whole, and thus on poverty; and it can be expected to evolve systematically over time. This evolution therefore needs to be taken into account[29].

Equity investments can be divided broadly into privatizations, new issues by existing private companies, and the purchase of existing shares on stock exchanges. Within a particular market, the first can be expected to decline progressively over time as the process of privatization is completed. The balance between new equity issues and secondary market transactions is also likely to shift towards the latter, as the volume of existing shares increases (swelled by privatization issues). New issues can be divided between those by large "blue chip" companies, and those by small and medium-sized enterprises (SMEs). Currently, the former are overwhelmingly predominant in most emerging markets. It seems possible, at least, that SMEs will become more acceptable to external investors as confidence in emerging markets increases, information systems improve, and markets become larger and more liquid.

This suggests a transition in the composition of equity investments over time. Initially, the benefits will accrue primarily to the government (in the form of privatization proceeds) and to large companies (in the case of new issues). The economic effects of the latter may be limited, however, as the availability of external equity financing for very large companies has relatively little effect on their cost of capital and few benefits for the rest of the market (Claessens and Gooptu 1994). Over time, government receipts (and the associated fiscal benefits) will progressively disappear as privatization is completed, and secondary market transactions (which benefit mainly the sellers) become more important. On the positive side, the balance of new equity issues may shift towards smaller companies, for which the effect on the cost of equity capital is greater.

The nature of investors is also an important factor, as the behaviour of different investors varies significantly according to their motivation. Gooptu (1993) identifies domestic residents with overseas assets and other private foreign investors as "the dominant category of portfolio investors who are currently active in the major emerging markets of Latin America". Together with managed funds and foreign banks and brokerage firms, they are "active...primarily because of expectations of short-term returns and have been observed to move funds among different ESMs frequently".

The largest *potential* sources of funds, however, are institutional investors and non-resident nationals, who are more risk-averse, and motivated primarily by longer-term considerations. This suggests that there may be a shift in the nature of investors from the former, more volatile, group to the latter, increasing the stability of flows. However, if a substantial proportion of flight capital (an important element of the former) is to be attracted into the emerging markets, this suggests that the transition is likely to be relatively slow. This is an important assumption underlying optimistic projections of future flows.

3.2.5 Conclusion

The major increase in direct and portfolio investment in recent years has provided much-needed relief from the liquidity restraints of the 1980s for a number of large and mostly middle-income developing countries. In some sectors, it may also bring significant benefits in terms of overall productivity and competitiveness.

However, it is not clear that these flows will be sustained over the long term; and they will be increasingly off-set by the corresponding outflows. In the event of a sharp decline in such flows, a new balance of payments crisis could be precipitated; and the domination of D/PI (and other non-reschedulable debts) in developing countries' liabilities would seriously complicate the process of adjusting to such a crisis.

The concentration of these flows leaves all but the largest low-income countries almost entirely dependent on official financing, increasing their vulnerability to the expected decline in aid flows due to political and budgetary pressures. It is in any case unclear whether D/PI is an appropriate form of external financing for low-income countries in view of its potentially high foreign exchange cost over the long term. In some sectors, this cost may be justified by the benefits, particularly where the net effect on trade flows is substantially positive. In other sectors, however, the net impact is likely to be substantially negative.

3.3 Structural adjustment and domestic liberalization

Structural adjustment, in the present context, can be divided broadly into three components: trade reform; liberalization of policies towards foreign investment; and liberalization of domestic economic structures.

3.3.1 Trade reform

Trade liberalization has been a key component of structural adjustment programmes, encompassing the lowering of obstacles to both imports and exports. While substantial progress has been made in this direction by developing countries as a whole, there are considerable variations in the extent of such reforms between different countries and regions.

Dean et al (1994) review the experience of trade reform in 32 developing countries since 1985. The following is a summary of their general findings, on a regional basis.

- **East Asia** as a whole already had a relatively liberal trade regime in the mid-1980s. Since then, policies have focused on "real exchange rate depreciation, and direct inducements to exporters initially, with reduction in QRs and tariffs on imports of final goods later". By the early 1990s, all the countries considered except China and Vietnam had moved on to this second stage.
- In **Latin America**, "reductions in trade barriers have been very large and in some cases surprisingly rapid". This was the only region to have made large tariff cuts over the period considered. Incentives to exporters were also increased.
- In **South Asia** (apart from Sri Lanka, which already had a relatively liberal trade regime), some progress has been made in reducing QRs, although much less than in Latin America. Tariff reductions were limited until 1991, but then accelerated in India and Bangladesh, in parallel with foreign exchange reforms. Import barriers remain high, but "reform is now rapid and strong".
- In **Sub-Saharan Africa**, there has been some (incomplete) foreign exchange reform, and QRs have been reduced; but "there has been virtually no change in the level of tariffs", with reductions in some countries off-set by increases in others. "African trade reform has been

halted or reversed in many cases"; and overall there has been "little progress towards a liberalized trade regime".

This view of Sub-Saharan Africa is perhaps a little uncharitable. While the reduction in the overall level of tariffs was reduced only slightly (from 41.1 per cent to 37.6 per cent in the sample countries for which both pre- and post-reform data were available), the reduction in QRs implies a significant reduction in the overall level of protection. In five of the ten countries for which data are provided, QRs were actually or virtually eliminated; and in one other QR coverage was drastically reduced (from 100 per cent to less than 20 per cent). Only in Zaire (and possibly Côte d'Ivoire[30]) was QR coverage not significantly reduced. Post-reform, five out of ten Sub-Saharan Africa countries had QR coverage of less than 2 per cent, compared with five out of sixteen countries in other regions.

Progress was also made on the other components of the initial phase of trade reform: eleven of thirteen countries reduced tariff dispersion, and "at least four" reduced the number of tariff rates. This suggests that trade reform has been relatively slow, delaying the final phase (tariff reduction), but that significant progress has nonetheless been made on the earlier phases of tariffication and reducing dispersion.

An important factor limiting progress in reducing tariff levels is governments' dependence on them as a source of fiscal revenue. In East Asia and Latin America, Dean et al find this to have been of relatively limited importance, possibly reflecting the stronger potential tax base. In the poorer regions, where tax bases are weaker – South Asia and especially Sub-Saharan Africa – fiscal considerations appear to have been much more important, and those countries where fiscal dependence on tariffs was greatest generally made the least progress in tariff reduction.

The fiscal constraints on reducing export taxes and import tariffs in low-income countries are clearly considerable. In Sub-Saharan Africa, the latest available data show 25 out of 42 countries relying on taxes on international transactions for 30 per cent or more of total government revenues (excluding grants). In five cases[31], dependence on trade taxes was greater than 50 per cent. Moreover, those countries with the greatest dependency tended to have particularly low overall revenues: in 14 of the 25 countries where taxes on international transactions were more than 30 per cent of total revenues, overall revenue was less than 15 per cent of GDP, compared with only two the 17 countries which were less dependent (World Bank 1995a: Tables 7-6 and 7-

10).

In the South Asian low-income countries considered by Dean et al, import tariffs and duties were around 40 per cent of total revenues in Bangladesh and Pakistan in 1984, 30 per cent in India and 22 per cent in Sri Lanka. Of the twelve (middle-income) Latin American and East Asian countries considered[32], import tariffs and duties were 5 per cent or less of total revenues in 1984 in five cases, 11-17 per cent in four, and 22-29 per cent in the remaining three.

Other aspects of trade reform have also had a negative impact on public sector finances, particularly the general removal of export taxes in Sub-Saharan Africa, Latin America and East Asia; and the creation of fiscal incentives for exporters, particularly in South Asia.

3.3.2 Foreign investment regimes

As well as the external economic environment, the recent dramatic increase in D/PI has in part reflected a liberalization of regulatory regimes relating to FDI and international capital flows in developing countries, often undertaken as part of formal adjustment programmes. This typically entails some combination of removing or simplifying bureaucratic obstacles to investment; easing regulations such as restrictions on foreign ownership; increasing legal protection for investors (e.g. by forbidding expropriation, or providing for access to international arbitration); and removing restrictions on profit remittances and/or repatriation of capital.

In some cases, preferential tax treatment has also been given, in the form of tax credits and exemptions, tax holidays, reduction of duties, etc. While such policies have been included in structural adjustment programmes, the World Bank now advises against specific fiscal incentives for new foreign investors. Thus Bergsman and Shen (1995) argue strongly against fiscal incentives specifically directed towards FDI, which "have had little, if any, impact", "create distortions of tax regimes", discriminate against domestic and existing foreign investors, and create "complex and bureaucratic administrative procedures that encourage corruption". Instead, the Bank emphasizes the need to improve the general policy environment and reduce rates of corporate taxation for all investors.

Again, poor revenue performance, the weakness of the tax base and the importance of corporate taxation as a revenue source represent serious obstacles to progress in this direction for many low-income countries, particularly in Sub-Saharan Africa. Half of the 26 Sub-Saharan countries for which data are available depend on corporate taxation for more than 15 per cent of their total current revenue, four of them receiving 28-40 per cent of revenue from this source. The combination of corporate taxation and taxes on international transactions typically account for between 35 per cent and 60 per cent of total current revenue[33].

A particularly important manifestation of the liberalization of FDI regimes in developing countries is the establishment of export processing zones (EPZs). EPZs offer tax and regulatory advantages to (mainly foreign) investors, including duty-free access to imported inputs, provided that their output is exported, as a means of promoting exports and attracting FDI.

EPZs have proliferated in developing countries over the last 30 years: they now exist in at least 70 countries, with others in the process of establishment; and they account for around half of all FDI in developing countries (Romero 1995). Like FDI as a whole, however, investment in EPZs is heavily concentrated, with just twelve countries[34] accounting for 84 per cent of total EPZ employment (excluding China) (Johansson 1994).

While EPZs have generally been successful in attracting FDI in export production, they tend to limit its benefits to host countries. In particular, the tax concessions which are offered severely reduce the benefits to government finances; and the enclave nature of many EPZs limits forward and backward linkages with the rest of the economy.

Case-study evidence suggests the existence of demonstration, learning and catalytic effects in some of the more successful EPZs, although there has been little empirical attempt to evaluate their importance. Where such benefits do exist, they may depend substantially on atypical country-specific factors. The success of the Mauritius EPZ, for example, rested to a significant extent on the availability of substantial domestic financial capital for investment, from the booming sugar sector (which benefited from a large sugar quota in the EU market). As a result, domestic investment in the EPZ was significant from its inception; and a number of joint ventures established in the EPZ subsequently became fully locally-owned. This enhanced backward linkages, and facilitated demonstration effects, learning-by-doing, access to international markets and technology transfer.

Such benefits also have to be set against the costs of establishing and operating EPZs. As well as the opportunity cost of tax concessions, there may also be a direct financial cost to the government in raising the infrastructure to the level needed to attract foreign investors.

On balance, it seems likely that EPZs have had a significant effect in attracting additional FDI to the countries in which they operate. They may also have some positive effect on the host economy (although this will largely be limited to employment effects). Certainly, the rapid proliferation of EPZs would seem to confirm that this view is held by many developing country governments; and comparative growth performance is also consistent with this view, although causation is an open question (Johansson 1994).

However, there are two important caveats to this optimistic view.

- Firstly, investment in some of the more successful EPZs has been motivated at least partly by distortions emanating from developed country trade policies. Examples include Mauritius's under-utilised textiles quota in the EU market; the Dominican Republic's membership in the Caribbean Basin Initiative; and attempts by companies in the NIEs to circumvent restrictions on exports imposed by the US in the case of South East Asian EPZs. These factors have generally been highly country-specific in nature; and, to the extent that such distortions are reduced by globalization, the prospects for successful establishment of new EPZs are likely to be reduced.
- Secondly, benefits to each individual host country do not necessarily translate into benefits for developing countries (or even for countries with EPZs) as a whole, but will depend on the additionality of the FDI which is attracted. From a broader perspective, the benefits to the host country of FDI in an EPZ are partly off-set by the loss of the same investments in the countries to which they would otherwise have gone. This issue is discussed later.

3.3.3 Domestic liberalization

Domestic economic reform is a multifaceted process, whose emphasis and rate of progress varies significantly between individual countries. Broadly, this entails the establishment (or attempts to establish) a sound macroeconomic policy framework, with small budget and balance of payments deficits, and realistic interest and exchange rates; and a shift in economic structures towards a deregulated, enterprise-friendly system, with a small but efficient state sector.

Such reforms interact with the more outward-oriented reforms in a number of ways:
- domestic and external liberalization policies are typically combined in overall structural adjustment packages;
- external financing constraints are central to the objectives of the overall adjustment process, which aims primarily to generate economic growth compatible with a sustainable external balance;
- domestic liberalization policies are intended to increase economic efficiency and international competitiveness, as a means of attracting foreign investment and promoting exports;
- the greater opening of the economy increases its sensitivity to external economic developments, and thus requires a greater responsiveness of macroeconomic policy-making; and
- as noted above, privatization is often an important element of D/PI.

In consequence, domestic and external liberalization policies are not merely implemented together for institutional reasons. As their overall impact is dependent on their interaction, they are to a great extent mutually dependent for their success.

As with trade and FDI reform, the implementation of domestic liberalization policies has been very variable. Generally, Latin America and East and South East Asia are seen as having liberalized with particular vigour, and South Asia and Sub-Saharan Africa as having reformed more slowly and often erratically. There is, however, a substantial degree of variation within each of these groups.

3.3.4 Implementation of reforms and economic performance

While the purpose of structural adjustment is to generate economic growth consistent with external sustainability, its success in doing so has been mixed. The larger and more industrialised middle-income countries (notably in Latin America) have improved their economic performance substantially since the late 1980s; and this has been attributed in large part to the lagged effect of their economic reform programmes.

However, the improvement in economic performance should not be overstated. Real GNP per capita in 1994 remained below its 1980 level in 13 of the 18 countries for which data are available, representing 85 per cent of the total population. Even if recent growth rates were sustained indefinitely, six countries (68 per cent of population) would not regain their 1980 position in the next ten years. Moreover, per capita growth in 1990-94 remained slower than in the 1970s in ten countries (76 per cent of population), and by a margin of at least 1 per cent in all but one case. Only Chile had regained its growth trajectory of the 1970s, while ten countries (73 per cent of population) remained at least 30 per cent behind. In Brazil, Ecuador and Paraguay, growth was at least 5 per cent per annum slower than in the 1970s, and GDP per capita in 1994 remained 55-60 per cent lower than it would have been if 1970s growth rates had been sustained[35].

Sub-Saharan Africa has yet to experience any substantial recovery. Only nine of the 39 countries for which data are available (representing 11 per cent of total population) had positive per capita growth between 1990 and 1994, while thirteen (21 per cent of population) faced negative per capita growth of at least 3 per cent per annum. Of 34 countries for which data are available from 1980, real GNP per capita remained below the 1980 level in 27 (accounting for 95 per cent of population), and in many cases the shortfall was considerable – in the order of 40-50 per cent in Côte d'Ivoire, Djibouti, Gabon, Sao Tome and Principe and Togo. In 24 of the 34 countries, representing 63 per cent of population, the growth rate fell between 1985-90 and 1990-94[36].

A number of World Bank studies have put forward econometric evidence that structural adjustment has had a favourable impact on economic growth (e.g. World Bank 1988 and 1990a, de Melo et al 1991). However, closer scrutiny suggests that these results are driven mainly by the performance of a group of relatively large, rich and industrialised countries which are over-represented among countries defined as "intensively adjusting", leaving the effects on smaller, poorer countries more dependent on primary commodities open to question (Woodward 1992, Volume I Chapter 3 and Annex II). While the Bank has also sought to demonstrate a positive effect of structural adjustment specifically in Sub-Saharan Africa (World Bank 1994a), this analysis is based on macroeconomic rather than structural policy variables, and is subject to some methodological criticisms (Mosley and Weeks 1995, Woodward 1995a).

Casual observation clearly confirms that structural adjustment programmes have not been universally successful in improving economic performance in Sub-Saharan Africa. Among the countries with substantially negative per capita growth in 1990-94 are a number with long records of IMF- and World Bank-supported structural adjustment (e.g. Kenya, Côte d'Ivoire and Malawi). Proponents of adjustment generally blame such instances of weak performance in "adjusting" countries largely on weak implementation of adjustment policies"; and Mosley et al (1991) seek to provide econometric evidence for this proposition for a sample of developing countries with structural adjustment programmes. However, this analysis is subject to a number of serious methodological problems, which appear to invalidate its results (Woodward 1992, ibid).

Nonetheless, it is clearly true that the implementation of adjustment programmes in Sub-Saharan Africa has in general been significantly slower and less consistent than in other regions – as demonstrated by the discussion of trade reform above. However, this raises the question of *why* implementation has been so poor. This may be explained partly by political impediments, such as the difficulty of overcoming entrenched interests, the lack of mandate for sweeping reforms in non-representative political systems, etc. However, two other constraints are also of critical importance.

- Firstly, most Sub-Saharan governments face acute fiscal constraints and limited tax bases; and low and falling income levels in the economy as a whole limit the scope for raising additional revenues. This is a serious impediment to the implementation of adjustment measures which entail a loss of government revenue (e.g. reductions in import tariffs, export taxes and corporate tax rates, and increasing producer prices for agricultural produce).

- Secondly, administrative capacity is in many cases exceptionally weak, partly as a result of liquidity constraints (which have led to low civil service salaries, and thus shortages of highly-qualified staff, demotivation, absenteeism, corruption, etc.). Low general levels of education are also an important contributory factor in many cases. The considerable extent and complexity of reform measures which are necessary means that effective design and implementation is critically dependent on administrative capacity.

These constraints interact to a considerable extent. Not only is weak administrative capacity largely caused by the inadequacy of government revenues, it also represents a major obstacle to strengthening the resource base, by undermining the effectiveness of tax collection.

Even to the extent that liberalization policies are implemented, it is by no means clear that they are likely to be as effective in improving economic performance in Sub-Saharan countries as, for example, in Latin America. Low educational standards, poor infrastructure, weak industrial structures, unintegrated markets and weak supply responses can be expected to weaken the potential benefits considerably. The perception that liberalization will bring few benefits may also contribute to weak implementation.

3.3.5 Conclusion

Substantial progress has been made towards liberalization in developing countries over the last 10-15 years, not least in trade reform and FDI regimes. However, the extent and pace of liberalization has varied considerably between regions, being greatest in Latin America, and least in Sub-Saharan Africa. Slow progress in the latter region, in particular, largely reflects political factors, resource constraints and weak administrative capacity.

After the "lost decade" of the 1980s, it seems likely that structural adjustment policies have contributed to faster economic growth in Latin America in the first half of the 1990s. However, recent growth rates will need to continue for a considerable time (and in some cases to be increased substantially) if much of the region is to regain its previous growth trajectory. In Sub-Saharan Africa, there is no sign of such a recovery, largely because of the constraints on the implementation of liberalization policies, and on the responsiveness of the economy to them.

3.4 Globalization, liberalization and competition between developing countries

The positive view of liberalization and globalization largely rests on the view that export promotion and the attraction of D/PI are beneficial to economic growth (and thus to poverty reduction); and that this process can be stimulated by changes in economic policies. At the individual country level, a fairly strong case can be made for this view: a number of countries clearly have stimulated economic growth through policies aimed at promoting exports and foreign investment, and have thereby achieved a substantial reduction in poverty (although there is clearly a need to consider to what extent this experience can be extrapolated to other countries).

However, the validity of this view is less clear-cut at the global level, because of the interaction and interdependence of developing economies. If one country increases its exports, this will have some effect on the market for that export – for example by depressing international prices in the case of primary commodities, or by displacing exports from other sources or provoking a protectionist response in importing countries in the case of manufactured goods. Similarly, by attracting an investor to open a factory in its own country, a government may effectively be preventing its establishment in another country.

In effect, export promotion and the attraction of foreign investment are, to a greater or lesser extent, competitive; and the overall effect of a general shift in developing countries' economic policies in favour of exports or foreign investment may therefore be substantially smaller than the apparent effect implied by the experiences of individual countries. If the policies which are implemented have some negative social or economic impact, the net effect on the welfare of developing countries as a whole may be negative, even though the private costs and benefits of the policies to each individual country are such as to persuade it to implement them. In short, export promotion and the attraction of FDI may be a prisoner's dilemma.

3.4.1 Export promotion

This argument is made most frequently in the context of commodity exports, in the form of the "fallacy of composition" critique. For many primary commodities the price elasticity of demand is less than one, so that a general increase in supply results in a decline in the revenues received by exporters as a whole. Where production is also dominated by developing countries, the general application in these countries of policies directed towards general export promotion may be counterproductive: producing countries as a whole may divert resources away from other sectors to increase production, but receive less foreign exchange as a result[37].

This problem may be compounded by two other factors (Woodward 1992):

- general export promotion policies which rely on market mechanisms (e.g. devaluation) may in practice have a disproportionate effect on traditional primary commodity exports; and

- when a developing country's terms of trade deteriorate, the policy response advocated by the international financial institutions entails an intensification of export promotion policies which raises the risk of a vicious circle of increasing production and declining prices.

The fallacy of composition argument has been put forward as a possible explanation of the extreme weakness of commodity prices from the early 1980s until the early 1990s (e.g. Woodward 1992). The World Bank (1994c), however, contends that this problem applies, if at all, only to a few products, such as coffee and cocoa. However, this analysis applies only to Sub-Saharan Africa, and ignores production in Asia and the Western Hemisphere. Moreover, coffee and cocoa are critically important from the perspective of Sub-Saharan Africa.

A simulation by Goldin et al (1993) provides substantial support for the fallacy of composition argument in the context of export tax reduction. They find that a general 25 per cent reduction in developing countries' export taxes from their 1993 level would give rise to a reduction in world prices for coffee and cocoa in the order of 3-5 per cent. In the absence of increased wage flexibility, Africa's GDP would be reduced by around 2 per cent by 2002; and tax revenues by $110m (in 1985 prices). The reduction or elimination of export taxes is a standard component of orthodox trade reform, and, while data are patchy, most Sub-Saharan countries have already reduced them substantially since 1980 (World Bank 1995a: Table 7-12).

The fallacy of composition argument has also been put forward in the case of manufactured exports (particularly labour-intensive products such as textiles and leather goods). In this context, it is argued that developing countries are effectively competing for a developed country market of finite size; and that a substantial increase in their overall export volumes would result in a greater reduction in price (and hence a loss in overall revenue) and/or a protectionist response. Historically, there has been some basis for this view – the MFA being a clear illustration. There is also some evidence of such an effect during the 1980s (Faini et al 1989), particularly in response to exports from the NIEs and Latin America.

More recently, the problem of protectionist responses appears to have been eased somewhat, China having escaped more freely than might have been expected; and the abolition of VERs under the Uruguay Round removes one of the most commonly used mechanisms. Nonetheless, the safeguard provisions under the Uruguay Round agreements leave substantial scope for protectionist responses; the possibility of a price effect clearly remains even in the absence of such responses; and the size of developed country markets for labour-intensive manufactured products remains a potentially important constraint.

3.4.2 Foreign direct investment

The competitive nature of policy changes aimed at attracting FDI was acknowledged in a recent symposium on the subject, which highlighted "increasingly stiff competition for the limited amount of FDI worldwide" (Bachmann and Kwaku 1994: vii). As well as economic policies (which are discussed later), a number of other factors were seen as important in attracting FDI flows. These included, in order of importance, political stability; domestic and export markets; an equitable and efficient legal system; adequate physical and human infrastructure; a well-functioning and efficient banking and financial system; a large, active and efficient private sector; and "quality of life, including personal safety".

Bergsman and Shen (1995) emphasize that low labour costs are no longer sufficient to attract FDI, as investors are interested primarily in productivity, and "only in sites where they can produce to international standards of quality and price". Among the specific factors they identify as necessary to promote

FDI are:
- a stable macroeconomic environment (including an appropriately valued exchange rate);
- "rapid, sustained economic growth" and "strong, consistent growth in demand for consumer goods and services";
- sustained trade reform (and non-bureaucratic customs procedures) and domestic liberalization;
- adequate legal protection for investors, including well-functioning legal systems;
- "general education, industrial skill training and managerial discipline";
- "access to quality supplies of parts, components, and supporting services", with upstream and downstream linkages; and
- conditions that facilitate "just-in-time" delivery.

Against this background, it is entirely predictable that FDI flows have been concentrated in middle-income countries and larger Low Income Countries (LICs) such as India and China, as these score much more highly on most (if not all) of these criteria than most smaller LICs. The conspicuous absence of these conditions in most Sub-Saharan (and other smaller low-income) countries inevitably sets them at a serious disadvantage in competing with higher-income countries. Neither is this an unfortunate coincidence: most of the factors listed are systematically related to overall income levels (e.g. domestic markets), levels of industrialization and development (e.g. physical infrastructure, potential for upstream and downstream linkages, well-functioning legal systems, efficiency of the financial sector, political stability) and/or resource availability (e.g. raw materials, educated labour force).

While the policy environment may also be a significant factor, its importance lies primarily in its contribution to macroeconomic stability and sustained demand growth. The World Bank (1995f: 162) argues that "The meagre FDI flows to non-oil-producing countries in Sub-Saharan Africa can be explained in part by the small domestic markets in most of these economies, civil strife and political instability, and the lack of well-developed indigenous suppliers networks and modern infrastructure".

On a more optimistic note, Bachmann and Kwaku (1994) observe that income per capita in Sub-Saharan Africa now is broadly similar to that of some rapidly-growing East and South East Asian countries prior to their economic "take-off". However, it seems dangerous to extrapolate from this observation to a possible take-off in Sub-Saharan Africa.

- There is more to development than per capita income; and it is less clear that Sub-Saharan Africa compares so favourably with pre-take-off Asia in terms of, for example, infrastructure and human capital. Another important distinction is the debt overhang, which is extremely serious in many Sub-Saharan Africa countries, but did not exist in East and South East Asia.
- In the context of a competitive model of development, it is not the *absolute* but the *relative* level of development which matters to economic performance; and the very fact that East and South East Asia (and Latin America) have gone before means that Sub-Saharan Africa's relative position (and therefore its ability to compete) is worse.
- The predominance of structural adjustment and liberalization as a paradigm of development policy, and some aspects of the Uruguay Round have effectively foreclosed some parts of the strategies pursued by the NIEs to achieve development, particularly in respect of trade policy and FDI regimes.

Thus the ability of Sub-Saharan countries to attract FDI is severely impaired by a number of factors which are largely or wholly beyond their control, at least in the short term. This intensifies the changes necessary in areas *within* governmental control (especially policies directly related to FDI) if FDI is to be attracted. The effort required is all the greater because these policies come well down the list of investors' priorities – fifth in Bachmann and Kwaku's (1994) prioritized listing of factors influencing FDI decisions. Appropriate labour policies (training, productivity, industrial relations and labour costs) featured still later in the list, also after physical and human infrastructure.

Among such policies, the order of priority given was:
(1)   ability to acquire full or majority ownership in the local company;
(2)   investment guarantees;
(3)   absence of exchange controls;
(4)   liberal policies for the employment of expatriate staff;
(5)   tax incentives.

Excluding their effects on FDI, some of these policies have potentially significant costs in social, economic or developmental terms. They (1) may tend to reduce local ownership and thus limit forward and backward linkages (cf. the Mauritius EPZ, as discussed above); (4) may reduce local employment, particularly in senior and technical positions, thus limiting human capital development; and (2) and (5) have fiscal costs, especially if general corporate taxation is reduced rather than exempting FDI[38].

There is also a long time-lag between policy changes and FDI flows, in the order of 6-8 years even in more favoured regions such as Southern Europe and South East Asia (Bachmann and Kwaku 1994). These time-lags are likely to be substantially longer in Sub-Sahara and other LICs, because of the prevalence of other negative factors and perceptions. Even if countries are successful in attracting FDI, there is likely to be a long gap between incurring the costs of competing and enjoying the spoils of winning.

A particular area of concern, though one of indirect relevance to the present paper, is the environmental implications of competition for FDI. The need to make conditions conducive to foreign investors may provide a strong incentive for governments to allow laxer environmental regulations (e.g. in the case of manufacturing industry) or to under-price natural resources (e.g. in mineral production and forestry). The latter sectors have been of particular importance in FDI to many smaller low-income countries, particularly in Sub-Saharan Africa. Increased pollution could have a significant impact on living standards in the short and medium term, and under-pricing of natural resources on economic development in the long term.

In short, the need to compete for FDI flows tends to shift the balance of advantage from host countries to investors; and this effect is likely to be most marked in those countries where non-policy factors are most adverse – primarily smaller, economically weak countries with poor infrastructure, low human capital and/or political instability.

3.4.3 Portfolio investment

In the case of equity investment, there is clearly a significant element of competition between the major recipient countries. As noted above, Gooptu (1993) identifies the major sources of equity flows to emerging markets as motivated primarily by short-term returns, and moving funds frequently between emerging markets. Thus Howell and Cozzini (1992)[39] contend that there was an active shift of funds from Latin America to East Asia during 1991, in response to changes in relative rates of return. In effect, the success of East Asia in attracting equity investment at this time occurred partly at the expense of Latin America.

As discussed earlier, the composition of equity flows may shift progressively towards more committed and stable sources over time. Nonetheless, initial investment decisions will still be as much about which emerging market to invest in as whether to invest in an emerging market at all, leaving a significant degree of competition between markets.

In parallel with this competition, there is also a process of contagion. While this is most conspicuous as a negative phenomenon (as when the Mexican crisis of December 1994 triggered a general sharp decline in foreign investment in emerging markets), it has also operated in a positive direction. The rapid increase in equity flows to emerging markets in recent years was at least partly prompted by the high rates of return secured in the more established emerging stock markets. Once such contagion, whether positive or negative, is established, it becomes self-perpetuating, as the inflow (or outflow) of funds generates higher (or lower) rates of return.

In some respects, competition for equity investment is less potentially damaging than competition for limited export markets. The factors which favour equity investment – particularly political and macroeconomic stability – are broadly favourable to the country concerned; and there is much less use of (or scope for) policies geared specifically to attracting equity investment than in the case of FDI. Competitive efforts to improve the environment for equity investment in these respects are therefore, on the whole, beneficial rather than harmful. Nonetheless, there are some more specific policies (e.g. reducing rates of corporate taxation, labour market liberalization, etc.) which may have significant economic or welfare costs, excluding their potential effects on financial flows and investment. There may also be some social costs entailed in the dynamic process of achieving macroeconomic stability.

3.4.4 Conclusion

To a great extent, developing countries have to compete for the fruits of globalization (exports and D/PI); and this competition very largely takes the form of liberalization and other, more specific, economic policies. This competition can be costly, depressing the prices received for exports, limiting the developmental benefits of FDI for host countries and reducing tax revenues; and it is almost inevitable that those least able to compete will lose. The key factors which inhibit effective competition – social and political instability, weak government revenues and tax bases, lack of administrative capacity, inadequate physical, economic and human infrastructure, etc. – are generally most acute in smaller and poorer countries.

3.5 Regional linkages and spill-overs

In parallel with the process of globalization, there has been a substantial increase – initially *de facto*, but increasingly *de jure* – in economic regionalism. This has taken three distinct forms:

- informal linkages occurring through market forces – for example the regional focus of FDI by Japanese firms in response to rising domestic labour costs, and the concentration of Latin American exports on the US market;
- formal regional groupings of developing countries, such as ASEAN and Southern Cone Common Market (MERCOSUR), aimed at increasing intra-regional trade through preferential market access and/or promoting other economic linkages; and
- regionally-based preferential trade arrangements between developed and developing countries, such as North American Free Trade Agreement (NAFTA) and (prospectively) Asia Pacific Economic Cooperation (APEC).

These factors provide an additional important dimension to the effects of globalization. The linkages between developing countries can be expected to allow some countries which might otherwise gain relatively little from the process (e.g. Bolivia, Paraguay, Myanmar, Cambodia) to gain indirectly from the contagion of the benefits to their neighbours. The linkages with developed countries will tend to skew the benefits of increased FDI and trade opportunities arising from globalization towards those countries which benefit from them.

In addition, regional *perceptions* are a critically important factor. In part, this may relate to the implicit guarantee of a major developed country's regional interests (particularly the US in Latin America). In part, it unquestionably operates on a less rational level: a country in South East Asia may be perceived as being a potential Malaysia; one in Sub-Saharan Africa as a potential Somalia. Being in Latin America has moved from being a disadvantage to being clearly advantageous, and even the Mexican crisis appears to have done little to dent the new-found enthusiasm for the region.

In all of these dimensions, Sub-Saharan Africa is at a disadvantage relative to other developing regions. Informal linkages mainly relate to past colonial ties with European countries, and are limited primarily to aid flows rather than commercial transactions. Regional trade arrangements have generally had a minimal impact in the region (Woodward 1993); and preferential trade arrangements with developed countries are limited to the Lomé Convention and GSP preferences, which have brought few benefits (Harrold 1995) and will be further eroded by the Uruguay Round. Perceptions of the region are also singularly negative. Thus Bachmann and Kwaku (1994: viii) found that, to attract FDI, African countries needed to overcome a "largely unsubstantiated but deep seated prejudice", quite apart from substantive economic policy changes.

3.6 Macroeconomic effects of globalization and liberalization

The most important channel through which changes in the international economy are transmitted to the household level is through their effect on macroeconomic variables, and the economic policy changes associated with these effects. This occurs primarily in two dimensions: effects on the balance of payments (and thus on the exchange rate); and effects on the fiscal balance (and thus on government spending, taxation and/or monetary policy).

3.6.1 Foreign exchange effects

In the context of G/L, a country's balance of payments, and thus its exchange rate, are affected primarily by its own and other countries' trade policies, and by the size and nature of external financing flows. These effects will vary substantially between countries and over time, and will often operate in conflicting directions.

Trade reform within a particular country can be expected, other things being equal, to worsen the balance of payments current account; and this requires a strengthening of policies designed to achieve a balance of payments improvement (primarily devaluation). Such a linkage is often made directly in adjustment programmes. Conversely, other countries' trade reform measures should help to increase export opportunities, and thus foreign exchange earnings. This may be used to allow slower import reduction (e.g. through slower devaluation), or to increase payments on external liabilities.

To the extent that the fallacy of composition problem is encountered (whether for primary commodities or manufactured goods), this can be expected to have a negative impact on foreign exchange earnings. Not only do export revenues for the goods affected decline, but resources may be taken away from the production of other exports and import substitutes, thus compounding the effect.

Renewed capital flows, in the form of D/PI, also increase a country's import (and/or debt-servicing) capacity, although this effect may be substantially less than the amount of the inflow. In the case of FDI in new productive capacity, part of the investment may be in the form of imported equipment, or other inputs which are paid for in foreign exchange, which reduces the amount available for other imports. In the case of secondary market equity investment and bond sales, the capital inflow is received by the original owner of the equity or bonds. This may be invested externally, or spent on imported consumer goods, in which case the beneficial impact on the domestic economy will be limited. In the case of privatization and other new issues of equity, however, the foreign exchange leakages are likely to be more limited.

Where D/PI inflows are artificially inflated by stock adjustments by investors, privatizations, etc, there is a risk that the resulting exchange rate appreciation will be excessive, leading to over-valuation. This will reduce competitiveness, possibly quite severely; and this may result in a subsequent need for adjustment. The latter may weaken confidence, and thus reduce future foreign (and domestic) investment.

Where the net foreign exchange effect of FDI is increasingly negative over the long term, this will progressively off-set and ultimately reverse the initial positive impact thereby, limiting the resources available for imports. There is also a risk of a general outflow of equity investment in a particular country, in response to deteriorating economic conditions, external shocks, political factors or market perceptions. This could precipitate a major balance of payments crisis (and associated macroeconomic adjustment), particularly if it coincided with other adverse developments. As noted earlier, the increasing predominance of non-reschedulable liabilities, particularly in middle-income countries, is likely to make the adjustment process in such circumstances more difficult than would otherwise be the case. This might also be further compounded by the procyclical nature of FDI flows.

Clearly, there is no such thing as a "typical" country. However, the case of Mexico serves to illustrate the processes described above. An account of Mexico's experience, and the effects of this experience on income distribution and poverty, is presented in Ms. Correa's paper in this volume entitled *Mexico's financial crisis and its effects on income distribution and poverty.*

The various balance of payments effects of G/L operate in different directions, and are phased differently over time. Accordingly, the nature of the impact will vary considerably between countries, both in the short term and the long term, according to the sequencing and relative importance of the different components.

In **Latin America and the middle-income countries of East Asia**, trade reforms are well advanced, and their foreign exchange effect has largely occurred already. The foreign exchange impact associated with changes in other countries' trade policies has as yet been limited, and, because of the phasing of the Uruguay Round commitments (particularly on agriculture and the MFA), will be felt mainly in 5-10 years' time. The effect of D/PI flows has probably peaked; and, while it is likely to continue over the medium-term, it will be progressively off-set by profit remittances with net transfers ultimately turning negative.

Thus the overall effect of G/L is likely to remain positive for the next ten years or so, though with the balance of benefits shifting from D/PI flows to increased export revenues. Thereafter, however, in the absence of substantial further trade liberalization in the developed countries, increasing profit remittances on portfolio and especially direct investment can be expected to turn the net foreign exchange effect increasingly negative. The ability of the economies to bear this additional cost will depend heavily on the extent to which D/PI has contributed to the development of the indigenous economy rather than competing with it. In the worst-case scenario, increasing foreign exchange pressure could contribute to a renewed balance of payments crisis, spread through the region by contagion effects.

At the other extreme, in **Sub-Saharan Africa**, the outlook is more consistently negative. The trade reform effect will occur as and when substantial trade liberalization occurs; but it is by no means clear that this can be expected in the near future because of fiscal constraints. As for other countries with access to preferential trade arrangements, the net effects of the Uruguay Round are likely to be negative, again coming into effect mainly in 5-10 years' time. There is also a serious risk that net export earnings will be further diminished by the fallacy of composition problem.

As noted earlier, net transfers on FDI are already substantially negative for Sub-Saharan Africa; and while this could be reversed by a renewed inflow, there is little sign of this at present. In view of the obstacles to the region in competing effectively for FDI flows, it is more likely that its current high level of dependence on aid flows will continue, which implies severe and tightening external financing constraints.

3.6.2 Government finances

As well as the effect on the balance of payments, G/L has a potentially important impact on both government revenues and government borrowing. Where this impact is negative, it can be expected to prompt a reduction in government expenditure and/or increases in taxes which are relatively unconstrained by the G/L process (e.g. taxes on consumption).

On the revenue side, trade reform has a direct effect, through the reduction of import tariffs and duties and export taxes. In the initial stages, however, it may be neutral (e.g. reducing the number or narrowing the range of tariff rates), or even generate additional revenues (converting QRs into tariffs). Similarly, any reduction in taxes or extension of tax concessions to foreign investors (or to export producers) is likely to reduce tax revenues, unless the additional transactions generated are enough to off-set the reduction in average tax rates. Such losses may be off-set by tax reform programmes, which aim to broaden the tax base; but in general these have been slow to materialise.

Most Sub-Saharan African countries have broadly completed the revenue-increasing component of trade reform (tariffication), and many have gone some way towards the revenue neutral component (simplification and narrowing the range of rates). Significant further progress would entail substantial revenue losses which could constrain the reform process. In general, South Asian countries (apart from Sri Lanka) are passing through the revenue-reducing stage now, as is China, while most Latin American and South East Asian countries have largely completed this process.

On the borrowing side, the shift towards D/PI represents a shift from financing directed primarily to the public sector to financing directed entirely to the private sector (with the exception of privatizations). This limits the external financing available to the government to official flows. These are generally either tied to specific investment projects (which may or may not reflect the needs and priorities of the recipient country) or are subject to strict policy conditionality. In the case of project finance, the requirement to provide an element of domestic funding may absorb the limited domestic resources available for capital spending, and thus virtually eliminate the discretion of the government in investment decisions[40].

The result is a significant tightening of the fiscal constraints facing governments, unless and until the tax base can be broadened through tax reform. In low-income countries, the scope for this may be limited, both by relatively low levels of income and consumption, and by limited administrative and enforcement capacity. The fiscal constraint is further tightened by the limited scope for non-bank domestic financing in most LICs; and by the need to keep inflation (and thus inflationary financing of the budget deficit) low, in order to attract D/PI (inflation control would in any case be desirable from a macroeconomic perspective).

In countries where the government's revenue base is relatively strong, this tighter fiscal discipline is arguably not unhelpful. In many low-income countries, however, this premise is clearly not fulfilled. In sixteen countries in Sub-Saharan Africa, government revenues (excluding grants) represent less than 15 per cent of GDP; and in the great majority of these countries as noted earlier, taxes on international transactions represent a particularly important source of revenue. This implies that domestic trade liberalization (in the form of tariff reductions) can be achieved only at the expense of exacerbating an already serious shortage of government resources. Essentially the same argument applies to reductions in general rates of corporate taxation, which are also a critically important revenue source in many countries (although there is less correlation with the overall fiscal situation).

Moreover, the trend in government revenues in Sub-Saharan Africa has been strongly downwards in recent years, having declined from 21.3 per cent of GDP in 1991 to 18.2 per cent in 1993. Coupled with negative per capita growth, this represents a fall of 18 per cent in real revenue per capita in just two years, to its lowest level for at least a decade (based on data from World Bank 1995a). The subject of government revenues in Africa, as well as in Latin America, is further examined in Mr. Mehrotra's paper on *Domestic liberalization policies and public finance: poverty implications* in this book.

To the extent that government revenues and the potential for external borrowing are further reduced by G/L, the effect will be some combination of a reduction in government recurrent expenditure, an increase in real interest rates, and an increase in inflationary financing of the fiscal deficit.

3.6.3 Conclusion

The effects of G/L on the balance of payments and on government finances are a critical component of its effects on poverty. In countries which are well-advanced in the process of liberalization, and likely to benefit from globalization, the fiscal effect is likely to be reflected mainly in increased fiscal discipline. While this may be a constraint on social expenditure, it should be broadly beneficial to economic performance; and, if economic growth is sustained, real expenditure per capita should still increase. The balance of payments effect should also be positive over the next ten years, but there is a risk that it will turn increasingly negative thereafter.

In Sub-Saharan Africa, the picture is once again less optimistic. The balance of payments effect is more consistently negative; and the potential fiscal effect will be a major constraint to trade liberalization, and may contribute to a further reduction in expenditure, increased interest rates and/or faster inflation.

3.7 Globalization, liberalization and development: an overview

From the above discussion, it seems likely that the overall impact of G/L on the economic prospects for developing countries *as a whole* is likely to be mildly positive over the medium-term. Trade liberalization under the Uruguay Round is expected to bring significant overall benefits (although not immediately); increases in D/PI have provided a renewal of capital flows, bringing a much-needed relaxation of liquidity constraints on investment and economic growth; and domestic liberalization and opening under structural adjustment programmes appear to have allowed an improvement in economic performance in many of the countries where they have been implemented.

However, this overall pattern conceals four critical points which could seriously undermine the apparent benefits, as summarised below.

3.7.1 Limitations to the benefits to developing countries

The first problem with the optimistic view outlined above is that **the benefits of each component of G/L are heavily concentrated in a relatively small group of countries**; and the type of economies concerned is essentially similar in all cases – larger, richer and more industrialised economies (LRIEs). The residual of smaller, poorer and more commodity-dependent economies (SPCEs) appear to face limited benefits, or even net costs, from the effects of the Uruguay Round; with one or two minor exceptions, they have no access to portfolio investment, and have mostly received limited FDI flows; and the track record of structural adjustment programmes in these countries has – again with one or two exceptions – been very poor. For these countries, it is difficult to escape the conclusion that the overall economic impact of G/L is likely to be negative.

Secondly, while there are highly visible benefits to the LRIEs, these are **off-set by potentially important, but less obvious, costs**. In the case of trade, the benefits of increased access to export markets in the long term are off-set by the short term costs of adjustment to the change in incentives – particularly the consumption forgone to finance investment, and the risk of frictional unemployment in the adjustment process. (A similar process is likely in the case of structural adjustment; but, in Latin America and East Asia at least, the greatest adjustment costs have probably already been incurred.) In the case of D/PI, the short-term benefits of increased inflows are off-set by longer-term costs in the form of the high cost of capital entailed.

These costs and benefits are to some extent complementary: the inflow of D/PI will off-set the need to reduce consumption to finance productive investment; and the benefits of increased export revenues will off-set the long-term cost of D/PI. However, the balance between the positive and negative elements in each case is unclear, and is likely to vary substantially between individual countries. Securing a positive balance over the long term is likely to require substantial further trade liberalization by the developed countries.

Thirdly, there are additional costs associated with the **competition between developing countries to secure the benefits of G/L**, through export promotion and efforts to attract D/PI flows. These may well be substantial, but are obscured in country-level analyses. These effects are likely to have the greatest impact on those countries least able to compete – again, primarily the smaller, poorer and more commodity-dependent countries.

The fourth caveat, from a poverty perspective, relates to the **distribution of the costs and benefits between different income levels**. This will, to a great extent, be determined by the economic policies which are necessary to secure the potential benefits of G/L, or which are prompted by its economic effects. If these policies make the income distribution more unequal, it cannot be assumed that a positive net impact on the economy will necessarily be translated into a reduction in poverty. Again, this may vary substantially, both between countries and over time.

Since the LRIEs account for around 70 per cent of total poverty in developing countries (excluding Europe and the former Soviet Union), any reduction in poverty here would probably be translated into an overall reduction in global poverty, notwithstanding any negative impact on the SPCEs. However, this depends crucially on the effects on China and especially India: According to one estimate India represents 30-50 per cent of overall poverty in developing countries, China 10-20 per cent, and the other LRIEs a further 10-20 per cent (in each case depending on the poverty-line used)[41].

Nonetheless, the SPCEs represent a substantial proportion – around 30 per cent – of developing-country poverty, 16-24 per cent of this being in Sub-Saharan Africa (again depending on the poverty-line used). If G/L indeed has a negative impact on poverty in these countries, this would therefore have a material effect on the rate of reduction of overall poverty.

3.7.2 The global division of labour: the World Development Report scenario

The 1995 World Development Report (World Bank 1995g) presents an optimistic "convergent" scenario, together with a more pessimistic "divergent" scenario. Even the former represents a remarkably slow reduction in the degree of inequality in the world economy.

Diwan and Revenga (1995) offer a regional interpretation of the "convergent" scenario. This envisages an orderly progression up the production ladder by different regions. The industrial countries move into the production of high-technology goods and services; the transition economies, East Asia and Latin America develop their medium- and high-technology sectors, Latin America also "extend[ing] its lead in mining and agriculture"; the Middle East and North Africa develop exports of low-skill products, and progressively upgrade their production to higher-skill sectors thereafter; South Asia and China expand low-skill production rapidly; and Sub-Saharan Africa focuses on commodities and labour-intensive production.

This is, no doubt, in line with the dictates of economic efficiency and static comparative advantage. It also appears broadly internally consistent, as each country group progresses up the ladder, leaving room for the next tranche. Even so, it is not clear that the envisaged expansion of agricultural production in both Latin America and Sub-Saharan Africa could be achieved without further substantial falls in commodity prices, in view of the overlap in their current production and the relatively low income- (and price-) elasticity of demand for most major agricultural commodities. The same problems may also apply to a lesser extent to mineral production.

Moreover, the achievement of this scenario is critically dependent on each successive wave of countries willingly relinquishing its current place on the ladder; and history suggests that this is unlikely in practice, particularly in agriculture and labour-intensive industry. It is by no means obvious that high-technology goods and services can provide adequate jobs in the developed countries for their governments to view the continued (or accelerated) decline of labour-intensive industries with equanimity, particularly given their current historically high rates of unemployment and the prospect of intensified competition in these sectors from the transition economies, East Asia and Latin America. It also seems unlikely that Asian countries will allow their agricultural sectors to wither, to the detriment of their rural populations and at the expense of a potentially destabilizing level of rural-urban migration, to allow room for expansion in both Latin America and Sub-Saharan Africa.

Such a blockage at any point in the process would discourage and hinder advances at lower points on the ladder. The greatest risk is therefore for those countries at the bottom; and once again, these are the countries of Sub-Saharan Africa.

3.8 Implications for poverty

The effects of G/L on poverty can be divided into four broad categories:
* effects on real incomes;
* effects on relative prices;
* effects on the social sectors (primarily health and education); and
* effects extending beyond individual consumption of goods and services (social effects).

Once again, these can be expected to vary considerably between countries. These types of effect are discussed in turn in this section, after a more general discussion of empirical analyses of the effects of liberalization on poverty at the national level. The section concludes with a brief discussion of the gender aspects of the social impact of G/L.

3.8.1 Liberalization, income distribution and poverty: data and interpretations

Widespread and vociferous concern has been expressed about the impact of structural adjustment on poverty, particularly by NGOs and many observers in developing countries. The World Bank, however, through multi-country statistical comparisons, has concluded that structural adjustment is, on the whole, benign in terms of its social impact, at least over the longer term; and that poverty has not varied systematically with structural adjustment status (e.g. World Bank 1990a and 1990c).

However, the analysis underlying this position is somewhat limited, and a closer inspection of the data on which this finding is based suggests that it is consistent with the existence of such a relationship (Costello et al 1994).
* In terms of the incidence of poverty, all "non-adjusting" countries performed either better than or worse than *any* of the "adjusting" countries. This suggests that, even at the level of the individual country, the current liberalization-based approach to structural adjustment is not the least effective policy option for reducing the incidence of poverty; but neither, more importantly, is it the most effective.
* Structural adjustment was also strongly and positively related to the rate of increase in the intensity of poverty.

Analysis based on a larger data set, adding further data from World Bank sources (Chen et al 1993), also suggests a possible negative relationship between structural adjustment and the rate of poverty reduction in the initial phase of the adjustment process, with no off-setting improvement relative to "non-adjusting" countries later in the process. Moreover, the results appear particularly unfavourable for low-income countries (Woodward 1995c).

Clearly, these results need to be treated with extreme caution, in view of the small (and unrepresentative) sample of countries, the short observation periods in some cases, the discrepancies between the policies actually pursued and adjustment criteria based on World Bank lending, and the potential importance of non-policy factors. However, it does give some cause for concern in relation to the World Bank's own policies (Woodward 1995b).

A particular analytical problem resorted to by the World Bank is the counterfactual argument: in order to assess the effects of structural adjustment, it is necessary to compare actual developments with what would have happened if no structural adjustment had taken place. This argument has often been applied in assessments of the effects of adjustment on economic performance, although questions may be raised over the models used for counterfactual simulations (Woodward 1992). In the context of the social impact of adjustment the criteria used have been absolute (improvement in indicators), historical (acceleration in the rate of improvement) or relative (the rate or acceleration of improvement in indicators in "adjusting" countries relative to "non-adjusting" countries). In some cases – for example, the use of absolute and historical criteria for health outcome indicators[42] – these may seriously weaken the validity of the results (Costello et al 1994).

Two more general problems arise from the conventional approach to the counterfactual problem. First, it presupposes that the burden of adjustment to shocks which have largely arisen from the economic policies of the developed countries should be borne overwhelmingly by the developing countries (Khan 1993). Second, while it may be relevant to the decision of an individual government to adopt an adjustment programme, it offers no valid evidence on the application of orthodox structural adjustment as a development paradigm for the developing countries as a whole. The latter would require consideration of the "wider counterfactual" – a comparison, not of the situation if one country adjusts or does not adjust, but of actual developments during the period of adjustment with what would have happened if an alternative model of adjustment had been generally applied (Woodward 1992).

In response to concerns about the social and poverty impact of orthodox structural adjustment since UNICEF's seminal *Adjustment with a Human Face* (Cornia et al 1987), the World Bank has increasingly advocated the use of "safety nets" and "compensatory programmes" as an adjunct to its structural adjustment loans. Such programmes have become increasingly widespread in adjusting countries, and, despite some limitations and practical problems, have probably improved to some extent the poverty situation in the countries where they have been applied. However, the extent to which this constitutes an improvement in the relationship between structural adjustment and poverty is questionable. Since a social programme could, in principle, be implemented to similar effect without structural adjustment, the appropriate analytical approach would be a counterfactual comparison of the situation with and without adjustment, but with a social programme in both cases (Costello et al 1994).

In terms of the relationship between growth, income distribution and poverty, a fairly clear pattern has emerged in the period since the mid-1980s. According to data presented by Demery et al (1995), in middle-income countries, the effects on poverty of changes in the distribution of income have generally operated in the same direction as economic growth: where growth has been positive, distributional changes have provided an additional reduction in poverty; where growth has been negative, the resulting increase in poverty has been compounded by a shift in the distribution of income away from the poor. In low-income countries, all of the sample exhibited a favourable effect of growth; but in twelve of seventeen cases (six of seven in Sub-Saharan Africa, and six of ten elsewhere), redistribution was away from the poor, limiting the benefits in terms of poverty reduction.

While this adverse trend in income distribution in low-income countries has coincided with the era of adjustment and liberalization, this does not imply causation: data are not available for an equivalent analysis of earlier periods, and other changes in the global economy may also be relevant. However, it seems reasonable to suppose, as a working assumption, that a similar pattern will apply over at least the medium-term.

If this is the case, this will further limit the potential benefits of G/L for poverty. Not only is the associated growth likely to be heavily concentrated in middle-income countries (where poverty is, on the whole, less prevalent), but even to the extent that economic benefits do arise for low-income countries, the translation of faster growth into poverty reduction will be relatively limited.

An important consideration is the effect of liberalization on the relationship between growth and income distribution, in both low- and middle-income countries. Views on this differ markedly: the proponents of liberalization emphasize the potential for generating labour-intensive growth, thus favouring a more positive association (e.g. World Bank 1990c and 1995g); critics, however, emphasize, e.g. the reorientation of prices and incomes towards market levels, increasing the returns to scarce and internationally tradeable assets (financial, physical and human capital) held mainly by the non-poor, and away from the non-scarce non-tradeable assets (unskilled labour and land) held mainly by the poor (e.g. Woodward 1992). Unfortunately, the available data remain wholly inadequate to resolve this question empirically, quite apart from the daunting methodological problems which would be entailed in such an analysis.

3.8.2 Income effects

In those countries which stand to gain from G/L, there should be significant benefits in terms of additional employment. Increased trade opportunities and FDI increase economic activity, which creates jobs; and in low-income countries the increase should be primarily in labour-intensive production, thereby intensifying the favourable impact. The extent of such benefits will depend to a significant extent on the marginal propensity to import and the extent of forward and backward linkages in the economy. The greater the proportion of any increase in income spent on domestically-produced goods, and the greater their local content, the greater will be the multiplier effect.

However, even where there is a significant positive effect on employment, the effect on wage levels may be more limited, or even ambiguous in the medium term. The liberalization of labour markets may reduce real wage levels in the short term, particularly where this encompasses a reduction in the real value of minimum wages, a narrowing of their scope, or less rigorous enforcement. Reduced job-security may also shift market conditions towards lower wage levels (as well as have a direct negative effect on welfare through increased uncertainty). Over time, the creation of additional demand for labour will tend to reverse this process; but the effect is likely to be limited until surplus labour has been fully absorbed. In many cases, particularly where there is a large, inefficient and labour-intensive agricultural sector, this could take a considerable time.

The agricultural sector is critical to poverty in both rural and urban areas, especially in low-income countries. The benefits of G/L to low-income agricultural producers are likely to be very limited. As discussed earlier, although the principles underlying the Uruguay Round agreement on agriculture are potentially beneficial to agriculture in developing countries, the actual terms of the agreement and the details of its implementation severely weaken its effects. The greatest scope for increased trade is in relatively high value-added sub-sectors such as horticulture; but their relative capital intensity and the importance of effective marketing networks and good transport facilities limit the scope for low-income producers to benefit.

The direct benefits of FDI to the agricultural sector are also limited. However, some FDI can be expected in processing industries and the production of agricultural inputs, increasing marketing (and particularly export) opportunities and improving access to inputs. There may also be some investment in plantation agriculture in some countries, increasing rural employment opportunities, although this has tended to be relatively limited. (It may also result in the displacement of small-scale producers, in which case the net effect on agricultural employment is ambiguous.) Investment in forestry (which is more widespread) may have similar effects, often on a very substantial scale relative to the local economy. However, the environmental sustainability of such operations is in many cases questionable.

In general, the effect of G/L on the agricultural sector in developing countries should be favourable. The GATT agreement on agriculture should improve international market conditions for producers of temperate products (and competing crops such as cane sugar), although these benefits will be more limited and uneven than they might initially appear, for the reasons discussed earlier. At the same time, the net effect of protection and subsidization is in most cases to skew relative prices against agriculture, so that the removal of these distortions by structural adjustment will increase agricultural incomes.

However, there are some important caveats to this general picture. Firstly, there may be some important costs to small producers as a result of liberalization in the short term. These include, for example, reductions in input subsidies; increases in the cost (or reductions in the availability) of credit, due to financial liberalization; and intensified import competition as a result of trade liberalization. At the same time, the potential benefits of liberalising marketing arrangements may be limited in practice by reduced access to the market (as in Zimbabwe) or the monopolistic practices of commercial traders (as in Mali). Input costs may be further increased to the extent that prices for improved seed varieties are increased by the TRIPs agreement.

Secondly, there are important obstacles to small-scale producers in responding to changing patterns of incentives by increasing or changing their production methods or the composition of their output. These relate primarily to limited availability of capital; limited access to credit, technology and inputs (e.g. seeds); and often low quality of land. Many of these factors are compounded by the potential short-term costs of liberalization (and of stabilization where this occurs at the same time). This gives rise to a risk of small-scale producers being locked into declining sectors.

Thirdly, increased commercialization of the agricultural sector may result in a consolidation of land holdings in the hands of larger producers. This depends to a considerable extent on local circumstances (particularly the existing pattern of production, the crops and production methods suitable to local conditions, relative factor prices, etc.). Where there is initially a large smallholder sector, this could result in a substantial concentration of land ownership. Bouis and Haddad (1990), for example, found strong evidence of this in Mindanao in the Philippines.

Fourthly, to the extent that production of tradeable crops (particularly tropical products) are increased by the relative price changes associated with liberalization, this may compound the fallacy of composition problem. This will limit the potential increase in real prices received by producers.

Ultimately, if agriculture in developing (and especially low-income) countries is to be internationally competitive at current levels of production and world prices, while generating incomes above the poverty line for those engaged in it, it can employ no more than a fraction of those currently engaged in it. Against a background of price inelastic demand, attempts to resolve this problem by increasing output would be largely or wholly self-defeating: the main effect would be to drive down prices, especially for tropical products. In the case of temperate products and sugar cane, developed country producers might be driven out of the market; but as yet there is little sign that developed country governments are willing to let this happen. At the same time, liberalization has the potential to unleash pressures for increased concentration of land ownership in some contexts; and this may be compounded where short-term costs of liberalization increase pressure on small producers to sell or mortgage their land.

Thus, while overall agricultural incomes should in general be increased by G/L, the effect on rural poverty will depend on the distribution of these gains, which may well benefit larger and richer producers disproportionately. If rural poverty is to be reduced substantially, this is likely, in many cases, to imply a substantial reduction in the number of people engaged in agriculture, thereby creating a labour surplus which will need to be absorbed elsewhere in the economy.

Although part of this surplus labour could be absorbed by an expansion of non-agricultural activities in rural areas, which would be fuelled by increasing aggregate agricultural incomes a substantial supply-led acceleration in rural-urban migration would also result which would create an additional pool of labour to be absorbed by expanding industries.

The above effect should be limited in most middle-income countries with relatively small or efficient agricultural sectors, as the displaced labour should be fairly readily absorbed in expanding industries. In many low-income countries, however, the bulk of the population is engaged in agriculture. This suggests that the process of absorption will take a very considerable time, even with relatively rapid industrial growth. Furthermore, it is by no means clear that G/L will generate substantial industrial growth in most such countries.

In China, while a major consolidation of landholdings is expected[43], it is possible that the current rapid pace of industrial growth, if sustained, could accommodate a substantial proportion of surplus agricultural labour. In India, Pakistan and Bangladesh, expanding industrial production, helped by the Uruguay Round and FDI flows, should also at least partly off-set the problem. In Sub-Saharan Africa, however, the increase in urban formal sector employment opportunities is likely to be much more limited, and the implications commensurately more serious.

If, as seems likely in many cases, the generation of surplus labour exceeds the rate of job-creation, this will substantially increase supply (and thus depress incomes) in the urban informal sector – the main locus of urban poverty. It will also limit or delay any substantial benefits of increased formal sector employment on real wages, and could well reverse this process. The decreasing importance of labour costs as a criterion for FDI decisions, coupled with chronically weak domestic investment in most LICs, will limit the responsiveness of labour demand to falling real wages, thus further compounding the problem.

Where rural poverty is substantially reduced by G/L, through increased smallholder incomes and rural employment, the above caveats imply only that this reduction may be partly off-set by an increase in urban poverty. However, where additional agricultural income is concentrated in the hands of larger producers and/or liberalization gives rise to an increase in the concentration of land ownership, an increase in overall poverty is possible.

For most middle-income countries, the greatest risk arises in the long term. In the event of the worst-case scenario – a balance of payments crisis due to a sudden loss of confidence, with limited scope for rescheduling to ease the pace of adjustment – there could be a need for drastic macroeconomic adjustment. The potential effects of such a scenario are illustrated by recent events in Mexico, but would almost certainly be compounded by the absence of the large financial safety net provided in that case.

A more specific concern raised in some quarters is that of wage rates and working conditions in export-processing zones (EPZs). However, such concerns often tend to be over-simplified and/or exaggerated: in many (if not most) cases, wages and working conditions within EPZs compare favourably with those outside. Nonetheless, there are many instances of wage rates or average incomes below those in the mainstream economy (e.g. in the Dominican Republic, Barbados and Jamaica); or where working hours are excessive (e.g. Costa Rica, the Philippines, the Republic of Korea, Sri Lanka and the Dominican Republic). Poor occupational safety and health conditions exist in some EPZs, particularly in smaller facilities and certain sectors (e.g. garment manufacturing and gem cutting). These problems variously reflect weaknesses in legislation or its enforcement, the exclusion of EPZs from national labour regulations, and limited unionization[44] (Romero 1995).

As well as incomes and working conditions within EPZs, any assessment of their impact must take into account the potential effect on conditions in other countries, and in the mainstream economies of countries with EPZs. In the latter case, the impact is likely to be favourable overall: the positive effect on the absorption of surplus labour should outweigh the need to compete with the EPZ for FDI flows. In countries without EPZs, however, the effect is negative (though unquantifiable). The more favourable conditions for investment in other countries' EPZs is likely not only to attract FDI away from other countries, but also to increase the need to provide more favourable terms for investors (including lower labour costs and tax rates, laxer regulatory standards and greater freedom to repatriate profits).

It is also important to take account of the nature of investment in EPZs. This is disproportionately directed at "foot-loose" sectors such as the assembly of imported components; it typically operates as an enclave, with few forward and backward linkages to the rest of the economy; and it makes a limited contribution to government revenues, due to tax concessions. As a result, the benefits are largely limited to the creation of employment and absorption of surplus labour, possibly on a temporary basis. This may be very helpful in reducing poverty over the medium-term, providing a valuable palliative, particularly at times of high unemployment; but its effect on long-term development and permanent poverty reduction may be more limited. From a global perspective, taking account of the limited additionality of EPZ investment, the benefits may be still more limited.

3.8.3 Price effects

A major component of the price effects of G/L arises from the effects on imports (and indirectly on import substitutes and exportables) of the combination of trade reform and exchange rate changes. The cost of tradeable goods is increased by devaluation and reduced by exchange rate appreciation, while the relative prices of non-tradeable goods by definition change in the opposite direction[45]. The effects of exchange rate unification (or narrowing differentials within a multiple rate system) are more complex, essentially implying different rates of devaluation for different categories of transaction.

At the same time, tariff reduction reduces the cost of imports (directly) and import substitutes (indirectly); but this effect is moderated by the associated devaluation, which also increases the cost of exportables. The tariffication of QRs should be broadly neutral with respect to relative prices (apart from the indirect effects of its fiscal benefits).

Reducing the dispersion of tariffs affects the relative prices of different imports and import substitutes, in much the same way as narrowing the differentials in a multiple exchange rate system: abstracting from any change in the overall level of protection (or the exchange rate), the prices of goods with relatively low initial tariffs (or over-valued exchange rates) will be increased, while those with higher initial tariffs (or under-valued exchange rates) will be reduced. Goods in the former category may include, for example, productive inputs, capital equipment and "essential" goods such as basic foods, drugs and medical equipment – or at least goods in these categories which are not produced domestically on a significant scale.

The distributional impact of these relative price changes clearly depends heavily on which goods fall into each category, and the relative importance of each in the consumption baskets of different income groups. Coupled with differences in the extent and direction of the potential effects of G/L on exchange rates in different countries over different periods, variations in the phase of trade liberalization and exchange rate reform which has been reached as well as differences in the relative tradeability of and levels of protection afforded to different products in different countries make the likely impact of trade reform- and exchange rate-related price changes related to G/L-extremely complex, and beyond the scope of this paper to analyze.

However, in countries which are dependent on imports as a major source of staple foods, the prices of such foods are likely to be increased by devaluation. Where initial tariff levels on such foods are low, reducing tariff dispersion would further increase this effect; and, while this would be progressively reversed by a reduction in overall tariff levels, the associated exchange rate adjustment would result in a significant increase in prices overall. Essentially the same argument applies to imports of essential drugs.

These effects are of particular concern because they coincide with the expected effects of the Uruguay Round agreements. Reduced agricultural export subsidies by developed countries are expected to contribute to a small increase in world prices for cereals (among other temperate products); and the strengthening of patent protection under the TRIPs agreement is expected to increase the prices for generic drugs in developing countries that have significant pharmaceutical industries. While the latter applies to a relatively small number of countries, the effect on prices (and thus on access to essential drugs and/or health budgets) in those countries could be considerable.

The reduction of government expenditure on subsidies tends to be particularly affected by liberalization, as fiscal pressure is intensified by the principle of removing price distortions. While this process is well advanced in many countries, further movement in this direction can be expected where significant subsidies remain. Thus in Sub-Saharan Africa, the real value of government expenditure on subsidies and transfers fell by 26 per cent in per capita terms between 1986 and 1991 (based on data from World Bank 1995a); but this still represented more than 9 per cent of total government expenditure and net lending. Price liberalization may also result in disproportionate increases in the prices of basic goods, as these are often held at particularly low levels, due to political pressures.

In all these case, however, it is important to note that increased prices for "essential" goods, whether as a result of subsidy reduction or changes in trade policies or exchange rates may affect poverty to only a limited extent. In many cases, the subsidized goods are consumed primarily by non-poor households (petrol is a common example); and, even where this is not the case, the access of poor households to goods at directly or indirectly subsidized prices may be limited.

These effects primarily relate to low-income countries, as most middle-income countries have largely completed the liberalization process, and the exchange rate effects of globalization and liberalization are likely to be positive rather than negative over the medium term. In the event of a reversal of the net foreign exchange rate in the longer term, however, import prices would be likely to rise. In the worst-case scenario of a balance of payments crisis, with limited scope for reducing the need for adjustment through rescheduling, the price rises could be dramatic.

In many cases such an event would have a disproportionate effect on basic goods; and, in a liberalized economy, this would translate much more directly into lower incomes for poor households engaged in the non-tradeable sector. This could have a very substantial impact particularly with respect to the urban informal sector, which is the main locus of poverty in many middle-income countries.

Privatization of state-owned enterprises (SOEs) may also have significant effects on the prices for utilities. The combination of fiscal adjustment and the preparation of SOEs for privatization typically leads to substantial increases in prices, where SOEs were previously subsidized or loss-making. Again, however, the impact on poverty will depend on the extent to which poor households have access to these services, which in many cases is limited. (This may, however, be more important for the "new poor", e.g. retrenched public sector workers.) After privatisation, this process may be partly reversed, and quality and reliability enhanced, if efficiency is increased. It is also likely that access to utilities will be increased overall, although it may be more closely related to ability to pay, so that the effects on poor households are ambiguous. (Illicit access, e.g. to electricity supplies, may be more important to the urban poor in some areas. This is likely to be reduced by firmer policing after privatisation.)

Another important area of relative price increases under liberalization is the introduction of, or increases in, user charges for health services, and a shift in the costs of education towards households (through payment for text books, learning materials, etc. as well as fees). This is discussed in the next section.

3.8.4 Effects on social sectors

The key effect of G/L on the provision of health services and education arises from its effects on government expenditure constraints. In those countries which benefit overall, and have largely completed the tariff-reduction process (e.g. most of Latin America and middle-income East Asia), this effect should be positive, provided faster growth and higher incomes are sufficient to off-set reductions in tax rates and the need for increased fiscal discipline. In other beneficiary countries, the effect is more neutral and may be negative over the medium term, due to the additional loss of revenues from taxes on international transactions. In both cases, however, the worst-case scenario would once again have a severe impact. In Sub-Saharan Africa and other smaller low-income countries, the effect is likely to be more clearly negative, as continued stagnation compounds the expenditure-reducing effects of liberalization.

As noted above, G/L may also have important effects on the cost of inputs, particularly in the health sector, especially for imported essential drugs. In Sub-Saharan Africa, drugs typically represent around 20-30 per cent of total recurrent costs at the facility level which is, second only to personnel expenditure (World Bank 1994b). Any increase in the international mobility of health professionals could also force an increase in their salaries, and increasing training requirements to allow departing staff to be replaced.

Where D/PI flows cause an appreciation of the exchange rate, the effects on imported inputs may be neutral or even positive overall. Where pressures for devaluation are predominant, however, as in most low-income countries, the effect may be substantially negative, compounding the effect of declining resources for social expenditure.

An important element of the response to increasing financial pressures on social sectors is the introduction of (or increases in) user charges. These may help to ease financial pressures on schools and health facilities, as well as be in line with the objective of "getting the prices right". Since even free services tend to be used disproportionately by non-poor households, the distributional impact of user charges on household expenditure may be neutral or in some cases progressive (Jimenez 1987 and Griffin 1988); and progressivity may be further enhanced by the operation of exemption mechanisms in many (though by no means all) cases. It is also often argued by proponents of user charges that the potential negative effects of increased financial cost are largely or wholly off-set by the positive effects of increased quality of service.

However, the revenue-raising potential of user charges is at best very limited. Even without deducting the costs of collection and administration, Creese (1991) found an average yield in Sub-Saharan Africa of around 5 per cent of total operating costs[46]. There is also widespread evidence of a negative impact on utilisation, particularly because effective exemption mechanisms for low-income households have yet to be found. While improvements in quality have helped to limit (or in some cases to avoid) declines in utilisation, these have generally been funded mainly by additional external financing rather than from the revenues generated. They may also be partly off-set by adverse incentive effects on patients and providers (e.g. delays in seeking treatment, non-completion of treatment, over-prescription and unnecessary or inappropriate treatment).

At best, user charges may moderate to some extent the impact of resource constraints in social sectors; it is by no means clear even that their net effect (abstracting from the benefits of external support which could have been provided without them) is positive (Woodward 1995d).

As well as the supply side, it is important to take account of the demand side in assessing the impact of changes in health and education (Woodward 1992 and Costello et al 1994). To the extent that incomes decline, particularly among lower-income households, the ability to bear direct and indirect financial and non-financial (e.g. time) costs of education and health-service utilization will be reduced. This may be compounded by the increased financial costs of health services and education associated with user charges. There is some evidence of declining primary enrolment ratios due to demand-side pressures in adjusting countries during the 1980s (World Bank 1990a).

3.8.5 Social effects

Beyond the effects of G/L on the income and consumption of individual households (and their time use, discussed in the next sub-section), G/L may also have important wider effects. These arise in part from the G/L process itself, and in part as side-effects of the associated changes in household incomes. In the latter case, in particular, there will be considerable variation between individual countries, according to the specific economic effects and income and price effects of G/L, as discussed above.

A particularly important social effect of G/L is on **urbanization**. This is to some extent a general result of economic disruption, particularly where it affects rural areas. When rural households face substantial real income losses, for whatever reason, a common response is to seek alternative opportunities in urban areas. On the other hand, liberalization is intended, in part, to reduce incentives for rural-urban migration by correcting the "urban bias" in economic policies. However, if it results in income losses for a significant proportion of rural households, it may nonetheless lead to an acceleration of urbanization, irrespective of the overall change in the rural-urban terms of trade. Up to the late 1980s, it appears that structural adjustment not only failed to slow the pace of rural-urban migration, but may have increased it, both relative to "non-adjusting" countries and, at least for low-income countries, in absolute terms (Woodward 1992).

With regard to globalization, as discussed earlier, the main benefits relate to industrial goods, with more limited benefits for agriculture. In practice, if G/L is to generate economic growth, the likely scenario is for expanding industrial production, partly financed by foreign investment, to absorb the surplus labour generated by a liberalising agricultural sector. This implies a rapid rate of rural-urban migration.

Apart for the implications for the urban informal sector (as discussed above), the welfare effects of urbanization are twofold. First, there is an important effect on the welfare of migrating households themselves. They will generally expect to improve their income prospects as a result of migration (although their expectations may not be realised, and if they are responding to an income loss, they may not regain their original level of income). However, any income gain is likely to be off-set by the financial and non-financial costs of migration, and by any differential in living conditions between the two locations. The welfare effects may be particularly severe when it is only the head of household who migrates (as is often the case, e.g. in Southern Africa), even if this is temporary. Second, rapid urbanization may contribute to urban over-crowding, thus causing a general deterioration in the living environment, and imposing additional stress on the urban infrastructure and facilities (e.g. housing, schools, health facilities, transport, etc.).

G/L also has potentially important **environmental effects** at both the local and the global level. At the local level, potential environmental effects include the impact of increased rural-urban migration, as discussed above. Where poverty is increased, this is also likely to erode living environments, with the opposite effect where poverty is reduced. Working environments may deteriorate as a result of deregulation and/or expansion of the informal sector; but they may, on the whole, be improved where FDI generates a shift towards production by transnational corporations (TNCs).

However, G/L seems likely to increase industrial pollution. Investment in polluting industries may represent a major component of FDI, as developed country sensitivities increase; and investment in chemicals industries, in particular, may be further encouraged by the TRIPs agreement[47]. Deregulation may also result in laxer controls on emissions; and, where fiscal constraints are tightened, this may result in less rigorous enforcement of environmental regulations, as well as a reduced provision of environmental services.

Overall, the local environmental effects are ambiguous among the middle-income beneficiaries of G/L, as the benefits of falling poverty should at least partly off-set increasing industrial pollution. In the smaller low-income countries, however, the effects are almost certainly negative, unless the reduction of pollution associated with deindustrialization outstrips the negative impact of increasing poverty.

At the global level, there are two key environmental issues which may be affected by G/L, and which are likely to affect low-income households in the long term[48]: deforestation, which may reduce future employment opportunities directly, and agricultural productivity through its effects on soil fertility and micro-climates; and the depletion of natural resources, which will reduce future production and exports.

As noted above, competition for FDI may have an adverse effect in both of these areas, as it creates an incentive for under-pricing of environmental goods. In low-income countries in particular, such FDI as there has been has tended to be concentrated in extractive industries and forestry; and in the latter case in particular, concerns have often been expressed about environmental sustainability. A shift towards more extensive agricultural production may also contribute to deforestation, as, in some cases, may industrial expansion (e.g. the Carajas development in Brazil).

A third social impact of G/L is on **administrative capacity**. To a great extent, this will vary in accordance with the net fiscal impact: where public sector resources are increased, administrative capacity should be improved; where fiscal pressures are intensified, the impact is likely to be negative. This is particularly important in low-income countries which are already well advanced down the spiral of inadequate resources and weak administrative capacity. There is also some concern that the prolonged application of conditionality by the international financial institutions as a means of achieving liberalization may further sap administrative capacity, by removing effective control of an increasing range of policy areas to Washington and increasing reliance on expatriate advisors. Increased international mobility of high-level staff could further compound the problem; and where the educational system is weakened, there could be an additional negative impact in the long term.

Finally, it is almost inevitable that major changes in the economic environment, such as those embodied in G/L, will entail some degree of **social dislocation**. This may contribute to a weakening of community and family structures, as households (or individual household members) relocate in response to changing economic incentives, particularly where poverty is increased. Periods of severe economic dislocation may also impose intolerable strains on traditional family and community support networks[49]. Other possible (though unquantifiable) risks include social unrest, political instability and crime, particularly where urban poverty is increased.

3.8.6 Gender dimensions

The gender dimensions of the effects of G/L are ambiguous. On the one hand, there is little doubt that some aspects of the process have increased income-earning opportunities for women – and often disproportionately so. According to Romero (1995: 249), "Young unskilled and semi-skilled women generally account for at least half of all workers and make up between 70 per cent and 90 per cent of the workforce in certain EPZs (e.g. Jamaica, the

Republic of Korea, Mauritius, Sri Lanka and El Salvador)". This represents a significant contribution to women's financial autonomy, potentially strengthening their position in household decision-making.

On the other hand, where structural adjustment and liberalization have an adverse effect on households, the burden of adjustment may fall disproportionately on women. Examples include the additional burden on women's time as a result of the need for increased income (Elson 1994), the impact of user charges on utilization of health services (Gertler and van der Gaag 1990), and, in some cases at least, reductions in household nutritional intakes (Behrman and Deolalikar 1988). While concern has also been expressed that declining school enrolment may widen gender disparities, cross-country evidence appears to provide little support for this hypothesis (Rose 1994). This may reflect the emphasis placed on girls' education by the World Bank (e.g. World Bank 1993b).

At the heart of this issue is the distinction between demand and supply factors in the level of employment of women. To the extent that increased employment is demand-generated, it is likely to be beneficial: women will be able to be more selective in their choice of work, wage levels will be increased, and those who wish to work (and are in a position to do so) will be able to increase their welfare. Conversely, to the extent that it is supply driven, women effectively pushed into paid work by pressure on household budgets are likely to enter lower-paid occupations with worse working conditions; the increase in supply will depress wages; and income will be generated only at the cost of increased pressure on women's time, to the detriment of their own and their households' welfare.

The latter process is unlikely in any sense to be enabling. While the former effects may be beneficial to the position of women in the long term, in the short term "the paid work of women still takes place within a context whose parameters are defined by men. Economic hardship...does *not* appear to have changed men's ability to set the limits on what their wives do; and to set limits on male contributions to the household budget" (Elson 1994: 43, original emphasis).

A second broad area of concern from a gender perspective is the commercialization inherent in liberalization policies. This entails a shift of emphasis away from traditional non-commercial economic relations (e.g. subsistence production, family and community support networks), social support (e.g. transfer payments) and subsidized or free basic goods and services, and towards commercial markets and economic pricing. This inevitably increases the importance of money as a means of access to goods and services.

In many societies, most notably in South Asia and Sub-Saharan Africa, control of financial resources is heavily concentrated in the hands of men. Income-generating activities such as employment and the production of cash crops are conducted mainly by men, while the traditional role of women is unpaid work in the home and production of food crops, mainly for home consumption. Such activities contribute critically, not only to the household's welfare, but also in many cases to its purchasing power, by reducing the need to buy goods and services (e.g. subsistence production, making or repairing clothes and other items, food preparation, health-care within the home, etc.). As a result, the need for such activities, and thus the pressure on women's time, increases when household income declines.

Against this background, it is to be expected that women's interests will be under-represented in decisions about how to adjust to economic shocks that affect the household, and that their welfare will be disproportionately affected as a result. It also seems almost inevitable that a movement from traditional to commercial economic relations will reduce women's control over access to goods and services, unless it is accompanied by an increase in money-generating activities by women (and they are able to retain control over a significant part of the proceeds).

This may, in part, explain the disproportionate impact on women of reductions in access to health services: by shifting the basis of access from time to money, the balance of decision-making is effectively shifted from women towards men. Increasing the financial cost of health care and education may also increase the need for a compensating financial gain in the future, which, in male-dominated societies, is substantially greater for men and boys than for women and girls, because of their greater role in the money economy. This is consistent with the finding that the effects of user charges for health care are least negative for non-poor men of working age, for whom the financial gains are greatest and most immediate.

In very general terms, it would therefore seem reasonable to conclude that, where liberalization has negative effects at the household level, the resulting burden will fall disproportionately on women, particularly in societies where the money economy is predominantly a male preserve. Conversely, globalization may benefit women, by generating a supply-led increase in income-earning opportunities for women. However, this will occur only in countries which benefit economically; and an entrenched gender division of labour will be a critical constraint on this process. In East Asia and Latin America, where the liberalization process is largely complete, and significant economic benefits can be expected from globalization, the overall effect should be positive. In Sub-Saharan Africa, once again, a negative impact seems inevitable.

3.8.7 Conclusion

In most middle-income countries, where G/L may be expected to bring significant economic benefits over the medium term, the effect on poverty is likely to be broadly favourable. The recent pattern of changes in income distribution suggests that poor households in these countries have benefited disproportionately from growth (and suffered disproportionately from economic decline); and there is a reasonable prospect that employment creation will successfully absorb the relatively limited amount of labour displaced from a liberalising agricultural sector. In the long term, however, the worst-case scenario of a serious balance of payments crisis could have a serious adverse effect on poverty, if it happens.

In the bigger low-income countries, including India and China, the larger potential surplus of agricultural labour may off-set urban employment generation, limiting the effect of G/L on poverty in both rural and urban areas. In small low-income countries, including most of Sub-Saharan Africa, the overall effect is more clearly negative. These countries will face most of the negative impacts of globalization but stand to receive few of the benefits.

3.9 Policy options

The policy areas relevant to the effects of G/L may be divided into three broad categories:
- possible modifications to the G/L process itself, through the policies of the international institutions and developed country governments;
- changes in economic policies in developing countries (relative to the predominant paradigm embodied in IMF- and World Bank-supported adjustment programmes); and
- social policies and "safety nets" designed as an adjunct to economic policies, to modify their social impact.

These are discussed in turn in this section.

3.9.1 International institutions and developed country governments

In practice, whatever the shortcomings of the **Uruguay Round agreements**, it is probably not realistic to propose modifications at this stage. However, pressure should be applied on developed country governments, where necessary, to ensure that they comply with their commitments, both bilaterally and in international organisations (the IMF and the World Bank as well as the WTO). They should also be urged to resist the temptation to minimise the effects of their commitments (e.g. in the phasing of MFA liberalization); to use safeguard provisions and anti-dumping measures only where this is legitimate and has a limited impact on developing-country exporters; and to refrain from circumventing the agricultural export subsidy restrictions by labelling subsidized exports to developing countries as food aid. Some tightening of regulations in these areas may also be desirable, but would probably be difficult to achieve in practice. It also appears that further action may be necessary to eradicate the threat of VERs.

If the potential benefits of globalization to developing countries as a whole are to be sustained beyond the Uruguay Round implementation period, it will be important to **continue the process of liberalization of developed countries' trade policies**. This should in particular encompass trade in long-distance service provision and agricultural goods, and take substantially greater account of the interests of developing countries than have previous rounds of **MTNs**. The position of the smaller low-income countries – especially, but not exclusively, in Sub-Saharan Africa – is a matter of particular concern in this context.

The Uruguay Round does not augur well for this process. It took six years for agreement to be reached; the negotiations and the terms and content of the agreements concluded were overwhelmingly dominated by the developed countries (Watkins 1992); and, as discussed above, there were in consequence serious limitations to the benefits for developing countries. Resolving this problem would be likely to require substantial **institutional changes in the WTO negotiation framework** as compared with the foregoing GATT framework. However, since the problem arises from relative economic power rather than institutional structures (such as the weighted voting system in the IMF and World Bank), this would be difficult to achieve. It should, nonetheless, be a priority area for consideration.

As discussed earlier, the current process of globalization, while benefiting many developing countries, will have adverse economic and social consequences for many low-income countries, partly because of their marginalization in the negotiation process. If it is not possible to give them equal weight in future negotiations, serious consideration should be given to devising **alternative approaches, in parallel with the broader globalization process**. This would be consistent with the GATT principle of "special and differential treatment". Some measures can and should be implemented immediately; others would need to be incorporated in future multilateral negotiations; and a third category (discussed in the next section) would entail policy changes at the national level.

The problems in low-income countries arise to a great extent from their reliance on existing **preferential trade arrangements**, their disproportionate dependence on primary commodities, and structural weaknesses in their economies which limit their ability to respond to new trade opportunities. In respect of preferential trade arrangements, the ideal would be to allow all least-developed countries unrestricted duty-free access to developed country markets. A more limited (and more politically feasible) alternative would be for developed country governments to undertake, where possible, to maintain preference margins to least-developed countries, and to broaden existing preferential arrangements to cover least-developed countries which do not currently benefit from them. Rules of origin could also usefully be modified, to apply to the value-added in all beneficiary countries rather than in the individual exporting country.

The disproportionate dependence of least-developed countries on exports of primary commodities, and the structural problems in their economies, need to be addressed largely by policy measures at the national level, as discussed in the next sub-section. However, two actions would be highly desirable at the global level.

In respect of **commodity exports**, there is an urgent need to avoid the fallacy of composition problem. Currently, this gives rise to a serious risk of a vicious circle, in which developing countries lose foreign exchange earnings when they (collectively) increase their export volumes, and respond to a loss of foreign exchange by policies which increase their export volumes further. The sole beneficiaries are consumers, who, for most tropical products, are on the whole much better-off than producers. During the 1980s in particular, but also to some extent in the 1990s, the structural factors underlying this problem were actually reinforced by the policies embodied in IMF and World Bank adjustment programmes.

To circumvent this problem, it is necessary to promote cooperative rather than competitive responses to balance of payments problems. The problem, as in any prisoner's dilemma situation, is how to ensure collusive behaviour. In this case, the answer would seem to be to **use IMF and World Bank conditionality to promote the application of optimal export taxes**. In principle, this could contribute to resolving the two key economic constraints on least-developed and Sub-Saharan countries: the foreign exchange constraint and the fiscal constraint.

There are two problems with this approach. Firstly, the very fact of relieving the foreign exchange and fiscal constraints on governments would relieve the pressure on the governments concerned to comply with IMF and World Bank conditionality. It would therefore be desirable (but difficult) to devise alternative mechanisms for enforcing conditionality in this particular instance[50]. Even without such mechanisms, there should, nonetheless, be some benefits: if nothing else, the process would impose a floor to commodity prices; and it would provide a source of advice on (and of pressure to pursue) mutually beneficial policies among commodity-producing countries.

The second problem is that the incomes received by producers would fall as a result of the tax. This suggests a need to spend some of the proceeds on schemes to promote diversification of production in the affected areas, and to provide compensatory assistance to poor producers who lose as a result. This in turn would require the development of an adequate administrative infrastructure to implement such policies, which would increase the fiscal cost. Again, however, there should be net benefits even after taking account of these costs.

Politically, there would in principle seem a reasonable prospect of achieving changes of this nature. The potential benefits to commodity-exporting countries would be considerable and greatly needed, while the costs to importing countries and consumers would be relatively limited and easily afforded. The costs to developed countries would also be at least partly off-set by the prospect of a declining need for aid flows in the long term. The main obstacle is essentially ideological – the preference of the major developed-country governments and international institutions for competitive and market-based, rather than collusive and interventionist, policies. At the very least, this option should be given serious and objective consideration.

Foreign exchange and fiscal constraints in least-developed and Sub-Saharan countries could also be relieved by **increasing the scope for debt reduction**. This could also act as an important spur to investment, by relieving the debt overhang and allowing the reallocation of aid flows, at present effectively absorbed by debt-servicing, for more productive uses. The most pressing need is for effective mechanisms to allow a reduction of debts owed to multilateral institutions. However, there is also a need for more reduction of bilateral debts than is possible under existing Paris Club rules, either by increasing the extent of debt reduction on eligible debts, or by increasing the proportion of total debt which is eligible (e.g. by including post-cut-off-date debt).

Although multilateral debt reduction is currently under discussion, there remains considerable resistance, both from the multilateral institutions themselves (particularly the IMF), and from some of their major shareholders. *Relative* protection of multilateral debt (i.e. preferred creditor status, as opposed to complete exemption) is in itself a tenable position. However, it must be accepted that multilateral debts can only be protected from reduction if the debt reduction available on other debts is adequate to make them serviceable without seriously undermining development or imposing high social costs. At present, this is clearly not the case in a substantial number of low-income countries[51].

The 1996 Spring meetings of the IMF and the World Bank suggest an important move in this direction, with the proposal that the extent of bilateral debt reduction be increased to 90 per cent, as a means of limiting the need for multilateral debt reduction. However, it is far from clear that this will be accepted by bilateral creditors; and the long delay envisaged before multilateral debt reduction could be offered is potentially damaging, especially for those countries whose multilateral debts themselves are unsustainable.

An alternative to the formal reduction of multilateral debts is their continued refinancing on concessional terms, through **IDA** and an enlarged and permanent ESAF. Over the long term, it is argued, the net present value of multilateral debt will be progressively reduced, without compromising the principle of preferred creditor status. While this is correct in terms of financial flows, however, it is far from clear/that this is the best option (Woodward, forthcoming).

- It assumes that it is the net present value (NPV) of debt which is relevant to economic performance rather than the nominal value. Since the economic effect depends critically on the perceptions and psychology of economic agents, this is not necessarily the case; and regressions of investment suggest a closer relationship with nominal debt than with the NPV measure.

- There is a much longer time-lag before concessional refinancing reduces debt than with outright debt reduction. This would extend the interim period of weak economic performance, with potentially serious implications for development and poverty.

- The concessional refinancing option would extend IMF and World Bank conditionality, potentially for another twenty years. Given the all-encompassing nature of this conditionality, and the one-sided nature of the "negotiation" process in smaller and poorer developing countries, this would effectively mean that most of the policy-making process would have been largely removed to Washington, in some cases for nearly two generations. This is not conducive to achieving the political maturity required for democratization and good governance.

To the extent possible, the financing of any additional reduction of bilateral or multilateral debts should be additional to existing (or currently projected) official financing. There is a strong case for this, in that the risk of non-payment on debts likely to be reduced should long-since have been borne by creditors in any rational accounting system. In practice, however, in view of current political pressures and budgetary constraints, this objective may be only partly achieved. In the case of multilateral debts, the best option from the perspective of additionality would appear to be to finance debt reduction through the sale of part of the IMF's gold reserves. Again, however, there is a substantial amount of opposition to this proposal (Woodward 1994a).

As well as maintaining (or if possible increasing) the value of their aid commitments, it would be very helpful if developed country governments were to institute improvements in their **aid policies**. A priority, particularly for the US, is to ensure more effective targeting on low-income countries. In terms of modalities, the changes required largely represent an extension of processes which are already underway or under consideration. This would include, for example, a continuation in the shift away from projects and tied aid towards more general financial assistance; and, within the latter category, from balance of payments support to budgetary support (Foster 1995). The latter would contribute to improved donor coordination, increasing the effectiveness of aid[52] (e.g. by moving away from vertical programmes in the health sector) and reducing the often very considerable administrative burden on recipient governments.

More specific attention to donor coordination is also needed on a sectoral basis. Coordination should be kept firmly in the hands of the recipient country, and strengthening the capacity of governments to carry out the coordinating role effectively should be a priority for technical assistance. Again, there has already been some movement in this direction, but this needs to be greatly strengthened and accelerated. This requires some forbearance on the part of donors, not least the World Bank.

There is a risk that the untying of aid and movement away from visible (and therefore politically useful) projects towards general financial support will further weaken the resolve of developed country governments in protecting their aid budgets. However, while a movement in this direction should be resisted as far as possible, this is probably a price worth paying for the potential benefits.

The highly particular subject of aid to Sub-Saharan Africa is taken up in Mr. Mosley's paper in this volume entitled *Globalization and liberalization in Sub-Saharan Africa: implications for growth and poverty.*

In addition to action on existing debts, the Mexican crisis suggests a need to review **international monetary and financial arrangements** in the light of recent changes in the structure of financial flows to developing countries. The risk is that shorter maturities on commercial liabilities, coupled with continued instability in export markets could give rise to a balance of payments crisis; that this could be compounded by the potential instability and procyclical nature of portfolio equity flows; and that the increasing domination of external liabilities by assets which are not at present subject to renegotiation could seriously limit the flexibility available in dealing with such a shock.

This means, in particular, the need for a review of surveillance mechanisms and data collection on the accrual of external liabilities (including short-term and "non-debt-creating" flows); consideration of possible mechanisms for limiting the risk of a crisis situation developing; and contingency planning and the development of mechanisms (and, if necessary, sources of financing) for limiting the impact of financial shocks and spreading the burden of adjustment.

With regard to foreign direct investment, there may be a case for a more cautious approach in low-income countries, in view of its potentially high foreign exchange cost. Apart from overt profit remittances, transfer pricing and under-pricing of natural resources imply be important (though unquantifiable) costs. The extent of competition for FDI flows, and the policies which have been adopted to attract them (including the establishment of EPZs) have the potential to limit the benefits to developing countries, in social, economic, developmental and environmental terms.

These problems, coupled with the growing importance of FDI as a source of external financing, investment and trade, suggest that there is a case for a **global institutional framework for dealing with issues relating to FDI** and the operations of transnational corporations (TNCs). In principle, such an institution could apply a code of fair practice for TNCs (e.g. minimum health and safety and environmental standards, avoidance of transfer pricing) while ensuring that would-be host countries do not compete away the potential advantages of FDI (e.g. through tax concessions and under-pricing of natural resources). There might also be a case for a coordinated phasing out of EPZs, limiting them to countries in exceptional need of the (possibly temporary) employment creation they can offer, while improving their design to maximise developmental benefits (e.g. through forward and backward linkages).

Again, however, there are some critically important political obstacles to such proposals. Any effective scheme of this nature would necessarily entail significant costs to (or at least restrictions on the behaviour of) some TNCs; and the political strength of TNCs, and their importance to the economies of the major developed countries (whose governments dominate the international institutions) would probably enable them to prevent or circumscribe any effective action in this direction.

3.9.2 Economic policies in developing countries

As discussed earlier, there is cause for serious concern that the current process of globalization, while benefiting many developing countries, will have adverse economic and social consequences for most low-income countries. Since the prospects for changing the nature of the globalization process are limited, this suggests a need to consider what changes in policies at the national level would be more conducive to a favourable outcome.

The key shortcoming of the national economic policies embodied in orthodox structural adjustment programmes is their exclusive focus on the national level. The design of adjustment programmes is aimed at the maximization of overall economic growth within external financing constraints, taking the external economic environment as given, with little direct reference to issues of distribution and welfare. Welfare considerations are essentially limited to the relative protection of government expenditure in the social sectors and parallel "compensatory" or "safety net" programmes. The current approach to adjustment is also heavily predicated on the validity of neoliberal economic theory in the developing economies.

In reality, economic policies operate within a global context: each country's economic policies represent a part of every other country's external environment. They also have major implications for the distribution of income as well as its level, and for the allocation of resources between uses with very different welfare implications. Both the economic effects and the social impact of adjustment policies will depend critically on the nature of the direct impacts on households, and their responses to them. Understanding the interactions between policy changes at the macro level and outcomes at the household level is critical to successful and socially benign adjustment; but economic theory has proved relatively weak in its analysis of these linkages.

If the objective of economic policy is to maximise poverty reduction (the goal proclaimed by the World Bank) or long-term welfare, this must be the central goal of policy, and the basis of policy design – not, as at present, an incidental by-product of the prior objective of economic growth. Equally, if similar economic policies are to be advocated and supported in a large number of developing countries, their effects on other countries must be taken fully into account.

This suggests a need for **a fundamental, and above all objective, review of the economic policies currently being supported in developing countries by the international institutions**. Serious consideration should be given to the development of a policy approach based explicitly on social objectives (poverty, health, education, etc.) and empirical analysis of the linkages between economic policies, economic process variables and welfare outcomes on a country-by-country basis. Given the current paucity of analysis on many of these linkages (and often the lack of reliable data on which to base such analyses), this would require substantial further research (Costello et al 1994).

Overall economic performance should be regarded strictly as an intermediate variable, and not as the central objective; and the direct and indirect economic linkages between developing countries must be taken fully and explicitly into account. The latter implies that policies relating to international transactions (e.g. with regard to export promotion and FDI regimes, as discussed above) may need to be subject to stronger international coordination, in the collective interests of low-income countries.

Within the current framework, the apparent ineffectiveness of orthodox structural adjustment policies in most smaller, poorer and more commodity-dependent countries, most notably in Sub-Saharan Africa, is a matter of particular concern from a developmental perspective. Casual observation suggests that one important characteristic distinguishing these countries from those in East Asia and Latin America, which appear to have benefited more from liberalization, is that the latter had reached a substantially higher level of industrialization and economic diversification prior to the beginning of the adjustment process, generally through development strategies based on import-substitution.

This suggests as a hypothesis that **import substitution may be more effective than export promotion to achieve the level of development required for a country to compete effectively in international markets, and thus to benefit from G/L**. If this is the case, then the application of orthodox structural adjustment programmes in most Sub-Saharan (and other least-developed) countries may be misconceived and harmful. This hypothesis should be investigated.

Even if this interpretation is correct, however, the implications for policy are not immediately clear, as import-substituting industrialization has been attempted in many Sub-Saharan countries, with little apparent success[53]. It is possible to envisage an import-substitution strategy based on regional trade groupings (to overcome the inadequate domestic markets in many countries). This would be compatible with Uruguay Round commitments, as agreed tariff ceilings are generally well above current levels, and the GATT provisions specifically permit regional trade arrangements (RTAs). Again, however, RTAs generally have a very weak track record in the region (Woodward 1993). If this path were to be pursued, it would therefore be necessary to consider the obstacles which have applied in these areas in the past, and, to the extent that they remain relevant, how they could be overcome.

If protection were to be permitted to foster the development of "infant industries", whether on a national or a regional basis, it should be based on tariffs rather than quantitative restrictions, to minimise distortions and generate revenues; and it should be strictly temporary, with a binding timetable for its elimination, deviations from which would be limited to clearly-defined and legitimate anti-dumping safeguards. The loss of revenue resulting from the progressive reduction of tariffs should be factored into fiscal plans.

Such a policy would also need to be highly selective – i.e. based on a realistic appraisal of potential comparative advantage. Protection on other goods should continue to be phased out, although in many cases the pace of tariff reduction would inevitably be influenced by the extent to which fiscal revenues were strengthened from other sources.

There may also be a case for **a greater degree of selectivity in export promotion policies and liberalization of FDI regimes**. In the case of exports this relates to the objective of diversification and the avoidance of the fallacy of composition problem. As noted above, there is a risk that blanket export-promotion policies (e.g. devaluation) may disproportionately favour traditional commodity exports; and these are often products for which the fallacy of composition problem is particularly important. This could be at least partly resolved by coordinated export taxes; but unless and until this is achieved (and for products not covered), there may be a case for investigating complementary measures to skew export promotion efforts towards products which contribute to economically viable diversification and away from those whose increased production may adversely affect developing countries as a whole (on a negative list basis).

In the case of FDI, investment in different types of activities has different implications, in terms of employment generation, foreign exchange effects, forward and backward linkages, input costs and overall competitiveness, environmental effects, natural resource depletion, etc. The social benefits of FDI will be heavily dependent on the nature of the investment; and, in view of the potentially high foreign exchange cost of FDI, not all investments will necessarily bring net social benefits. Thus a labour-intensive, export-oriented investment using local inputs in an area of limited employment opportunities is likely to be much more beneficial than, say, a soft-drinks bottling plant producing for the domestic market using mostly imported inputs and largely substituting for existing locally-owned production. Another priority area is likely to be in the provision of productive services (e.g. transport and communications) which could contribute to overall competitiveness. Such differences in social benefits will not, in general, be fully reflected in relative profitability.

Such considerations could be included in the coordinated approach to FDI policies proposed above. Again, however, there may be a case for implementation by individual countries in the interim, or for adaptation of general principles to national conditions. Such policies could be implemented on a collective basis by regional trade groupings, although it would be important to avoid an excessively directive or bureaucratic approach (cf. the Andean Pact in the 1970s).

In many low-income countries, **fiscal policy** is a matter of particular concern. In many cases, particularly in Sub-Saharan Africa, fiscal constraints and the paucity of public sector revenues are a critical factor limiting development potential, the scope for liberalization and the potential benefits of globalization. Some of the policy proposals discussed earlier will bring some benefits in this respect, particularly the coordinated application of optimal export taxes, debt reduction and measures to increase the efficiency and flexibility of aid flows. However, further action will also be necessary in a number of cases.

Specifically, **tax reform** should be treated as a matter of priority within structural adjustment programmes, primarily to broaden the tax base and improve collection. This is already regarded as an important objective, but practicalities – particularly constraints on administrative capacity – mean that the process has been completed at best slowly. A priority use of the additional revenues generated by export taxes, etc. (and of technical assistance) should be to strengthen capacity in tax policy and collection, to provide a more solid and sustainable revenue base.

A second critical component of fiscal policy, particularly from a welfare perspective is the **inter-sectoral reallocation** of resources. Again, this has become an explicit objective within structural adjustment, the key constraints being political. If it were possible to increase the resources available for non-interest expenditure, this should facilitate the reallocation process: it is easier to allow a relatively small real increase in the budget of a powerful ministry than to impose a disproportionate reduction.

Defence expenditure is often a particularly contentious area. The instinctive desire of donors and international agencies to reduce defence spending is often matched by an equal and opposite view on the part of the government concerned. In practice, there are both political and practical considerations to be taken into account. Politically, an excessive reduction in defence spending may raise the risk of political intervention by the armed forces, to the detriment of the long-term objectives of democratization and good governance. Practically, there may be genuine external and/or internal threats; and under-paid soldiers are not conducive to social and political stability. A relatively large army may also be useful as a means of absorbing surplus labour at times of adjustment (cf. national service in some European countries in the post-War period).

Perhaps the most beneficial area for reductions in military spending is in imports of defence equipment – not least because they represent an unproductive drain on scarce foreign exchange resources as well as on the budget. Here, the governments of arms exporting countries could usefully reduce their sales efforts, particularly towards low-income countries, preferably on a multilateral basis. However, the importance of arms exports to some countries (notably the US, the UK and France) will continue to be an important constraint.

3.9.3 Social policies and safety nets

The most effective way of reducing poverty and increasing welfare in developing countries is to design economic policies explicitly around these objectives, as proposed above. Such an approach would imply the incorporation of social policies (subsidies, transfers, public employment schemes, health and education expenditure, etc.) as an integral part of economic policy, where they would promote long-term welfare, taking account of economic costs.

However, the achievement of this objective is, at best, some way off. Accordingly, this sub-section is premised on the continuation of the current approach to structural adjustment. It should, however, be emphasized that some of the proposals outlined above (particularly coordinated export taxes) may require parallel compensatory measures to avoid an adverse impact on some groups.

Policies directed towards incomes can be divided broadly into three categories:

- compensatory programmes, designed to off-set the potential negative impacts of economic policy changes on targeted groups who are adversely affected;
- market-based programmes, designed to change market conditions in favour of low-income households, for example by absorbing surplus labour; and
- facilitation measures, aimed at enabling low-income households to benefit from potential economic opportunities arising from economic changes.

Such measures have been included, in varying combinations in a number of World Bank social dimensions of adjustment programmes, in parallel with structural adjustment. The three types of programme have different implications and limitations (although there may be a significant degree of overlap between them).

The direct benefits of pure **compensatory programmes** (e.g. targeted nutrition programmes, exemption schemes for user charges, etc.) are essentially limited to the recipients[54]. In some cases, however, hybrid programmes have been implemented, for example based on public employment targeted explicitly on particular groups. Such programmes may have additional benefits, as discussed below.

The targeting of compensatory programmes may be on the poorest (as those most vulnerable to even limited adverse effects), or on those most directly affected. The latter category is generally limited to retrenched public sector workers. While these are not normally among the poorest, and therefore may not, from a strict economic perspective, be priority recipients, their inclusion may be necessary to political stability and the effective implementation of adjustment measures. (The inclusion of redundant tin miners as a major target group in Bolivia's Emergency Social Fund is a case in point.)

Effective targeting is critical to the effectiveness of compensatory programmes; and explicit targeting is by no means always the most effective means of reaching those in greatest need. There is a particular danger of focusing benefits on those most *directly* affected by economic changes rather than those for whom the effects are *greatest* in terms of welfare. The latter requires a greater understanding of the indirect effects of adjustment than often exists (including, for example, the effects of household coping strategies on household time, incomes in the urban informal sector, etc.); and an implicit evaluation of the effect of given changes in real income, relative prices, time-use, etc. at different levels of per capita income. These problems, coupled with the inadequacy of information at the household level (and the high cost of collecting it) makes explicit targeting inherently difficult and unreliable – hence the reliance on sectoral targeting and self-targeting measures.

Self-targeting compensatory programmes broadly correspond with the **market-based** category. These most commonly comprise public employment schemes, with wages fixed at very low levels, so that participation is not worthwhile for households which are not in need of assistance. In addition to the benefits of additional income to the beneficiaries, such schemes can create a floor (albeit a very low one) to wage levels and informal sector incomes, and may increase wages to some extent by absorbing surplus labour, providing benefits to other low-income households. Where participants are engaged on the development, rehabilitation or maintenance of infrastructure, this will bring additional economic benefits in the longer term.

There is, however, some danger in the nature of the self-targeting mechanism. For many low-income households, not only income but also the time available to household members (particularly women) for expenditure-reducing or welfare-related activities (food preparation, child care and feeding, in-home health care, etc.) is of critical importance. Setting wage levels at very low levels makes the trade-off between income and time particularly unfavourable; and the welfare benefits of increased income may be largely off-set by the associated time costs.

Nonetheless, public employment schemes are likely to be beneficial, irrespective of economic policies, where there is substantial or rapidly increasing surplus labour and rural wages and urban informal sector incomes are very low. However, the time-cost factor, coupled with the problems of targeting in compensatory programmes suggests that the two should be operated in parallel, self-targeting public employment effectively operating as a safety net below explicitly targeted compensatory programmes.

The direct benefits of compensatory programmes and public employment schemes last only as long as resources continue to be put into them. However, they also have important indirect benefits in the long term, in terms of the effects of the improvements in health and nutritional status and educational attainment associated with higher incomes, as well as improvements in infrastructure (in the case of public employment). These effects, coupled with the potentially important role of such programmes in reducing poverty, suggest that such schemes should be maintained as long as poverty would persist without them, although their scale should diminish as development proceeds and economic opportunities increase.

The operation of compensatory and public works-based social dimensions of adjustment programmes has often, in practice, been less than wholly satisfactory. Problems have included shortcomings in the design of targeting and the translation of appropriate targeting objectives into practice; and frequently implementation has been very slow and patchy, largely reflecting the delays in donor funding, a weak administrative capacity, and in some cases the failings of implementing NGOs (Costello et al 1994 and Marc et al 1993). There is a need for further work to investigate ways of overcoming these problems.

Facilitation measures, if successful, offer much more durable benefits than compensatory and market-based approaches, as they should establish beneficiaries on the path towards a viable long-term income. The benefits may also extend beyond the recipients of assistance, through the stimulation of local economies, forward and backward linkages, etc. Examples of such policies include, in particular, retraining programmes, credit schemes, agricultural extension and support to microenterprises in the informal sector.

There is an important trade-off in the targeting of facilitation programmes. While the greatest benefit from the point of view of poverty reduction would in principle be achieved by targeting the poorest, the attributes necessary or conducive to future economic success (education, entrepreneurial and other skills, capital, access to land, etc.) are primarily concentrated in less poor households. Since unsuccessful facilitation brings few benefits, if any, this suggests that feasibility should predominate over social objectives in targeting, so that the primary target group would be significantly above the bottom of the income distribution.

It is important, in establishing facilitation programmes, to take account of the implications for the supply of the good or service whose production is supported, and hence on market prices and the incomes of existing suppliers. By way of illustration, supporting the establishment of petty traders would in most cases be likely merely to compound an existing pattern of over-supply in a market already dominated by poorer households. As such, the net effect on poverty might well be negative. Similarly, promoting the production of tropical products subject (or potentially subject) to coordinated export taxes would, in aggregate, be counterproductive. It is therefore important that facilitation programmes be designed to be compatible with the broader objective of economic diversification, on a negative-list basis.

Overall, compensatory, market-based and facilitation measures can play a significant role in poverty reduction, and can thus help to off-set any negative impact of G/L on particular groups and sectors. The three categories are essentially complementary in nature, and the appropriate balance between them will depend on local economic conditions (e.g. needs, administrative capacity, the feasibility of targeting, economic opportunities and scope for facilitation, etc.). As such, they should be a priority area for donor support in the short term, particularly in countries where G/L is expected to have an adverse effect on poverty or to require a substantial adjustment process, and domestic resources are not available. As resources become available, funding should shift to the budget[55], to avoid the delays and disruptions which could be associated with declining official financing and bureaucratic delays[56]. The subject of compensatory and facilitation measures is further addressed in this volume in the paper by Ms. Graham entitled *Safety nets and compensatory measures*.

Another key element of the current approach to limiting the social impact of adjustment is the **protection of health and education spending** from budgetary pressures. This is strongly endorsed, although, as noted above, increasing the social sectors' share of public spending would be easier politically in a context of increasing total (non-interest) expenditure. As a result, increasing budgetary resources should have a disproportionate effect on health and education spending.

A major benefit of increasing the public resources available for health and education would be to reduce the pressure for the imposition of user charges. As discussed earlier, these are likely to have a significant negative impact on the utilization of health services, particularly for those in greatest need. This should be a priority use of any increase in resources available to health services. There is also a strong case for reducing the cost to households of primary school education, e.g. by increasing subsidies on learning materials as well as reducing or removing fees. At higher levels of education, however, the arguments are more finely balanced.

Another form of social expenditure which has been accorded some respectability in the context of liberalization is **"self-targeting" food subsidies**. While state subsidies in general have been reduced or eliminated as distortionary and expensive, a case has been made (e.g. IMF 1986 and World Bank 1990c) for retaining subsidies on the cheapest calorie source in a particular country, where this is consumed disproportionately by poorer households. While there are some caveats to this approach (e.g. with respect to the implications for protein and micronutrient intakes, energy-density, etc.), it is likely to bring substantial benefits (Costello et al 1994). There may also be a case for extending the definition of eligible staple foods, as not all countries have a commodity which fulfils the "self-targeting" criteria. Again, where appropriate to local conditions, basic food subsidies should be a priority use of government resources.

Notes

1. A conspicuous exception is the TRIPs agreement, whose provisions extend well beyond the scope of most structural adjustment programmes.

2. However, Mr. Drabek in his paper in this volume, argues that this is not the case if the fish and textiles sectors are excluded.

3. In Guyana, for example, exports of sugar to the EU under the Sugar Protocol represent virtually all of the country's sugar exports; and the reform of the EU's sugar régime prompted by the Agreement on Agriculture may require a reduction in either the price or the volume of imports under the sugar protocol. Sugar represents 45 per cent of Guyana's total exports, 30 per cent of GDP, and 10 per cent of employment (Woodward, 1994b).

4. See "Rotten Tomatoes", *The Economist*, 10 February 1996, pp. 98-9 (UK edition).

5. Hong Kong is also projected to lose, by $1.1bn; but this is much less significant in terms of the impact on global poverty.

6. This is based on Goldin and van der Mensbrugghe's Simulation II, which compares the nearest approximation of the expected implementation of the Uruguay Round, as compared with the average level of protection in 1989-93.

7. This is illustrated by the effects on the EU's sugar régime, and their implications for exporting countries, as discussed in Woodward (1994b).

8. However, this argument does not apply to Sub-Saharan countries, as their commitments within the Uruguay Round do not represent a reduction in trade barriers from their current level.

9. Financial instruments are not included in the following discussion, due to lack of data.

10. The figures for financial flows are taken from, or estimated on the basis of, World Bank (1995f).

11. GDP data are taken from World Bank (1995g). This analysis excludes European countries and countries which were part of the Former Soviet Union. The one country with GDP greater than $40bn but no recorded equity inflow is Iran.

12. The exceptionally high equity flows to Liberia would appear to be a statistical anomaly.

13. Only 10.4 per cent of the net resource flow to China in 1980 came from official sources, and this had increased slightly (to 12.1 per cent) by 1993.

14. As measured by the unit value of G5 manufactured exports, weighted by the volume of exports to developing countries (World Bank, 1995b).

15. Debt-equity schemes have also been a very important source of foreign equity investments in some developing countries (most notably Chile and Argentina); and this source has also dried up with the completion of Brady packages for debt and debt-service reduction. However, debt-equity

conversions are not included in the World Bank data used here.

16. Regulatory changes in developed countries regarding outward flows of equity finance (e.g. the US SEC Rule 144A) have a similar effect.

17. Ugandan flight capital, for example, is put at around 80-85 per cent of GDP at end-1990, the seventh highest in the developing world (World Bank, 1993a). It is likely that a substantial proportion of this represents the savings of Asians who left the country in the 1970s.

18. Examples include Cameroon (1989-93), Cape Verde (1989-92), Central African Republic (1988-92), Iran (1986-93), Jamaica (1982-6), Mali (1986-92), Panama (1986-93), Senegal (1983-7), Sierra Leone (1985-8), Somalia (1982-9), Tanzania (1986-90), Zaire (1987-90) and Zimbabwe (1982-90). (Data are from World Bank, 1990c and 1995f.)

19. Based on data from World Bank (1990c). Note that the group of seriously-indebted middle-income countries at the time differed somewhat from the current group. However, the earlier group corresponds more closely with the countries which experienced problems with commercial debts in the 1980s, and is therefore more relevant to the current discussion.

20. This includes bonds issued under Brady deals for debt and debt-service reduction.

21. This is an unweighted arithmetic mean, estimated from World Bank (1995c), Figure 8. Countries receiving equity inflows are determined on the basis of World Bank (1995f). It is assumed that such inflows occurred to Taiwan, Province of China, which is not included in the latter source. The two EU members included in the data (Portugal and Greece) are excluded from this estimate.

22. Price earnings ratios in recipient countries in 1994 are shown as between 18 and 30 (Figure 2), and average dividends as ranging between 30 per cent and 40 per cent of earnings in 1986 and 1994 (Figure 5).

23. It should be noted that the average rate of return estimated above is estimated over a 17-year period, from 1976 to 1992.

24. This estimate is based on data from IMF (1992a), for Colombia, Republic of Korea, Swaziland, Thailand and Venezuela (all 1985-91), Malaysia (1984-8) and Panama (1984-7). The average rate of return in these cases was 18 per cent per annum, but this excludes reinvested profits in a number of cases. A very strong negative relationship exists between the rate of return and GNP per capita at purchasing power parity in 1987 (based on UNDP, 1990), ranging from Republic of Korea (7.8 per cent per annum at $4,832 per capita) to Swaziland (31.9 per cent per annum at $2,110 per capita). The only exception to this pattern is the higher rate of return in Colombia (25.0 per cent per annum at $3,524 per capita) than in Thailand (19.5 per cent per annum at $2,576 per capita). Even here, the Thai figure is understated by the exclusion of reinvested profits; and Thailand's GNP per capita had moved ahead of Colombia's by 1992 (UNDP, 1995).

25. This point was made to me by Ms. Mallampally of the UNCTAD Secretariat, during the course of the inter-agency seminar.

26. Transfer pricing is suggested by Yeats (1991) as one possible reason for the substantially higher prices paid by Sub-Saharan countries than other developing countries for iron and steel imports between 1962 and 1987. The additional import cost for the products considered was estimated at $1bn (in 1987 NPV terms); extrapolating to all iron steel products would roughly double this figure, and extrapolation to all manufactured imports would increase it to around $25bn. This represents around 15 per cent of the region's total external debt in 1987.

27. Based on weighted average data for 51 developing countries, from IMF (1992a). There is little obvious pattern in the rates for different countries in terms of regions, income per capita or size of economy.

28. The existence of a large net transfer even in 1970 suggests that this may in part reflect the stock of foreign-owned productive assets inherited at Independence.

29. It should be noted that the following discussion is something of a caricature. It may nonetheless provide some insight into the longer-term implications of equity investment.

30. Côte d'Ivoire is shown in Figure 6.1(a) as having made no reduction in QR coverage, but described in the text as "having reduced Qrs".

31. Comoros (54.0 per cent in 1987), Guinea (74.4 per cent in 1990), Lesotho (51.8 per cent in 1991), Swaziland (56.6 per cent in 1992) and Uganda (57.7 per cent in 1991).

32. No data are provided for the other two low-income countries in the sample (China and Vietnam).

33. Based on data from IMF (1992b).

34. Mexico, Singapore, the Dominican Republic, Hong Kong, Malaysia, Mauritius, Brazil, Taiwan Province of China, Macao, Sri Lanka, Indonesia and Tunisia.

35. Based on data from World Bank (1994d, 1995e and 1995g). The exceptions are Chile, Colombia, Costa Rica, the Dominican Republic and El Salvador. Data are not available for Cuba or Haiti, but in both cases real GNP per capita almost certainly also declined between 1980 and 1994.

36. Based on data from World Bank (1994d and 1995e).

37. The same argument applies to a lesser extent even where the price elasticity of demand is less than one, and/or developing countries represent a minority of production. In these circumstances, overall developing country export revenues will increase, but by less than the increase in export volume; and the loss of production of other goods resulting from resource reallocation could, in principle, outweigh the benefits associated with increased export revenues.

38. However, while offering preferential terms to foreign investors is cheaper in fiscal terms, it is likely to have adverse developmental effects by discriminating against local investors.

39. As reported in Gooptu (1993), p. 56.

40. In the case of Mozambique, for example, 80 per cent of the development budget was externally funded in 1993. Of the remaining 20 per cent, more than half represented the government's contribution to donor-funded projects. Overall, 96 per cent of programmed investments were partly or wholly donor-funded (Woodward et al, 1994, p. 71).

41. The figures in this paragraph and the next are based on Chen et al (1993), Tables 3 and A4.

42. This is particularly problematic because of major changes in health delivery technologies (particularly the widespread development of primary health care, mass immunisation campaigns and oral rehydration therapy) which roughly coincided with the beginning of the adjustment period.

43. *The Economist*, for example, anticipates "a further brutal rationalisation of its farm sector, to create a few big farms where many small ones now stand. That will imply...more shedding of labour" ("A Vacancy Awaits: a Survey of China", *The Economist*, 18 March 1995, p. 25).

44. While independent trade unions are legal in almost all EPZs, membership is limited (or in some cases prevented) by a number of *de facto* obstacles.

45. However, the pattern of price changes is likely to be much more complex than is suggested by the simple tradeable/non-tradeable dichotomy (Woodward, 1992).

46. Revenues from user fees are often diverted, in whole or in part, to the Ministry of Health or the Ministry of Finance. To the extent that this occurs, the potential benefits in terms of quality will be still more limited, and the effect on utilisation more negative.

47. Chemicals companies feature particularly prominently among those for whom intellectual property considerations are important to FDI decisions; in Mansfield (1994 and 1995).

48. There may also be important effects on carbon dioxide and other emissions relevant to global warming. However, they are not discussed here, as the effect on low-income households is very indirect and may be relatively limited. The effects of G/L in this context are likely to be similar to those on industrial pollution more generally.

49. In the case of Peru, Glewwe and Hall (1995) found that "transfer networks that may assist the poor in relatively stable periods do not appear to protect them during a major shock, with the exception of transfers that originate from outside Peru". It is not clear whether this effect was purely temporary, or whether there has been some permanent weakening of informal transfer mechanisms.

50. In the view of the author, this argument does not extend to conditionality with respect to economic policies more generally, but is limited to the enforcement of policies which are in the interest of all implementing countries collectively, but would not occur in the absence of effective mechanisms to enforce collusive behaviour. Any more general strengthening of IMF and World Bank conditionality would further weaken the autonomy of developing country governments, raising serious concerns about sovereignty and the development of the political maturity essential for successful democratization.

51. There is also cause for some concern about the extent of debt and debt-service reduction actually achieved under the Brady Initiative for a number of middle-income countries, particularly in Latin America (EURODAD, 1995). However, this is of more limited relevance in the current context.

52. Tied aid may significantly increase the cost of the imports it pays for. Yeats (1991) suggests tied aid as an alternative (or complement) to transfer pricing as an explanation for the higher prices paid for imports of iron and steel products by Sub-Saharan countries.

53. Zimbabwe and South Africa are the most notable exceptions. It is interesting to observe that these are also the two countries in the region which had import-substitution forced on them for some time by external forces (i.e. trade sanctions).

54. There may, however, be some indirect benefits to others, for example through an improvement in public health associated with improved nutritional status reducing the prevalence of communicable diseases.

55. It should be noted that infrastructure developed through public works schemes will also entail some recurrent costs for operation and maintenance, which may need to be financed from the budget where projects cannot be made self-financing.

56. The point was made to me at the inter-agency seminar by Mr. R. van der Hoeven of ILO that their research has found that compensatory programmes established prior to structural adjustment and without external support had proved better targeted and more sustainable than externally-financed programmes introduced in parallel with formal adjustment programmes. This would appear to reinforce the case for maximizing local financing and responsibility.

References

Bachmann, H. and K. Kwaku. 1994. *MIGA Roundtable on Foreign Direct Investment Policies in Africa: Proceedings and Lessons.* Washington D.C.: World Bank, MIGA Policy and Advisory Services Research Paper.

Barratt Brown, M. and P. Tiffen. 1992. *Short Changed: Africa and World Trade.* London: Pluto Press.

Behrman, J. and A. Deolalikar. 1988. Health and Nutrition. In H. Chenery, and T. Srinivasan (eds.) *Handbook of Development Economics,* Volume I. Amsterdam: Elsevier.

Bergsman, J. and X. Shen. 1995. Foreign Direct Investment in Developing Countries: Progress and Problems. *Finance and Development* 32(4):6-8, December.

Bouis, H. and L. Haddad. 1990. *Effects of Agricultural Commercialization on Land Tenure, Household Resource Allocation, and Nutrition in the Philippines.* Washington D.C.: International Food Policy Research Institute, Research Report No. 79.

Chen, S., G. Datt and M. Ravallion. 1993. Is Poverty Increasing in the Developing World? Mimeo. World Bank. April.

Claessens, S. and S. Gooptu. (eds.) 1993. *Portfolio Investment in Developing Countries.* Washington D.C.: World Bank, Discussion Paper No. 228.

Claessens, S. and S. Gooptu. 1994. Can Developing Countries Keep Capital Flowing in? *Finance and Development* 31(3):62-5, September.

Coote, B. 1992. *The Trade Trap: Poverty and the Global Commodity Markets.* Oxford: Oxfam.

Cornia, G., R. Jolly and F. Stewart. 1987. *Adjustment with a Human Face.* Oxford: Oxford University Press.

Costello, A., F. Watson and D. Woodward. 1994. *Human Face or Human Façade? Adjustment and the Health of Mothers and Children.* Occasional Paper: Institute of Child Health, London.

Creese, A. 1991. User Charges for Health Care: a Review of Recent Experience. *Health Policy and Planning,* 6:309-19.

Dean, J., S. Desai and J. Riedel. 1994. *Trade Policy Reform in Developing Countries since 1985: a Review of the Evidence.* Washington D.C.: World Bank, Discussion Paper No. 267.

de Melo, J., A. Senhadji-Semlali and J. Stanton. 1991. Macro Performance under Adjustment Lending. In V. Thomas, A. Chhibber, M. Dailami and J.

de Melo (eds.). *Restructuring Economies in Distress: Policy Reform and the World Bank.* New York: Oxford University Press.

Demery, L., B. Sen and T. Vishwanath. 1995. Poverty, Inequality and Growth. Education and Social Policy Department Discussion Paper No. 70, World Bank.

Diwan, I. and A. Revenga. 1995. The Outlook for Workers in the 21st Century. *Finance and Development* 32(3):10-11, September.

Elson, D. 1994. Household Responses to Stabilisation and Structural Adjustment: Male Bias at the Micro Level. Gender Analysis and Development Economics Working Paper No. 6, University of Manchester, November.

EURODAD. 1995. *World Credit Tables, 1994-5: Debtor-Creditor Relations from Another Perspective.* Brussels: European Network on Debt and Development.

Faini, R., F. Clavijo and A. Senhadj-Semlali. 1989. The Fallacy of Composition Argument: Does Demand Matter for LDCs' Manufacturers Exports? Centro Studi Luca d'Agliano/Queen Elizabeth House Development Studies Working Paper No. 7, March.

Finger, M. and P. Messerlin. 1989. *The Effects of Industrial Countries' Policies on Developing Countries.* Washington D.C.: World Bank, Policy and Research Series No. 3.

Foster, M. 1995. Financing Structural Adjustment via the Budget. Paper for the Structural Adjustment Forum, Nottingham University, 13-14 November.

Francois, J., B. McDonald and H. Nordström. 1995. Assessing the Uruguay Round. In W. Martin and A. Winters, (eds.) *The Uruguay Round and the Developing Economies.* Washington D.C.: World Bank, Discussion Paper No. 307.

Gardner, B. 1993. The GATT Uruguay Round: Implications for Exports from the Agricultural Superpowers. Briefing Paper, CIIR/SAFE Alliance, London, December.

Gertler, P. and J. van der Gaag. 1990. *The Willingness to Pay for Medical Care: Evidence from Two Developing Countries.* Baltimore: Johns Hopkins.

Glen, J., Y. Karmokolias, R. Miller, and S. Shah. 1995. *Dividend Policy and Behaviour in Emerging Markets: to Pay or not to Pay.* Washington D.C.: World Bank, International Finance Corporation Discussion Paper No. 26.

Goldin, I., O. Knudsen and D. van der Mensbrugghe. 1993. *Trade Liberalization: Global Economic Implications.* Paris: OECD/World Bank.

Goldin, I., and D. van der Mensbrugghe. 1995. The Uruguay Round: an Assessment of Economywide and Agricultural Reforms. In W. Martin and A. Winters (eds.) *The Uruguay Round and the Developing Economies.* Washington D.C.: World Bank, Discussion Paper No. 307.

Gooptu, S. 1993. Portfolio Investment Flows to Emerging Markets. In Claessens and Gooptu (eds.) *Portfolio Investment in Developing Countries.* Washington D.C.: World Bank, Discussion Paper No. 228.

Griffin, C. 1988. *User Charges for Health Care in Principle and Practice.* Washington D.C.: World Bank, EDI Seminar Paper No. 37.

Harrison, G., T. Rutherford, and D. Tarr. 1995. Quantifying the Uruguay Round. In W. Martin and A. Winters, (eds.) *The Uruguay Round and the Developing Economies.* Washington D.C.: World Bank, Discussion Paper No. 307.

Harrold, P. 1995. The Impact of the Uruguay Round on Africa: Much Ado about Nothing? Paper for the Conference on the Uruguay Round and the Developing Economies, January.

Hertel, T., M. Martin, K. Yanagishima and B. Dimaranan. 1995. Liberalizing Manufactures Trade in a Changing World Economy. In W. Martin and A. Winters (eds.) *The Uruguay Round and the Developing Economies.* Washington D.C.: World Bank, Discussion Paper No. 307.

Howell, M. and A. Cozzini. 1992. *International Equity Flows.* London: Baring Securities.

IMF. 1986. *Fund-Supported Programmes, Fiscal Policy and Income Distribution.* Washington D.C.: International Monetary Fund, Occasional Paper No. 46.

Ingco, M. 1995. Agricultural Trade Liberalization in the Uruguay Round: One Step Forward, One Step Back? World Bank, International Trade Division Working Paper.

Ingco, M. and D. Hathaway. 1995. Agricultural Liberalization and the Uruguay Round. In W. Martin and A. Winters (eds.) *The Uruguay Round and the Developing Economies.* Washington D.C.: World Bank, Discussion Paper No. 307.

Jimenez, E. 1987. *Pricing Policy in the Social Sectors: Cost Recovery for Education and Health in Developing Countries.* Baltimore: Johns Hopkins.

Johansson, H. 1994. The Economics of Export Processing Zones Revisited. *Development Policy Review* 12(4):387-402, December.

Khan, A. 1993. *Structural Adjustment and Income Distribution: Issues and*

Experience. Geneva: International Labour Organisation.

Madden, P. 1993. Brussels Beef Carve-up: EC Beef Dumping in West Africa. Viewpoint No. 3, Christian Aid, London.

Marc, A., C. Graham and M. Schachter. 1993. Social Action Programmes and Social Funds: a Review of Design and Implementation in Sub-Saharan Africa. Mimeo. Human Resources and Poverty Division, World Bank.

Mosley, P., J. Harrigan and J. Toye. 1991. *Aid and Power: the World Bank and Policy-Based Lending.* London: Routledge.

Mosley, P. and J. Weeks. 1995. Assessing 'Adjustment in Africa'. *World Development.*

Page, S. and M. Davenport. 1994. *World Trade Reform: Do Developing Countries Gain or Lose?* London: Overseas Development Institute.

Pryke, J. and D. Woodward. 1994. The GATT Agreement on Agriculture: Will it Help Developing Countries?. Background Paper, Catholic Institute for International Relations, London, March.

Romero, A. 1995. Labour and Export Processing Zones: Situation and Pressures for Change. *Development Policy Review* 13(3):247-276, September.

Rose, P. 1994. Female Education and Adjustment Programmes: a Cross-Country Statistical Analysis. Gender Analysis and Development Economics Working Paper No. 5, University of Manchester, November.

Sader, F. 1995. *Privatizing Public Enterprises and Foreign Investment in Developing Countries, 1988-93.* Washington D.C.: World Bank, Foreign Investment Advisory Service Occasional Paper No. 5.

Trebilcock, M. and R. Howse. 1995. *The Regulation of International Trade.* London: Routledge.

UNCTAD. 1994. *Trade and Development Report, 1994.* New York/Geneva: United Nations.

_____. 1995. *World Investment Report, 1995.* New York/Geneva: United Nations.

Watkins, K. 1992. *Fixing the Rules: North-South Issues in International Trade and the GATT Uruguay Round.* London: Catholic Institute for International Relations.

Woodward, D. 1992. *Debt, Adjustment and Poverty in Developing Countries.* London: Pinter Publishers/Save the Children (UK).

_____. 1993. Regional Trade Arrangements in Sub-Saharan Africa. Mimeo. Oxfam (UK), Oxford.

_____. 1994a. IMF Gold Sales for Debt Relief. Mimeo. Debt Crisis Network, London.

_____. 1994b. Reform of the EU Sugar Régime: Implications for Developing Country Exporters – a Study with Particular Reference to Jamaica, Trinidad and Tobago and Guyana. Occasional Paper, Catholic Institute for International Relations, London.

_____. 1995a. Assessing 'Adjustment in Africa': Comments. Mimeo.

_____. 1995b. Children and Poverty. Paper for Conference, Children and Poverty: towards 2000, Coventry University, 12 May.

_____. 1995c. Structural Adjustment and Poverty: some Indications from Limited Data. Paper for the Structural Adjustment Forum, Nottingham University, 13-14 November.

_____. 1995d. User Charges and the Health of Mothers and Children: a Conceptual Framework. Mimeo. Institute of Child Health, London, January.

_____. (forthcoming) Debt Sustainability and the Debt Overhang in the Highly-Indebted Poor Countries: some Comments on the IMF's View. In EURODAD: *World Credit Tables, 1995-6*. Brussels: European Network on Debt and Development.

World Bank. 1988. *Adjustment Lending: an Evaluation of Ten Years of Experience*. Washington D.C.: World Bank, Policy and Research Series No. 1.

_____. 1990a. *Adjustment Lending Policies for Sustainable Growth*. Washington D.C.: World Bank, Policy and Research Series No. 14.

_____. 1990b. *Trends in Developing Economies, 1990*. Washington D.C.: World Bank.

_____. 1990c. *World Development Report, 1990: Poverty*. New York: Oxford University Press.

_____. 1991. *World Debt Tables, 1991-92*. Washington D.C.: World Bank.

_____. 1992a. *Global Economic Prospects and the Developing Countries. 1992*. Washington D.C.: World Bank.

_____. 1992b. *World Development Report, 1992: the Challenge of Development*. New York: Oxford University Press.

_____. 1993a. *Global Economic Prospects and the Developing Countries, 1993*. Washington D.C.: World Bank.

_____. 1993b. *World Development Report, 1993: Investing in Health*. New York: Oxford University Press.

_____. 1994a. *Adjustment in Africa: Reforms, Results and the Road Ahead.* New York: Oxford University Press.

_____. 1994b. *Better Health in Africa: Experience and Lessons Learned.* Washington D.C.: World Bank.

_____. 1994c. *Global Economic Prospects and the Developing Countries, 1994.* Washington D.C.: World Bank.

_____. 1995a. *African Development Indicators, 1994-5.* Washington D.C.: World Bank.

_____. 1995b. *Commodity Markets and the Developing Countries, November 1995.* Washington D.C.: World Bank.

_____. 1995c. *Financial Flows and the Developing Countries, February 1995.* Washington D.C.: World Bank.

_____. 1995d. *Global Economic Prospects and the Developing Countries, 1995.* Washington D.C.: World Bank.

_____. 1995e. *Trends in Developing Economies, 1995.* Washington D.C.: World Bank.

_____. 1995f. *World Debt Tables, 1994-95.* Washington D.C.: World Bank.

_____. 1995g. *World Development Report, 1995: Workers in an Integrating World.* New York: Oxford University Press.

_____. 1996. *World Debt Tables, 1995-96.* Washington D.C.: World Bank.

4

Globalization and liberalization: an opportunity to reduce poverty

Ishrat Husain*

As noted in Mr. Woodward's concepts and issues paper, those countries that stand to gain from globalization and liberalization will, most likely, enjoy the benefit of additional employment, as a result of increased trade opportunities and FDI. The impact that either increase will have on the welfare of the poor will, of course, depend on a number of factors. The most important of these are (a) income changes in agriculture and the urban informal sector, where most of the poor reside, and (b) the allocation pattern of public expenditure. There might also be time-lags as the poor, in the short term, bear transitional costs due to dislocations caused by the liberalization of output and factor markets.

The two questions that need to be addressed are: (a) What will be the direction and magnitude of the aggregate effect of globalization and liberalization? Individual, or household, welfare is the most appropriate indicator for measuring this aggregate effect. This implies weighting by population, rather than by the number of developing countries. (b) How will aggregate gains be translated into net benefits for the poorer segments of the population? This conversion process is central to an understanding of how poverty is reduced in the countries that gain from globalization and liberalization. The channels for reducing poverty should not, however, be confused with those for lowering income inequalities. The objective is to improve the living standards of those living below the poverty line.

The first section of this paper analyzes evidence pertaining to the aggregate effects of globalization and liberalization on developing countries. The second

---

* Director, Poverty and Social Policy Department, the World Bank

section addresses the transmission channels through which the aggregate gains can be translated into net benefits for the poor. The third section challenges some of the assumptions and assertations made in the concepts and issues paper by Mr. Woodward.

4.1 Effects of globalization and liberalization

Contrary to what is indicated in Mr. Woodward's concepts and issues paper, the benefits of globalization and liberalization are not concentrated in a small group of larger, richer and/or more industrialized economies. The most recent World Bank estimates of the incidence of poverty, based on 67 actual household surveys covering 85 percent of the population of developing countries, show that 90 percent of the poor in the developing world are concentrated in India, China, Bangladesh, Brazil, Indo-China, Central America, Pakistan and Sub-Saharan Africa (Table 4.1).

Table 4.1: Number and Percentage of the Population Living Below US$l/day in Developing and Transitional Economies 1987-1993

Region	Cover-age *) (%)	Number of Poor (millions)			Headcount Index (%)			Poverty Gap (%)		
		1987	1990	1993	1987	1990	1993	1987	1990	1993
East Asia & the Pacific	88.0	464.0	468.2	445.8	28.2	28.5	26.0	8.3	8.0	7.8
(excl. China)	*(61.5)*	*(109.2)*	*(89.3)*	*(73.5)*	*(23.2)*	*(17.6)*	*(13.7)*	*(3.8)*	*(3.1)*	*(3.1)*
Eastern Europe & Central Asia	85.9	2.2	n.a.	14.5	0.6	n.a.	3.5	0.2	n.a.	1.1
Latin America & the Caribbean	83.9	91.2	101.0	109.6	22.0	23.0	23.5	8.2	9.0	9.1
Middle East & North Africa	46.7	10.3	10.4	10.7	4.7	4.3	4.1	0.9	0.7	0.6
South Asia	98.4	479.9	480.4	514.7	45.4	43.0	43.1	14.1	12.3	12.6
Sub-Saharan Africa	65.9	179.6	201.2	218.6	38.5	39.3	39.1	14.4	14.5	15.3
Total	85.0	1227	n.a.	1314	30.1	n.a.	29.4	9.5	n.a.	9.2
Total (excl. E. Europe & C. Asia)	85.0	1225	1261	1299	33.3	32.9	31.8	10.8	10.3	10.5

Notes: *) Percentage of population covered by at least one survey. *Source:* World Bank (1996a).

China and India, the two poorest countries in the world, account for more than half of the population of the developing world and have more than half a billion people living below the poverty line. Both countries, however, have benefited, and are projected to benefit, from globalization and liberalization – if nothing extraordinary happens. China has increased its exports more than 10 times in the last 15 years; is the largest single beneficiary of FDI; has doubled its per capita income in less than a decade; and has reduced its incidence of poverty from one third to one tenth[1].(The subject of FDI in China is further addressed in this volume in Ms. Mallampally's paper on *The importance of foreign direct investment for exports, economic growth and poverty reduction in China.*

Since its liberalization in 1991, India's exports have expanded by more than 50 percent; FDI flows are doubling every year; growth rates have exceeded 6 percent (in the last two years); and the incidence of poverty has been lowered. From all accounts, the economic prospects for India, despite recent elections and political changes, are promising. (This subject is taken up at greater length in Mr. Roy's paper in this volume entitled *What prospects does India have of benefitting from globalization?*).

Other large countries with substantial poverty, such as Indonesia, Brazil, Pakistan, Vietnam and Bangladesh, have also benefited from increased participation in the world economy and the liberalization of international trade and investment. It is true that Sub-Saharan Africa has not done as well. However, the growth performance of the countries in this region has also been quite impressive in the last few years (Chart 4.1). Of 42 Sub-Saharan African countries, 31 have recorded positive growth rates. In 1995, the GDP growth rate exceeded that of the population rate in these countries. On the basis of this mapping – between the countries benefiting from globalization and liberalization and the countries having the largest number of poor in the world

---

[1] Note that the decline in the incidence of poverty in China to an estimated one tenth of total population uses national poverty estimates that are comparable over time and a poverty line that is set lower than the poverty line, adjusted for Purchasing Power Parity (PPP) prices, that is utilized in Table 4.1; i.e. 60 PPP cents per person a day rather than one PPP dollar per person a day.

Chart 4.1: Annual GDP growth in Sub-Saharan Africa, 1992-94

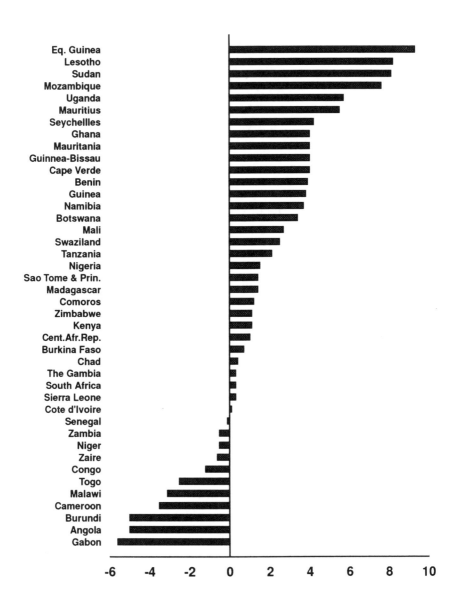

Source: World Bank (1996b) p. 18.

– it is safe to conclude that the aggregate effect of gains from liberalization and globalization would benefit 70-80 percent of the world's poor.

The argument in Mr. Woodward's concepts and issues paper, that the high foreign exchange costs of capital flows will offset the benefits of liberalization and globalization over the long term is not supported by the evidence. One of the most attractive features distinguishing debt financing from equity financing is the nature of payment. In debt financing, service charges are fixed. Irrespective of whether the enterprise or the project for which debt has been incurred makes profits or losses, debt service has to be paid. In the case of equity financing, foreign partners or shareholders will enjoy dividends and profits only if the enterprise or the project is able to generate positive returns and cash flows. Even in that best-case scenario, the reinvestment of dividends, tax payments and dividends to local partners reduces the amounts that are remitted abroad and that require foreign exchange transfers. If the foreign capital flows are destined towards labor-intensive export sectors that augment foreign exchange earnings, the net foreign exchange obligations will be insignificant.

The assertion in the concepts and issues paper that there are substantial costs associated with the need to compete for export markets and for direct and portfolio investment ignores the fact that growth in world trade has outstripped the growth in world output consistently over the last 25 years[2] (Chart 4.2). This expansion in world trade has benefited every region of the developing world, except Sub-Saharan Africa, as manifested by changes in real trade ratios (Chart 4.3). The same picture is true for FDI as a share of GDP. Except for the Middle East and North Africa – where oil and gas-related investments were exceptionally high in 1981-1983 – and Sub-Saharan Africa, all other regions of the world have gained from FDI, not only in absolute dollar volume but in relation to their increasing GDP (Chart 4.4). Over the coming decade, world trade volume is projected to grow at an annual average of 6.3 percent, i.e. the same pace that was achieved in the second half of the 1980s. With world output growing at 3.5 percent a year over the coming decade, global trade integration, as measured by the ratio of trade to GDP, is expected to continue rising at about 2-3 percent a year. Developing country export growth in 1995 was 13 percent.

---

[2] Except for 1975 and 1982.

Chart 4.2: World Exports/GDP and GDP, 1971-97

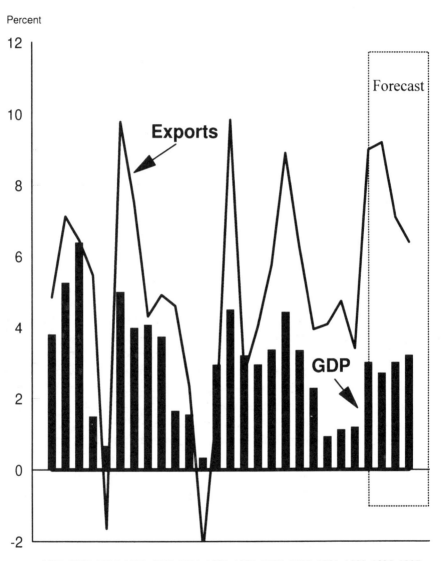

Source: World Bank (1996b) p. 13

Chart 4.3: Changes in Real Trade Ratios

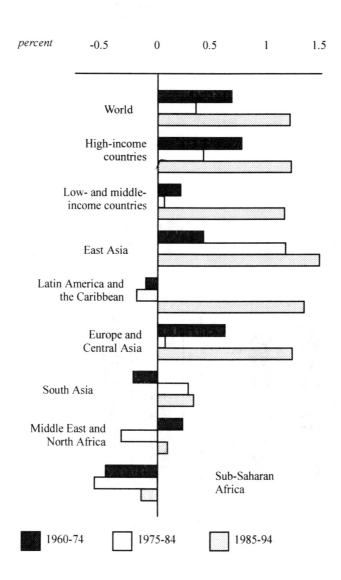

Source: World Bank (1996b) p. 21.

**Chart 4.4: Average Foreign Direct Investment
share of GDP 1984-93**

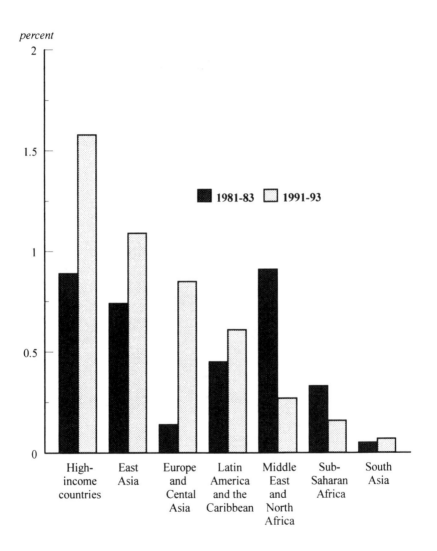

Source: World Bank (1996b) p. 22.

A survey of the literature shows that, except for coffee and cocoa, the fallacy of composition argument in the concepts and issues paper is not valid. As an increasing share of developing country exports is in the form of manufactured goods, it is not likely that there will be a decline in prices arising from a simultaneous expansion of exports. Cocoa and coffee exports account for only 10 percent of Africa's total exports.

Contrary to what is stated in the concepts and issues paper, it is important to note that increased fiscal discipline does not constitute a constraint on social expenditures and, thus, on the alleviation of poverty. A recent empirical study carried out by the Operations Evaluation Department of the World Bank (World Bank 1995) shows that the countries that have been able to reduce their fiscal deficits, bring down inflation and achieve macroeconomic stability were also the countries that did not abate their allocations to social expenditures. Countries with high and unsustainable fiscal deficits had no choice but to cut expenditures on social sectors more heavily than for other sectors.

Another point that needs to be emphasized, particularly for Sub-Saharan Africa, is that the budgetary and quasi-fiscal losses on parastatals, public enterprises and state-owned trading entities are twice, or sometimes three times as large as the overall allocation to the social sectors. Morover, household surveys from many African countries show that private expenditures by the poor on education and health are not insignificant. Thus, there is no *a priori* relationship between fiscal discipline and the level of social expenditures. It is the degree of political commitment by the country's leadership that determines the level and efficient utilization of social expenditures.

One also needs to correct the misconception that the scope of regional linkages and spillovers is limited outside the East Asian and Latin American regions. In fact, the replacement of the South-South regional trading arrangements of the early 1980s (which were a response to export pessimism) by outward-oriented trade policies, and a resurgence in global trade integration have led to an expansion in intra-developing country trade. There was a 12 percent annual growth in South-South trade between 1985-94 that was more buoyant than the 10 percent annual expansion in developing country trade with OECD countries during that period.

Chart 4.5: Integration and Growth

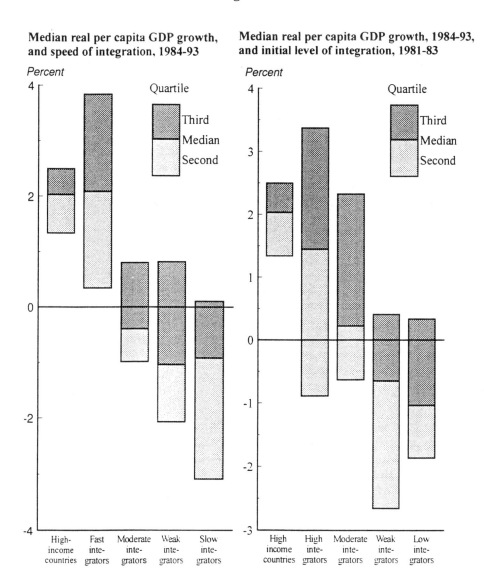

Median real per capita GDP growth, and speed of integration, 1984-93

Median real per capita GDP growth, 1984-93, and initial level of integration, 1981-83

Source: World Bank (1996b) p. 26

Finally, the World Bank (1996b) recently carried out a study relating the speed and initial level of integration of countries with their economic performance. As Chart 4.5 shows, the countries that have integrated themselves strongly with the global trade, investment and credit markets have grown relatively more rapidly than the weak integrators. For countries that have lagged in their integration with global markets, the message is somber: isolationism carries high costs in terms of foreign finance, inhibited investment and often misallocated credit.

4.2 Transmission channels and effects

Studies of the effects of the Uruguay Round have emphasized that countries with domestic liberal trade regimes will be able to benefit relatively more from global trade liberalization than those countries that have restrictive trade policies. Different types of transmission channels are presented below.

4.2.1 Globalization to poverty

(a) *International trade*

- In the medium- to long-term, trade will help the poor, since labour is the primary asset of the poor which is used in the exportables of developing countries.

- Increased trade will result in gains for relatively abundant factors (labour in most low-income countries).

- Consumers get cheaper products (nearer world prices), at least in the medium- to long-term.

(b) *International capital flows*

- Long-term capital inflows (FDI) are beneficial for labour in the developing countries if these are destined towards labour-intensive sectors.

- Short-term flows reward economic discipline and punish policy failures.

- External financial flows also lead to an appreciation of the exchange rate.

(c) *International labour flows*

- In both the long and short run, international migration generally helps the poor.
- With more trade and capital flows, the *need* for labour to move is, however, lower (Chart 4.6).

4.2.2 Liberalization (adjustment) to poverty

(a) *Domestic macroeconomic stability*

- Lower inflation helps everybody; but probably helps the poor more.
- Investor uncertainty is reduced.

(b) *Reduced overregulation and lower relative price distortions*

- The removal of price controls on agriculture helps raise the incomes of poor farmers, but higher food prices and the removal of consumer subsidies may hurt the rural landless (in the short term) and urban consumers.
- The removal of exchange rate distortions should help agriculture (in Asia and Africa, and many of the poor in rural areas) since producer incentives are improved.
- Reduced labour regulations will likely lower the price of labour and help employment growth. (This may reduce wages in highly regulated labour markets, but the poor do not usually constitute a large proportion of the formally employed.)

(c) *Changing public expenditure patterns*

- Expenditures on primary health care and education need to be protected as the revenue base falls (in some countries) over the short term.

(d) *Rural-urban migration*

- The reduced burden on agriculture implies a slower migration to urban areas.

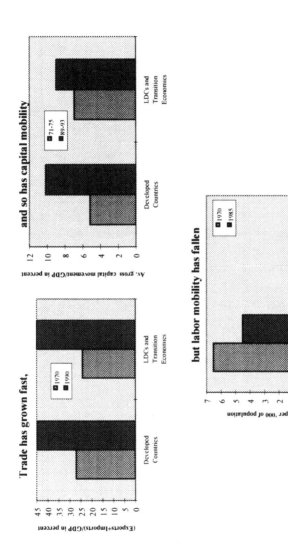

Chart 4.6: The progression of the three forms of global integration has been uneven

Note: Total inflows plus outflows over all the countries in the group divided by total GDP or population for all the countries in the group. *Source:* Migration data from Zlotnik (1993).

(e) *Effects through the external sector*

- Liberalization and structural adjustment encourage international flows of goods, services, and capital; the effects on poverty are outlined above.

- These effects and channels are not always unambiguous and clear, and a number of caveats should be kept in mind.

   (i)   Economic growth is the main transmission channel.
   The effects of globalization and liberalization often work on poverty through higher growth, and only then through the above transmission channels.

   (ii)   Poverty and inequality are not synonymous.
   We must always distinguish between the effects on inequality (relative income levels) and the effects on poverty (usually absolute income levels). Recent work by the World Bank's Poverty Monitoring Unit shows that poverty declines with growth, but the effect of growth on inequality varies across countries.

   (iii)   The effects differ over the long and short term.
   We must also keep in mind that economic analysis is a better guide to long-term effects than short-term effects, and that globalization and liberalization have both types of effects.

   (iv)   There are both partial and general equilibrium effects.
   The first order responses by economic actors to various liberalization measures are incomplete and do not necessarily capture the full effects, particularly any second and third order effects. A look at three exogenous stimuli – import liberalization (domestic trade policy), global agricultural liberalization, and the elimination of the Multifibre Arrangement (Uruguay Round) – helps to illustrate this point (Chart 4.7). In each case, it is possible that the final and total effect may be at variance with the initial effect, depending both on the public policy response and the subsequent actions of affected economic actors – consumers, producers, etc.

Chart 4.7: Uruguay Round

Agriculture liberalization

	Food importing countries	Food exporting countries
First order	Higher prices for food importers	Increased potential of exports by developing country net food exporters
Second order	Increased prices stimulate domestic food production reducing demand for imports	Allocation of resources at the margin to food production may slow down diversification of economy

Import liberalization

	Consumption imports	Investment imports
First order	Lower the prices for goods consumed by the poor, e.g. second-hand clothing for the poor	Labour-intensive manufactures and exports => increased employment and higher wages
Second order	Competition by imports leads to cost-efficiency in domestic textile manufactures	Inflationary pressures and loss of international competitiveness (if labour market is inefficient). Reduced exports (if exchange rate is overvalued).

Textile trade

	Efficient producers	Inefficient producers
First order	Low-cost textile producers would gain market shares, employment and wages expand	Monopoly rents accruing due to MFA quotas may make some current developing country exporters noncompetitive and render some employment redundant
Second order	Increased competition in world market may lead to demand for state subsidies which may negate the benefit of MFA liberalization	Market forces would compel restructuring of industry and reallocation to other sectors in accordance with country's comparative advantage

4.3 Evidence challenges some of the assumptions and assertions of the concepts and issues paper

In conclusion, certain assumptions made in the concepts and issues paper by Mr. Woodward are not substantiated by the evidence.

(a) *The evidence contradicts some assumptions.*

The implicit assumption that liberalization will affect agriculture adversely is contradicted by evidence carefully gleaned from countries across the globe in a recent World Bank study. The liberalization of domestic and exchange rate policies is shown in this study to reduce the burden that many developing countries have placed on agriculture. Schiff and Valdes (1993) call it the "blundering of agriculture in developing countries." From 80 to 90 percent of the poor in Sub-Saharan Africa, and the majority of the poor in South Asia, live in rural areas and depend on agriculture directly or indirectly for their livelihood. Agriculture price and marketing liberalization has been found to benefit these poor farmers.

(b) *The evidence contradicts some assertions.*

In chapter 3.9.3 of the concepts and issues paper it is stated that the most effective way of reducing poverty and increasing welfare in developing countries is to design policies that rely fundamentally on subsidies, transfers, public employment schemes, and the allocation of expenditures to health and education.

However, successful poverty reduction strategies have relied fundamentally on growth-enhancing policies – income growth, not income redistribution – and helping the poor acquire productive assets by allocating expenditures to primary health and education. Safety nets, such as public works, may be necessary but are not substitutes for growth and human capital formation. In fact, evidence shows that the decline in GDP growth in Latin America in the 1980s led to income inequalities (Chart 4.8).

Chart 4.8: Income inequality and economic growth in Latin America and former centrally planned economies

Where economies declined in Latin America during the 1980s, inequality rose

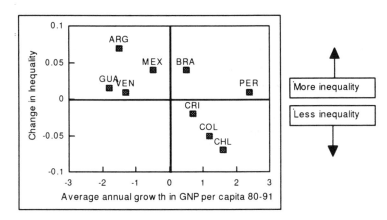

and almost all former centrally planned economies have seen inequality increase

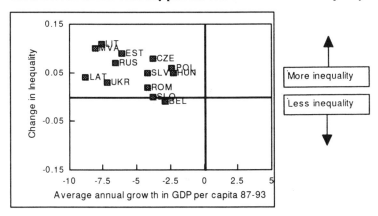

Sources: Psacharopoulos *et al* (1993) for Latin America, Milanovic (1994) for former centrally planned economies.

Furthermore, while some of the instruments mentioned in the concepts and issues paper may be necessary for alleviating poverty, there is evidence that they do so in large part by facilitating growth-oriented policies (e.g., public works in Chile) or directly increasing economic growth (e.g., investments in primary education and health in East Asia).

(c) *Some assertions are based on little or no empirical evidence.*

Finally, the concepts and issues paper opens with the disclaimer that it represents only "a discussion of the nature of the processes which may be involved." However, such terms as "substantially negative" and "strongly skewed" are used to describe the effects of globalization and liberalization. More evidence is required to support these assertions. For example, the claim that the poor will be hurt by liberalization because employment in urban areas will not grow, and employment in rural areas will fall, requires sophisticated studies that unfortunately do not exist. However, a casual look at the evidence shows that where exports have grown, so have wages (Chart 4.9).

Chart 4.9: Growth in real wages rises with export intensity

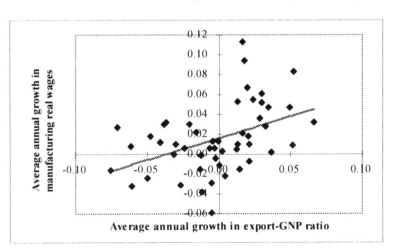

Source: World Bank estimates.

References

Milanovic, Branko. 1994. *Poverty in Transition.* World Bank Policy Research Department. World Bank. Washington, D.C.

Psacharopoulos, George, Samuel Morley, Ariel Fiszbein, Haeduck Lee and Bill Wood. 1993. *Poverty and Income Distribution in Latin America: The Story of the 1980s.* Regional Studies Program, Report No. 27. World Bank. Latin America and the Caribbean Technical Department. Washington, D.C.

Schiff, M. and C. Valdes. 1993. *Plundering Agriculture in Developing Countries.* World Bank. Washington, D.C.

World Bank. 1995. *The Social Impact of Adjustment Operations: An Overview.* World Bank. Operations Evaluation Department. Washington, D.C.

World Bank. 1996a. *Poverty Reduction and the World Bank.* Washington, D.C.

World Bank. 1996b. *Global Economic Prospects and the Developing Countries.* Washington, D.C.

Zlotnic, Hania. 1993. International Migration: Causes and Effects. In Laurie Anne Mazur (ed.) *Beyond the Numbers: A reader on Population, Consumption and the Environment.* Covelo. Calif.: Island Press.

5

Trade and the Uruguay Round: some misconceptions dispelled

Zdenek Drabek*

The main background paper of the seminar by Mr. Woodward contains much valuable information on international trade and other matters of concern to the seminar. However, there are also a number of misconceptions and alarmist views expressed in the paper that need to be clarified or put into proper perspective. Setting the record straight on international trade, the provisions of the Uruguay Round and the role of the World Trade Organization (WTO) is the purpose of the present note.

Clarifications concerning the implications of the Uruguay Round

To begin with, it is of course true that the developed countries, like all countries, protect access to their markets. However, the level of protection is very small. According to WTO estimates, average tariffs for industrial goods currently amount to 3.8 per cent, while the corresponding tariffs on developing country imports, at 4.3 per cent, are only slightly higher. This tariff level cannot be seen as burdensome in terms of developing countries' access. Moreover, the average tariff level is strongly affected by relatively high tariffs in two sectors – the fish industry and textiles and clothing. If one does not include these two sectors in the tariff calculations, the average tariff on imports to developed countries from developing countries is even lower than that on imports to the developed countries from other developed countries. In

---

* Counsellor, Economic Research and Analysis Division, World Trade Organization

short, allegations of excessive protectionism in the developed countries are often exaggerated, including in Mr. Woodward's paper.

Criticism in Mr. Woodward's paper concerning the end-loading of the MFA and agriculture agreements in the Uruguay Round is unfortunately well-founded. These agreements, needless to say, were the result of long and tedious negotiations. However, it is equally or even more important to note that, finally, countries have decided to do something about textiles, and that is a fact which should be adequately recognized and credited among the achievements of the Uruguay Round. The end-loading of the agreement, albeit unfortunate, is in a sense the price to be paid to give the textile industries of the developed countries time to adjust. On agriculture, several studies have shown that the Round has led to some increase in the tariffied level of protection, although not all observers agree on this finding. On the positive side, however, it should be acknowledged that there has been talk on agriculture and that this has resulted in the establishment of a system that is transparent. These achievements may provide the basis for future negotiations in this sector.

In his paper, Mr. Woodward also alludes to a number of "factors" which he believes limit the benefits of the Uruguay Round agreement for many developing countries. One of these is the erosion of preferences, which he sees as beneficial and instrumental for the economic growth of developing countries. However, it is by no means clear that preferences have been of all that much help to those countries. Indeed, preferences have the effect of encouraging the perpetuation of existing export production structures, when in fact an export diversification strategy would more likely help low-income countries grow out of "underdevelopment".

Another factor raised by Mr. Woodward is that there are adjustment costs incurred by developing countries and these should be weighed against the benefits that these countries can expect from the Uruguay Round agreement. It is, of course, true that adjustment is costly – all adjustments are. It is therefore true that adjustment implies that these countries forego some consumption. However, the purpose of such an adjustment is to generate savings which presumably are channelled into investment which, in turn, can lead to higher incomes of benefit to all, including the poor.

The third factor cited by Mr. Woodward is that the distribution of the gains from international trade has not been even. A more interesting question to raise, however, would be why have some countries gained less than others?

Most of the poorer performers are clustered in sub-Saharan Africa. More discussion is needed on why this sub-region has not been able to grasp the opportunities that have been created in the external environment.

Clarifications concerning the World Trade Organization

Turning now to policies concerning the work of the WTO, Mr. Woodward is right to emphasize the need of countries to honour the commitments that they made at the Uruguay Round. One of the weakest areas of the Round has been the "discretionary" elements of the Agreement; for instance, the endloading of the MFA, as noted above, and the provisions for contingent protection with respect to safeguards and anti-dumping. However, it is not only the developed countries that are the culprits in this respect. Developing countries themselves are also in the race to see which of them will have anti-dumping legislation first. In other words, Mr. Woodward's criticism holds for the developing as well as for the developed countries.

As for a stricter enforcement of the agreements made by member countries in the Uruguay Round with respect to liberalization and other commitments, the proper institution for settling any and all disputes is the WTO. Although Mr. Woodward has suggested a role for the IMF and World Bank as well is this area, the possibilities of these two institutions are very limited in this respect. Unlike the WTO, their mandates do not provide for the settlement of disputes, with the sole exception of the World Bank's provision for investment disputes. It is, therefore, hard to imagine any institution better suited than the WTO to enforce countries' commitments and to arbitrate dispute settlements.

From the perspective of the WTO, Mr. Woodward is absolutely wrong to propose any selective protection on the part of developing countries with respect to import liberalization or foreign direct investment. Economic counter-arguments are powerful and well-known. Moreover, the WTO rules are clear in this respect: interventions must not be selective; the principle of universality must apply.

In his paper, Mr. Woodward has also proposed to give more power in the WTO to the voice of developing countries. He goes on to suggest that this should be achieved by introducing a system of voting based on countries' shares. If implemented, however, such an approach could seriously backfire against the interests of the developing countries. Voting by consensus in the WTO, as is the case at present, protects better the interest of developing countries than a voting formula based on shares, which would undoubtedly give a disproportionate voice to the largest developed countries. Moreover, Mr. Woodward's proposal of parallel approaches to negotiations could prove in practice to be quite divisive and, as with his voting shares proposal, counterproductive.

Apart from these few observations and caveats, there is much of interest and relevance in Mr. Woodward's paper concerning the effects of international trade on poverty in the developing countries.

6

Global financial integration and related domestic liberalization policies

Peter S. Heller[*]

Global financial integration and related domestic liberalization policies are manifested at the national level by a greater openness of countries' financial sectors to capital flows. Basically, this financial integration has been a beneficial genie that is already out of the bottle, and which cannot be put back in easily.

Financial liberalization has contributed significantly to real growth through gains in employment; increased marginal efficiency of capital from technology transfers; more capital investment; and, in some countries, the reduction of inflation as a result of an appreciation of the exchange rate. Through its effects on the aggregate performance of a country's economy (vis. on employment, output growth, inflation, etc.), global financial liberalization can have a positive impact on poverty and, possibly, on the distribution of income. To the extent that the financial capacity of governments is enhanced and thus their capacity to pursue policies in the social sphere is fortified, there may also be beneficial indirect effects for poverty from financial integration. Such benefits include social and economic programmes, the promotion of education and health care, and other measure that reinforce the ability of the poor to take advantage of the opportunities presented by globalization. At the same time, global financial integration could have short-term adverse effects on some population groups (for instance, those employed in shrinking sectors of the economy), for whom safety nets and compensatory measures will be necessary.

It is important to note, however, that the extent to which global financial

---

[*] Senior Advisor, Fiscal Affairs Department, International Monetary Fund.

integration yields benefits depends on the accompanying macro and structural policies that a country pursues. External financial liberalization policies are only a subset – albeit a very important one – of the policies at the disposal of a government.

The present paper is focused on this last point, viz., the impact of global financial integration on macroeconomic policy management. This issue has posed severe challenges to national policy-makers in some countries, and will continue to do so in the future. For one, global financial integration increases pressure for rationalizing activities in both the real and financial sectors. It also imposes greater financial discipline on both public and business sector agents, which is important in terms of the macroeconomic implications particularly for the poor.

Principal problems for macroeconomic policy management

There are three principal problems for macroeconomic policy management that arise in the context of greater global financial integration.

The first concern regards the country's exposure to capital flows, which can lead to a temporary upward pressure on the exchange rate, a development which may be problematical for exporters. While potential benefits can result in terms of the effect of the exchange rate in dampening inflation (see Mr. Urani's paper in this volume), the implementation of export-promotion strategies is by the same token rendered more difficult. Dealing with this pressure is, of course, not easy, as evidenced by the efforts of many governments in Asia and Latin America to limit the degree of appreciation of their exchange rates. In limiting the appreciation, ought one put sand in the wheels of short-term capital movements? Should monetary policy be tightened by sterilizing the reserve accumulation that comes from capital inflows? Should further fiscal tightening be resorted to? All approaches obviously have their drawbacks. For instance, sterilization raises domestic interest rates, which intensifies pressure on banks with weak portfolios and potentially slows down the pace of domestic activity. Fiscal tightening is very difficult politically to implement, particularly when it involves cutting into bone rather than fat.

The second important concern consists of the procyclical tendencies associated with capital flows. Macroeconomic policy management is rendered especially difficult by the fact that when a country's economy is in trouble is the precise moment when external capital stops to flow in.

The third concern regards the risk of contagion effects. External developments, such as interest rate shifts in the major industrial countries, can critically affect capital flows. Because they lie outside of the macroeconomic policy manager's control, such factors make macroeconomic management more difficult.

Implications of global financial integration for macroeconomic policy management

What are the implications of global financial integration for macroeconomic policy management?

First and foremost, the maintenance of policy credibility in macroeconomic management is essential. The penalties of a perceived loss in credibility are likely to be swift and harsh.

Second, with respect to fiscal policy, it may be desirable for policy-makers to seek to insulate the fiscal sector to some degree from such pressures. This may necessitate shifting the fiscal structure over time to a position where the most critical economic and social expenditure categories are not subject to excessive or frequent pressures to be fiscally consolidated. Similarly, the extent to which tax rates, particularly on incomes, are varied should be limited. The economy should also ideally be in a position where the underlying or structural fiscal balance is strong enough to, when necessary, allow the use of fiscal policy to stimulate the economy.

Third, macroeconomic policy managers will need to evaluate whether significant capital inflows are matched by current account deficits that are associated with higher rates of real capital formation rather than higher consumption. When the latter is the case, it may be necessary to contemplate measures that would dampen speculative capital inflows. In this regard, it may be necessary to establish an appropriate matching and sequencing of the pace of the capital account liberalization process to policies that strengthen a country's financial sector.

Fourth, policy-makers will need to ensure that real investment incentives are not negated by excessive variability in real exchange rates resulting from financial flows. At the same time, speculative investors ought not to be given complete assurance that they can realize lucrative gains from high real interest rates without any down-side risk. There is also need, when opening up the financial sector, for adequate prudential supervision of commercial banks and transparency in financial markets.

Lastly, enhanced surveillance by the International Monetary Fund of countries' macroeconomic policies is important. Greater transparency by countries is also necessary and can be achieved by publishing a wide range of accurate financial and fiscal statistics. In that way, financial markets will be in a position to know what is going on in the economy, rather than acting on the basis of hearsay and speculation. Such statistics would also encourage players in the market to take into account longer-term trends, opportunities, and risks.

7

Implications of macroeconomic policies for equity and poverty

Rolph van der Hoeven*

What is new in the current process of globalization is not so much the increase in trade and capital flows but the ever increasing deregulation, both at the national and international levels, of trade and capital flows. Added to this deregulation is the unprecedented explosion in information technology, which allows financial markets to be global (see Mr. Heller's paper in this volume) and which allows decisions at distant places on production and trade to be linked all over the globe. A number of developing countries have profited from more outward oriented policies. However, many countries, despite various degrees of effort on their part, have not yet been able to profit from increased openness because the structure of their economics makes them unequal partners in international markets (see Mr. Woodward's paper in this volume). The challenge for these countries is to make their economies more robust in accommodating the process of globalization, and to include equity and poverty reduction as important policy objectives (ILO, 1995).

Deregulation or liberalization originated in many developing countries with the stabilization and adjustment policies that were adopted in connection with the debt crisis of the 1980s. The present paper begins therefore with a brief review of the effects that stabilization and adjustment policies have had on income distribution and poverty. The lessons derivable from this experience are pertinent to the adjustment or liberalization policies associated with the globalization process.

The remainder of the paper is focused on what has been learnt from stabil-

---

* Head, Employment Policies and Planning, International Labour Office.

ization programmes about the implications of macroeconomic policies for income distribution and sustainable long-term growth. In the light of those findings and postulates, modifications are proposed whereby macroeconomic policies could be made more equitable and poverty-reducing. In view of the significance of macroeconomic policies to the success of developing countries in liberalizing and adapting to the globalization process, such proposals are important if developing countries are to benefit from globalization in ways that will reduce poverty and not make the distribution of income more skewed.

Stabilization and adjustment policies, income distribution and growth

Adjustment policies – loosely called structural adjustment programmes – consist of stabilization policies and policies to change the structures of markets and production in order to foster more rapid growth and increased exports. Since stabilization policies constitute an integral element of almost all adjustment programmes, it is first necessary to review the theory regarding the effects of national stabilization policies on employment and poverty before examining the effects of structural adjustment policies.

The short-term effects of macroeconomic stabilization policies on economic growth have been the subject of a vast body of literature during the past ten years. It is widely agreed that fiscal and monetary policies that aim at reducing absorption in the economy have resulted in short-term declines in national income. Simulation models applied by Khan (1990) suggest that growth is reduced for usually one or two years as a result of stabilization programmes. How much and how long, however, depends not only on the amount of deflation but also on the capacity of the institutions of the economy to recover.

How do such deflationary policies affect income distribution in the short term? If one assumes that income distribution does not change in the short run, then a deflationary programme, by definition, has little effect on income distribution, although poverty may grow as per capita incomes fall. However, income distribution can change even in a very short period, depending on the weight and intensity of the policy instruments applied (Ndulu 1992). Rather than the deflationary part of the stabilization package, it is the switching part of the package, i.e. devaluations of the national currency that change the price ratio between tradeable and non-tradeable products, which is associated with changes in the income distribution. According to Stewart (1995), income distribution is likely to worsen as a result of devaluations in countries where (a) urban poverty is high in relation to rural poverty, (b) exports consist mainly of minerals or agricultural commodities the production of which is highly concentrated, and (c) a large oligopolistic modern sector exists that specializes in import-substituting production. On the other hand, income distribution may improve as a result of currency devaluations in countries where (a) agricultural and manufactured tradeables are labour-intensive relative to non-tradeables and (b) rural tradeables production is fairly evenly distributed and, at the same time, rural poverty is high in relation to urban poverty.

In evaluating the impact of macroeconomic stabilization programmes on poverty and employment in developing countries, Khan (1993) makes a distinction between countries according to (a) the efficiency of their institutions and (b) the degree of their income inequality. He classifies countries into four groups in accordance with their degree of efficiency (do they have suitable policies and institutions to adapt to world market conditions and changes?) and their degree of equity (do they have a fair distribution of income and assets?). In an efficient, egalitarian country, according to Khan, a balance of payments deficit which requires adjustment is typically caused by an external shock or by an overheating of the economy. In such a situation the correct solution is often a quick stabilization policy, of a deflationary nature, which will result in a temporary increase in unemployment and a short-term drop in real wages. The efficiency of the economy will enable it to resume its growth path quickly, while the egalitarian nature of the political economy will serve to minimize the short-term negative impact on lower-income groups. Few countries fall into Khan's typology of efficient, egalitarian countries.

A larger number of countries correspond to Khan's efficient inegalitarian grouping. Among such countries, a stabilization and deflationary policy will increase poverty and unemployment and several groups of the population will be made worse of after the implementation of the policy has run its course. Institutional and supplementary policy changes are needed to reverse such situations. Corrective measures should be taken in terms of retargetting public expenditure, providing compensation to the groups of citizens most effected, and altering production patterns and ownership structures so that lower-income groups – such as smallholders and the owners of micro- and small-scale enterprises – can augment their output and productivity.

A third group of countries is characterized by Khan as inefficient egalitarian economies. Stabilization programmes in such countries will not bring about a resumption of growth. There is also the risk that the egalitarian system may be eroded by the pressure of market-oriented macroeconomic reforms.

Khan's fourth category of countries combines high levels of both inefficiency and inequality. Some Latin American countries and most African countries fall into this category. The main challenge for countries in this group is to resume growth and reduce inequality, thereby allowing the population as a whole to benefit from growth. It is in these countries where conventional macroeconomic stabilization policies are least likely to lead to reduced inequality and growth. Such countries need to adopt policies that are conducive to overall and continuous development, which include industrial and agricultural policies for small- as well as large-scale producers and enterprises, together with land reform programmes and increased investment in human capital.

It is evident from the literature on the subject that *a priori* assumptions on the relation between stabilization policies, employment and poverty rest on the combined effect of fiscal policies (in general negative), monetary policies (usually negative), wage policies (usually negative) and devaluation (negative or positive depending on the specific situation). Combining these effects, it can be argued that stabilization policies usually decrease employment opportunities and increase poverty, at least in the short to medium term.

The impact of adjustment policies on employment and poverty, however, is more difficult to judge. For example, the effects of privatization or a shrinking in public sector employment on poverty depend on whether, for example, dismissed civil servants belong to poor groups or not, whether they can find other jobs, and whether the privatization process will result in a decline in the tax burden and free up resources for the creation of productive employment. Similarly, the effects of deregulation cannot be foreseen in advance. If deregulation reduces rent-seeking by wealthy and influential groups and this results in lower prices for products consumed by ordinary workers and the poor, then deregulatory policies can contribute to a decline in poverty. However, if deregulation results in the creation of private monopolies, then the net effect of deregulation on the poor may be negative. In short, the effects on poverty of adjustment policies aimed at opening up the economy depend on (a) the ways in which such policies are applied, (b) the initial situation in the country and (c) the extent to which adjustment policies will lead to faster growth and income equality.

Since low or zero growth is often responsible for increased poverty, the remainder of the paper first contains a review of various aspects of the relation between growth and macroeconomic policies, following which the relation between macroeconomic policies and income distribution is examined, and lastly recommendations are made with respect to poverty and income inequality reduction.

Macroeconomic policy and growth

When discussing adjustment policies, it is important to distinguish between short-term growth and long-term growth. As discussed above, periods of stabilization and adjustment are often characterized by a contraction in the economy, with a fall or marginal improvement at best in GDP per capita. Such a contraction is often accompanied by lower rates of capacity utilization. Several economists have therefore argued that a priority of macroeconomic policies in such situations is to increase capacity utilization, as this will contribute to non-inflationary growth. In this connection, Taylor (1993) has criticized the financial accounting in most stabilization packages of failing to take into account the importance of capacity utilization. Monetary and income policies can play an important part in helping increase capacity utilization and reviving non-inflationary growth.

Up until the 1970s, most economists looked to Keynesian demand policies as the most effective way to deal with short-term cyclical movements. However, inflationary pressures in the industrialized countries and the debt crisis in many developing countries largely precluded this policy option in the down-cycle of the 1980s, with the result that contractionary macroeconomic stabilization policies were instead adopted. In over a decade's experience with macroeconomic policies, a number of findings have emerged. Principally, it has been learned that macroeconomic stability may contribute positively to long-term growth, except for its effects on fiscal and public expenditure policies and on interest rates.

Cross-sectional analyses of recent years generally support the hypothesis that macroeconomic policies are good for sustainable growth. Research findings by Fisher (1991) and Serven and Solimo (1992) suggest that the increased certainty and stability that macroeconomic policies provide help encourage productive investment, which in turn leads to long-term growth. Beyond that, attempts to determine the growth implications of the impact of macroeconomic policy changes on the fiscal deficit, money supply, inflation rate, and other economic aggregates have not been strongly conclusive (Fisher 1991, Dornbush 1990). A methodological problem in this connection has been that variables like the debt ratio and the current account deficit are not necessarily exogenous to growth: the direction of causality is difficult to discern since those variables not only affect growth but are also affected by growth.

The fiscal implications of macroeconomic policies, however, have generally proved damaging to public expenditure policies, including those that are essential for long-term growth. For instance, Buffie (1994) found that fiscal contraction can have a negative effect on economic growth when essential investments in infrastructure and in human capital are neglected. Through a general equilibrium model, Buffie demonstrates that short-term contractionary policies may force an economy into a lower-level equilibrium trap.

The issue of public investment in infrastructure and human capital is at the core of the so-called new growth theory. In seeking to explain growth, this theory focuses on production-oriented structural phenomena as well as the policy climate. In essence, the new growth theory relates changes in structural factors – such as education, infrastructure, market access and human resource development – not only to a higher level of income, as in neoclassical theory, but also to higher growth rates. In endogenizing aspects of the "technical progress" residual of the neo-classical growth function, some economists have emphasized a production function called "knowledge industry" which combines (a) the human capital that results from education and training and (b) the increased productivity that results from, among other things, increased international trade and associated foreign capital inflows. According to the new growth theory, the marginal productivity of capital need not decline and therefore savings and investment should be encouraged (Pio 1994, Shaw 1992).

In short, the effects of macroeconomic policy on long-term growth are ambiguous: on the one hand, the more certain and stable environment created by macroeconomic policies serves to create an investment climate that is more conducive for attracting domestic and foreign capital; on the other hand, the effects of macroeconomic policies on public expenditure can be harmful to the development of the human capital and physical infrastructure that are among the necessary complements of private investment in the economy.

Macroeconomic policy and income distribution

While the implications of macroeconomic policy for long-term growth are ambiguous, the effects on income distribution are clear. Tight monetary policy, as far as interest rates are concerned, favours mainly upper-income holders of interest-bearing assets. At the same time, higher interest rates depress economic activity, which results in increased unemployment and lower wages. Therefore, in terms of primary income distribution (which concerns total income earned), strict monetary policies tend to make income distribution more skewed. On the other hand, the income-distribution effects of a more relaxed monetary policy that results in higher inflation are more ambiguous and difficult to discern (Dornbush, 1990). Such effects depend partly on whether wage income and pensions are properly indexed in order to keep real wages and pensions constant.

Fiscal policies have, by definition, an impact on income distribution since taxes determine the net disposable incomes of households. The effect of different tax measures on secondary incomes (income after taxes and transfers) depends in large measure on the composition of taxes. Macroeconomic policies associated with stabilization and adjustment have tended in practice to place greater reliance on indirect taxes than on direct taxes, which has made tax systems more regressive (see Mr. Mehrotra's paper in this volume).

By providing services to poorer groups, public expenditure policy affects a country's tertiary income distribution (which includes the imputed value of government services). A sizeable literature existed at the end of the 1970s and in the early 1980s on the distributive aspects of government expenditure (Paukert 1984). Short-term cutbacks in public expenditure as a result of macroeconomic stabilization policies have had ambiguous effects on the tertiary income distribution, depending on which income groups have been most negatively affected by reduced subsidies, entitlements and services. In accordance with the new growth theory (see above), the distributional impli-cations are even more difficult to unravel since the effects concern not only welfare but long-term growth. The answer will partly depend on the extent to which lower-income groups, as a result of income earning assets or higher factor rewards, will be able to profit from the change in the growth rate.

It has been argued above that macroeconomic stability is essential for regaining and sustaining economic growth. A critical question is whether it is possible to have sustained economic growth without increased income inequality. The case for growth with increased inequality has often been buttressed by the opposite postulate contained in the theory of accumulation, i.e. less income inequality would lower national savings rates and hence, hamper future growth. However, there is a body of research that has shown rather convincingly that the savings arguments for a trade-off between income equality and growth is not necessarily valid, and where it has been valid it is only a weak explanatory variable. Instead a number of country studies have shown that it is possible to have a combination of relative equity and satisfactory growth rates.

The debate on inequality and growth has recently received impetus from authors who combine the new growth theory – which endoginizes technical progress – with political economy models – which endoginize political decisions. Alesina and Perotti (1994) argue that inequality is harmful to growth because of the resulting sub-optimal composition of demand and inequality of factor endowments effecting the supply of human capital. A more equal income distribution leads to an increased demand (a) for goods, which induces more innovation and growth, and (b) for increased investment in education by low-income groups, which builds up more rapidly the stock of human capital. From a political economy perspective, it has been argued (a) that inequality encourages a voting behaviour which sanctions higher taxes and larger budget deficits, which negatively affects growth rates, and (b) that inequality creates political instability and prevents governments from effective management. However, Alisina and Perotti (1994) show that the argument that inequality causes higher taxes which harm growth is not sup-ported by empirical evidence. They find only a weak link between inequality and taxation. Moreover, as Burgess and Stern (1993) argue, taxation levels play a relatively small role as determinants of economic growth.

In short, both the empirical experiences of the 1980's and certain findings of the new growth theory cast a new light on the growth versus equity debate. It is widely agreed that higher taxes and some degree of deficit financing may distort growth and to some extent negatively affect saving and investment decisions. On the other hand, a higher level of government expenditure (as a result of increased taxes or deficit financing) can increase investment in human resources, support the development of markets and improve infrastructure which, according to the new growth theories, will increase growth. In the latter case, at least as far as the link between tertiary income distribution and the generation of future primary incomes is concerned, there can be a positive association between increased growth and reduced inequality. However, to the extent that such an approach would countenance deficit financing rather than resort to higher taxes, it would not correspond with the principle of sound macroeconomic stability. The matter of tax policies is taken up below.

Recommendations

Macroeconomic policies can make a potentially positive contribution to income distribution concerns if more attention is given to equitable tax and expenditure policies (van der Hoeven 1991). Macroeconomic policies can especially be more poverty-focused if "sound" macroeconomic policies are carried out in tandem with a set of incomes policies, including minimum wage policies, and mesopolicies that orient in a positive fashion the redistributive aspects of the macroeconomic policies. For example, an incomes policy, when based upon consultation with employers and workers, may contribute to a better social climate that can help reduce inflationary pressures in the economy. There is evidence of countries where the income gap has narrowed and economic growth has been strong as a result of, among other policies, income measures that include an active minimum wage policy.

Most developing countries are also in a position to consider adopting mesopolicies that are more equitable and pro-poor in areas such as the fiscal burden, targeted public expenditure, labour market intervention in product markets, and the distribution of assets ownership. Tax policies could be made more progressive, and tax receipts could be increased through more effective collection procedures, so as not to have to cut back on essential expenditures in physical and human capital formation (for an analysis of tax and public expenditure trends in developing regions, see Mr. Mehrotra's paper in this volume). Moreover, a larger share of public expenditure could be directed to poverty alleviation and reduction needs without impairing economic growth rates.

There will inevitably be severe political constraints to overcome if macroeconomic stability policies are to be made more equitable and pro-poor. Evaluations of tax and expenditure policies reveal that a progressive or regressive design of macroeconomic policies depends less on the macroeconomic policies themselves than on the prevailing social situation in the country in question – in particular, on whether a society is willing to give priority to distributional issues during times of economic crisis. The empirical evidence is not encouraging: macroeconomic policies in countries which have a more egalitarian society are more likely to contain elements that are socially equitable and sensitive to the needs of the poor than is true of countries that are less egalitarian. External funding can, of course, facilitate in periods of economic difficulty the move to a more egalitarian society; more commonly, however, such funding tends to perpetuate existing unequal patterns of income distribution (van der Hoeven, 1996). Explicitly formulated redistributive policies should therefore be part of any policy aiming at macroeconomic stability and further opening up to reap the benefits of the globalization process.

References

Alesina, A. and R. Perotti. 1994. "The political economy of growth a critical survey of the recent literature". *The World Bank Economic Review* 8(3).

Buffie E. 1994. "The long run consequences of short-run stabilization policy" in Horton S., R. Kanbur and D. Mazumdar. *Labour markets in an era of adjustment*. EDI Development Studies. Washington D.C.: World Bank.

Burgess, R. and N. Stern. 1993. "Taxation and Development", *Journal of Economic Literature* 31.

Dornbusch, R. 1990. "Policies to move from stabilization to growth" in World Bank. *Proceedings of the Annual Conference of Development Economics.* Washington D.C.

Fisher, S. 1991. "Growth, macroeconomics and development" in *National Bureau of Economic Research Macroeconomic Annual.* Cambridge, Mass: MIT Press.

van der Hoeven, R. 1991. "Adjustment with a Human Face: still relevant or overtaken by events? in *World Development* 19(12).

_____. 1996. "External dependence, structural adjustment and development in sub-Saharan Africa" in Jansen K. and R. Vos (eds). *External Finance and adjustment. Failures and success in the developing world.* London: MacMillan.

ILO 1995. *World Employment Report.* Geneva: ILO.

Khan, M. 1990. "The macroeconomic effects of Fund-supported adjustment programs" in *IMF Staff Papers* 37(2).

Khan, A. 1993. *Structural adjustment and income distribution: Issues and experiences.* Geneva: ILO.

Ndulu, B. 1992. "Enhancing income distribution and rationalizing consumption patterns" in Cornia, G. A., R. van der Hoeven and T. Mkandawire. *Africa's Recovery in the 1990s: From stagnation and adjustment to human development.* London: MacMillan.

Paukert, F. et al. 1984. *Income distribution and economic development.* Geneva: ILO.

Pio, A. 1994. "New Growth Theory and old development problems", *Development Policy Review* 12: 277-300.

Serven, A., A. Solimano. 1992. "Economic adjustment and investment performance in developing countries: The experience of the 1980s" in Corbo, V. et al. *Adjustment lending revisited: Policies to restore growth.* Washington, D.C.: World Bank.

Shaw, G.K. 1992. "Policy Implications of Endogenous Growth Theory", *Economic Journal* 102: 611-21.

Stewart, F. 1995. "Adjustment and poverty options and choices". London: Routledge.

Taylor, L. 1993. *The rocky road to reform.* Cambridge, Mass: MIT Press.

8

Domestic liberalization policies and public finance: poverty implications

Santosh Mehrotra[*]

The emphasis of domestic liberalization policies in the 1980s and early 1990s has been to reduce budget deficits by focusing more on demand-reducing public expenditure than on the tax side and resources mobilization. One of the main consequences of the liberalization process in Latin America and Sub-Saharan Africa – the two regions examined in the present paper – has been for the state to withdraw from the productive sectors of the economy and focus, instead, on financing and providing services in health, education and other social sectors. With respect to taxes, the Washington consensus has been that an increase in tax rates should be carried out only as a last resort; preferably, the tax base should be broadened and marginal tax rates kept moderate. Presumably, lower rates would ensure better compliance with tax laws, and the broadened tax net would raise the necessary revenues. So has this approach to public finance led to an increase in tax to GDP ratios in Latin America and Sub-Saharan Africa?

Government revenue

A comparison of the ratio of total tax revenue to GDP in Latin America during the 1980s and early 1990s (1980-85 versus 1986-92/3) provides a disconcerting image. Of 12 Latin American countries for which a reasonable series is available in the IMF's *Government Finance Statistics* publications,

---

[*] Planning Officer, Office of Social Policy and Economic Analysis, United Nations Children's Fund.

it can be seen that in 7 countries the tax/GDP ratio remained either constant or declined. Only in five cases has it increased. Overall, the tax ratio in Latin America fell by almost 1.3 points in the 1980s. It should, moreover, be noted that Latin American countries have had a lower level of taxation (almost 1.2 percentage points of GDP lower) than developing countries as a whole, despite the fact that regional per capita income is 29 percent higher.

What has been the role of trade liberalization policies in this process? Theory suggests that the elimination of quantitative restrictions (QRs) and the 'tariffication' process would, *ceteris paribus*, raise the international trade tax share in total taxes. On the other hand, the reduction of tariffs and export taxes as a result of liberalization would have an offsetting effect. Thus, the effect of the liberalization process on tax revenues from international trade appears indeterminate – at least in theory. But what has happened in practice?

In Latin America, where international trade taxes on average account for 18 per cent of tax revenue, the international trade tax share in total taxes fell in most of the countries concerned. Trade taxes as a per cent of total taxes even declined in three of the 7 countries where tax/GDP ratios declined or remained constant. Thus, tax revenues from international trade have had a tendency to fall in liberalizing Latin American countries.

How do the tax policies of Latin America relate to income distribution and poverty? Most of the developing countries in the world tend to follow a pattern in which income taxes, consumption taxes and trade-related taxes each account for roughly 30 per cent of total tax revenues; the remaining 10 per cent can normally be attributed to social security and other taxes. The shares for Latin America, however, have been different: income taxes have accounted for 23 per cent; trade-related taxes for 18 per cent; social security for 15 per cent; and consumption taxes for 36 per cent. In other words, there has been a greater reliance on regressive indirect taxes in Latin America than elsewhere in the developing world. Latin American countries thus report not only a lower level of taxation than developing countries as a whole; they also report a more regressive tax structure.

Have privatizations helped offset this decline in tax revenues? In Argentina and Mexico, privatizations contributed revenues amounting to 6 and 8.5 per cent of GDP, respectively, during 1991-93 (see also Mr. A. Urani's paper in this volume). A key reason for privatizing state enterprises, as stated by many who have studied the privatization process in Argentina, Brazil and

Mexico, has been to resolve the public debt problem. Moreover, privatizations have produced only one-off increases in government resources. None the less, by reducing the public debt burden, privatizations may help alleviate poverty over the long-run in countries where governments have shifted much of the additional, freed resources to the health and educational needs of the poor (see further on).

In Sub-Saharan Africa, out of 11 countries for which a reasonable series is available, tax/GDP ratios declined in 5 countries, were constant in 3 countries, and rose in only 3 countries if one compares the 1980-85 period with 1986-92/3. Between 1990 and 1993, government revenue on average declined from 21.3 per cent in 1990 to 18.2% in 1993. In 1990-91, the ratio of total revenues (including tax revenues) to GDP was about 18 per cent, the same as in 1981-86. Privatization revenues have accounted for less than 1 per cent of total tax revenues in the region.

International trade taxes in Sub-Saharan Africa have made up 35 per cent of total tax revenues, or 17 per cent more than in Latin America. In 4 countries (out of the 8 countries for which there is a continuous series) in which total taxes to GDP declined, the share of international trade taxes in total taxes also fell. However, the decline in international trade taxes does not fully explain the stagnant tax revenues situation in the 1980s and early 1990s. Liberalization policies played a role by failing to promote increased personal taxation as a source of government revenue; instead, increased levies such as user charges for health and education services were emphasized as a means of closing the revenue gap.

Government expenditure

Instead of promoting tax increases, orthodox liberalization policies have instead emphasized the compression of public expenditure to GDP ratios as a way to reduce budget deficits. An important question, therefore, is what have been the trends for public expenditure on health and education during the 1980s and first half of the 1990s? Since the overlap between people below the absolute poverty line and those who have inadequate access to basic services is large, if not complete, the answer to the above question may have significance both for short-term poverty alleviation and long-term poverty reduction in Latin America and Sub-Saharan Africa.

As is generally well known, per capita health and education expenditures fell consistently during the 1980s throughout most of Latin America. But what happened after economic growth picked up in the 1990s? According to ECLAC figures, real education expenditure per capita rose in 1990-93, compared with 1982-89, in only 2 out of 12 countries (Brazil and Colombia). In the rest it remained either stable (2 countries) or fell (8 countries). In health, the situation was better: per capita levels rose in 9 countries during 1990-93, compared with 1982-89. However, in the cases of 6 countries, the levels of health per capita expenditure were still lower in real terms in 1990-93 than they had been in 1980-81.

What about Sub-Saharan Africa? Average education and health expenditures as a proportion of GDP were lower in the region at the end of the 1980s than in the first half of the decade. The fall in expenditure was concentrated among countries that had experienced a deterioration in their macroeconomy. Countries with an improving macroeconomy experienced little change or a slight increase in social expenditures as a proportion of GDP. Social expenditures have generally risen in the 1990s in countries where macroeconomic conditions improved.

The shrinking of public expenditure on education and health in most of Latin America and Sub-Saharan Africa has in large part been due to the exigencies of domestic and, in particular, external debt servicing. In fact, debt servicing requirements have been rising as net barter terms of trade for both Latin America and Sub-Saharan Africa decline. Even though LIBORs have tended to fall through the 1980s and 1990s (in spite of some fluctuations), the debt overhang continues to be so large that discretionary public spending remain constrained. In addition, with most countries liberalizing their foreign exchange regimes, real devaluations have produced a large increase in government commitments on external debt. In Sub-Saharan Africa multilateral debt is the single-largest source of external debt servicing outflows. The combined effects of the huge stock of external debt and the depreciation of the exchange rate on government expenditures have thus been to crowd out social expenditures, including in countries which have managed to reduce their expenditures in defence and other nonproductive sectors.

Achievements in restructuring discretionary expenditures between and within sectors have generally been limited to date. Such restructuring – particularly in terms of intra-sectoral spending priorities – is of critical importance if public spending is to achieve a higher social rate of return and be pro-poor. Expenditure levels still continue to be biased toward higher education and hospital care despite the conditionality provisions and substantially increased share of World Bank adjustment lending that goes to primary education and primary health care. Spending per capita, moreover, will have to be considerably higher if these regions are to hope eventually to emulate the educational levels and growth rates of East Asia (see Mr. Rasiah's paper in this volume). In this connection, case studies have shown that high-achievers in education in all developing regions invested heavily early-on in primary and then secondary education.

A recent study by the World Bank of the social dimensions of adjustment over 1980-93 noted that in respect of education spending, the bias toward tertiary education appears to have worsened during the adjustment period. Of the 14 countries spread across all regions having data on allocations to both tertiary and primary education, the tertiary share rose in eight countries after 1980, while the primary share stagnated or fell in most of them. Evidence from the World Bank's country reports also indicates that in the health sector, there continue to be significant imbalances between hospital care and primary health care in most countries, even in adjusting countries. Furthermore, adjusting countries have tended to cut spending on material inputs for supplies and maintenance, while holding personnel spending constant because of employment concerns. The growing imbalance between spending on personnel and supplies has constrained public social services and possibly adversely impacted on physical infrastructure.

Conclusions and recommendations

Domestic liberalization policies, as conventionally practised, have not been favourable to the government revenue bases of either Latin America or Sub-Saharan Africa during the 1980s and early 1990s. Indeed, the evidence from these two regions makes clear that reductions in national budget deficits have been achieved mainly by cuts in public expenditure rather than the mobilization of additional resources. This is regrettable on the following two counts:

• If income taxes had been higher, the impact of declining output and income in the 1980s would have been counter-cyclical – given that income taxes are generally progressive in most countries. In a region such as Latin America where income and wealth distribution is highly skewed, this would have tempered the decline in growth and increase in income inequality and poverty that took place in the 1980s.

- Given the low primary completion rates of Latin America and Sub-Saharan Africa, the inadequate and stagnating levels of public spending for basic schooling in those regions do not augur well for preparing the next generation labour force to compete successfully in the global economy.

There are thus strong and sound reasons for reassessing the role of ortho-dox liberalization policies with respect to public finance and expenditure. In particular, a greater effort should be made to mobilize additional revenues by increasing income taxes (especially in Latin America) and by improving the efficiency with which they are collected. Likewise, public spending should be increased particularly in areas such as elementary education and basic health care that yield high social rates of return. Modifying the tax-ation and expenditure priorities of conventional liberalization policies is especially important if such policies are to be made more equitable and pro-poor.

9

Safety nets and compensatory measures

Carol Graham*

Adaptation to a more competitive world is not a short-term undertaking. For the poor, the challenge will be to increase their human capital through improved access to education, health care and nutrition. At the same time, the implementation of liberalization policies as can have short-term conjunctural effects on certain poverty groups that will require the provision of safety nets and compensatory measures. Globalization and liberalization can be based on the accumulation of existing experience with certain approaches, such as (a) "self-selection" public work schemes in connection with droughts and other calamities and (b) social development funds forming part of structural adjustment programmes, on which proposals in connection with globalization and liberalization can be based.

Safety net and compensatory measures should be seen as inseparable from macroeconomic reforms and the externally-oriented liberalization policies associated with a country's integration in the globalization process. In the absence of such economic policies, safety net measures are likely to be mere palliatives, and arguably wasteful at that. Moreover, safety nets should be understood as being complementary to regular basic needs programmes to reduce poverty. Where resource limits make necessary a trade-off, investment in basic education and health care should have priority over than safety net measures for the poor.

In principle, a timely and coherent phasing-in of liberalization policies ought to provide a policy framework in which the poor and vulnerable can be identified and more effectively protected. Delayed policy changes, on the

---

* Visiting Fellow, Foreign Policy Studies Program, The Brookings Institition, Washington D.C., and Adjunct Professor of Government, Georgetown University, Washington D.C.

other hand, are likely to produce haphazard effects and *ad hoc* measures which typically preclude any kind of well-conceived safety-net effort. For instance, a stalled or gradual introduction of policy measures may allow groups opposed to the liberalization process more time to coalesce, as well as to monopolize the benefits of public expenditure, whereas rapid and far-reaching policy action can provide unique political opportunities to redirect resources to previously marginalized groups. In the case of many low-income countries, however, both liberalization reforms and associated safety-net measures will no doubt prove difficult to implement for lack of administrative capacity and, often, suitable political institutions.

Experience has shown that safety net measures can both reach the poor and contribute to the political sustainability of liberalization policies. In this connection, the emphasis that globalization and liberalization place on market approaches is likely to provide a favourable context for the adoption of safety net measures that place a premium on beneficiary participation. The incorporation of beneficiary participation and private sector management techniques into safety net programmes (e.g reliance on local demand for project allocation; reduced administration; sub-contracting arrangements with NGOs and the local private sector, etc..) can make such programmes more effective and sustainable. Moreover, such demand-oriented approaches are not only more efficient in terms of sustainable poverty reduction; they will also increase the political voice of the poor. By encouraging the poor to participate in solving their problems and exercising their political voice, previously marginalized groups gain a stake in the ongoing process of economic and regulatory reform.

Besides their relation to market-oriented reforms, safety nets and compensatory measures are influenced and shaped by political considerations. Safety nets and compensatory measures can be of particular importance in making economic reform sustainable under democratic regimes. Generally speaking, these measures are more likely to be successful in open political environments than in authoritarian ones. That is because a democratic environment is more conducive to building a broad base of support for reform and change, and hence a policy environment in which poverty alleviation and reduction are countenanced. For example, more open environments allow the participation of a broader range of society, including NGOs, neighbourhood groups, and other groups that best represent the interests of the poor. However, effective government communication will be necessary to sell and explain the implications of globalization and the need for liberalization measures, if those measures are to be politically viable and sustainable. Moreover, success will more likely be ensured when the associated benefits of safety net programmes are delivered on a demand-driven basis and in a non-partisan manner.

On the other hand, experience has shown that in some cases safety net programmes can be effectively implemented under centralized, authoritarian forms of governance. If targeting and providing effective protection to the poorest of the poor is to be attempted on a wide scale, then centrally implemented schemes, such as the wide-scale emergency employment and health and nutrition programmes under the Pinochet regime in Chile, can be very effective. It should be noted, however, that many developing countries do not possess the sophisticated targeting and administrative capacity to duplicate Chile's experience. In the absence of such centralized targeting capacity, demand-based safety nets may be more viable as an approach.

Generally speaking, it has been seen that safety nets are more likely to be successful and sustainable when they are initiated domestically and have the political backing of the government authorities concerned. No amount of foreign aid can substitute for domestic commitment. Indeed, aid which is provided without such a commitment can prove unsustainable as there will be no political stakes in the long-term success of the programmes in question.

For mainly political reasons, there has been a tendency in many developing countries for safety nets not to be targeted to the most poor and vulnerable of the affected population groups. The non-poor have gained more than the poor because they have usually been more directly affected by economic reform measures, have been more politically vocal and organized, and have been more easily reached through compensation packages than the poor. The poor, however, have had less margin for shocks and have therefore been more vulnerable and needy. This accumulated experience in connection with structural adjustment programmes suggests how politically and institutionally difficult it can be to safeguard the interests of the absolute poor during the liberalization process.

It should be noted, however, that from a cost-effectiveness perspective, resources that are targeted at the poor may entail considerably less expenditure per head than severance payments and other compensatory measures directed at the non-poor. In fact, not all safety net measures imply significant budgetary outlays. There are some relatively "cost free" measures that governments can take which will favour the poor, such as (a) removing complex regulations which affect informal sector workers and (b) facilitating the poor's access to legal title of their urban plots and rural land.

In sum, if implemented well and linked effectively to broader economic and sectoral reforms, safety net and compensatory measures can have positive effects on poverty alleviation and the sustainability of liberalization policies. However, such measures must be properly implemented. The risk to be avoided is that such programmes become merely an expensive channel to support politically relevant groups that are less needy than the poor. There is no denying, however, that political constraints and the relative weight of various interest groups will influence the choices that governments will make in the safety net and compensatory arena.

Part II

Regional and national experiences: lessons from diversity

10

Globalization and liberalization in East and South East Asia: implications for growth, inequality and poverty

Rajah Rasiah*

East and South East Asia is the developing region of the world which has most successfully inserted itself into the globalization process during the past quarter century. Largely as a result, average annual GDP growth rates exceeded 7 per cent and 6 per cent in the periods 1970-80 and 1980-93 respectively in the five Asian newly industrialized economies (NIEs) that are examined in the present paper: Republic of Korea, Taiwan Province of China, Malaysia, Thailand and Indonesia (see Table 10.1). These economies have also enjoyed high export growth rates, increasingly full employment, falling poverty levels and relatively positive patterns of income distribution.

In the case of the East Asian economies in particular, this development process was fostered in large part by the market intervention strategies of the 1970s and early 1980s, and has continued under the economic liberalization regimes that were adopted in the mid-1980s. Pressures to liberalize imports originated from major trading partners and, more recently, have formed part of the commitments undertaken during the Uruguay Round and in other settings. While orthodox liberalization policies are often viewed with some scepticism by the NIEs, it is generally acknowledged that national conformity with international deregulatory agreements is necessary on the part of all countries if they want to benefit fully from international trade, technology and capital transfers, and other dimensions of globalization. Moreover, the East

* Professor, Institute for Malaysian and International Studies, Universiti Kebangsaan Malaysia. Contributing authors: Ishak Shari, Universiti Kebangsaan Malaysia, and Jomo K.S., Universiti Malaya.

Asian governments in particular recognize that many of their previously protected industries are for the most part mature enough now to withstand the competitive onslaught of import liberalization. As for the South East Asian countries, liberalization with respect to foreign direct investment and exports has been in place for a long while, but there is concern in some of these countries that import liberalization policies could negatively affect heretofore protected heavy industries that are not internationally competitive.

Table 10.1: Key Economic Indicators

	Per capita income (US$)	Average annual GDP growth (%)		Manufacturing/ GDP (%)	
	1993	1970-80	1980-93	1970	1992
Korea, Rep. of	7660	10.1	9.1	21	26
Taiwan Province of China	8788[a]	10.0[b]	7.5[c]	35[d]	42[d]
Malaysia	3140	7.9	6.2	12	30
Thailand	2110	7.1	8.2	16	28
Indonesia	740	7.2	5.8	10	21

Notes: [a] - for 1991; [b] - for period 1963-80; [c] - for period 1981-93; [d] - for industry. *Source:* World Bank (1995); Taiwan Province of China's figures from Yu (1994) and Lee (1994).

The purpose of the present paper is to review the factors that have contributed to the rapid growth and poverty reduction of the economies concerned and, in particular, to examine the implications of globalization and liberalization for growth, inequality and poverty. Three liberalization variables are particularly important in this connection: trade regimes, foreign direct investment rules, and financial deregulation.

1 From market intervention to economic liberalization

Industrial strategies

Extensive government intervention in the form of industrial policies has taken place in all five economies under consideration. Industrial policy focusing on manufacturing transformed in particular the economic structures of the Republic of Korea and Taiwan Province of China. Besides protectionist barriers, such policies entailed subsidized loans (see further on) and tax rebates subject to time-bound performance criteria and effective discipline. These industrial strategies have been applied successfully in sectors such as steel, electronics, ships and automobiles in the case of the Republic of Korea. They have made it possible for infant industries to mature and compete against imports, thus enabling governments to liberalize their import regimes without running the risk of destroying their initially protected industries.

While industrial strategies have played a significant role in the growth of the second-tier NIEs (Malaysia, Thailand and Indonesia), they have been less effectively utilized than in the Republic of Korea and Taiwan Province of China because of the lack of inter-industry coherence and the failure to use such strategies to discipline investors when necessary (Rasiah 1995). However, the second-tier NIEs' industrialization strategies have been pursued in generally pro-market settings where macroeconomic stability has been emphasized (Amsden 1989 and Wade 1990). Moreover, as part of their efforts to augment their exports of manufactured goods, Malaysia, Thailand and Indonesia have combined their industrial strategies with investment liberalization policies designed to attract foreign direct investment (Rasiah 1995, Rasiah 1994, Rasiah 1996 and Roemer 1994). Thus industrial policies have in certain respects complemented macroeconomic stabilization and outward-oriented liberalization policies in the second-tier NIEs. This integration of liberalization policies with industrial policies should make the shift toward enhanced liberalization easier.

Credit policies

As part of industrial strategies, commercial banks in the Republic of Korea and Taiwan Province of China were for many years directed to offer discounted credit to favoured investment projects. The emphasis was on heavy industries in the 1970s, but starting with the late 1980s, small- and medium-sized enterprises became the major target. In the case of the Republic of Korea, the subsidized interest rates have formed part of (a) direct loans from government funds allocated to banks and (b) indirect loans through central bank rediscounting (Amsden 1989, Wade 1990, Chang 1994, Landau *et al*,

1995: footnote 53 and Lee 1994). Subsidized credit was primarily directed to prioritized investments with export targets (Amsden 1989). Policy-based loans accounted for around half of all commercial bank loans in the Republic of Korea in the 1970s and 1980s (Nam 1993 and Landau *et al*, 1995). Taiwan Province of China has likewise provided subsidized credits as part of a strategy to promote exports (Wade 1990: 25-29). Its central bank, as in the case of the Republic of Korea, rediscounted loans to prioritized sectors (Landau *et al* 1995: 39).

Malaysia has provided subsidized credit to favoured, mostly state-sponsored ventures, as well as to small and medium-sized enterprises. However, due to weak control and disciplinary mechanisms, the results have often been less than satisfying (Jomo 1994, Rasiah and Ishak 1994). On the other hand, the array of incentives introduced to promote exports has been reasonably effective. An example is the export credit refinancing (ECR) scheme, which has offered financing at below-market rates to appropriate enterprises, irrespective of their ownership. Indonesia and Thailand have offered similar incentives, but principally to small enterprises, including agricultural smallholders. In recent years, the role and significance of subsidized credit schemes have diminished as the second-tier NIEs take steps to deregulate and liberalize their financial systems.

Savings and financial liberalization

The East Asian economic "miracle" is often in large part attributed to the high savings rates achieved by the first-tier NIEs. The Republic of Korea and Taiwan Province of China managed to generate saving levels which in the 1990s have exceeded 30 per cent of GNP. Corporate savings have played a much larger role than household savings in terms of the productive capital formation that has taken place in these economies (Akyuz and Gore 1996, Rodrick 1994). In decomposing savings and investment, it is evident that business savings have mainly been plowed back into investment (see Table 10.2).

In contrast, Malaysia, Thailand and Indonesia have been generally less successful in investing their domestic savings productively. For instance, although Malaysia enjoys high savings rates, savings became negative in 1989 because of the government's investment forays into heavy industries and "mega" development projects that have produced relatively low returns (You

1995a and Rasiah 1995a). Instead, foreign direct investment (FDI) has accounted for the bulk of the investment made in those countries' export manufacturing sectors.

Table 10.2: Sectoral Savings and Investment

Country	Household		Business		Government		Economy		
	Sh	Ih	Sb	Ib	Sg	Ig	Sd	Id	Sf
China	12.5	5.5	14.1	22.1	6.0	5.7	32.5	33.4	0.8
Korea, Rep. of	10.3	5.3	8.3	20.0	4.1	3.1	22.7	28.4	5.7
Taiwan Province of China	13.7	na	12.0	na	6.2	4.1	31.9	26.9	-5.0
Malaysia	19.7	2.9	9.1	16.3	-1.2	11.1	27.7	30.3	2.6
Thailand	10.4	3.6	8.7	15.2	0.2	4.5	19.2	23.3	4.0
Japan	16.9	7.8	10.8	15.6	6.4	8.3	34.2	31.7	-5.5

Notes: Sh - household saving/GNP; Sd - domestic saving/GNP = Sh + Sb + Sg; Id - domestic investment/GNP = Ih + Ib + Ig; Sf - foreign saving/GNP = Id - Sd; na - not available. *Source:* Honohan and Atiyas (1989; *Taiwan Statistical Data Book 1995*, cited in You (1995a).

Financial liberalization has been viewed with some apprehension in the region (e.g. Singh 1994) out of a concern that savings and capital could flow mainly into short-term, speculative investments. It is feared, for instance, that speculative investments might end up competing for the capital needed by small and medium-sized enterprises (SMEs) to develop. In the Republic of Korea in particular, a vibrant SME sector is viewed as essential if efforts to restructure the economy and reduce industrial concentration are to succeed.

Foreign direct investment

The role that foreign direct investment (FDI) has played in the economic growth and export-orientation of East and South East Asian countries has differed considerably in the cases of the first- and second-tier NIEs discussed in this paper. FDI has not been a major factor in the economic growth and exports of the Republic of Korea and Taiwan Province of China (Nayyar

1978, Amsden 1989, Chang 1994 and Wade 1990). During the period 1971-93 (see Table 10.3), the share of FDI in gross domestic investment in those two economies reached a maximum of 1.9 per cent (1971-75) in the case of the Republic of Korea and 3.5 per cent (1986-90) in the case of Taiwan Province of China.

**Table 10.3: Share of Foreign Direct Investment in
Gross Fixed Capital Formation, 1981-93 (%)**

	1971-75	1976-80	1981-85	1986-90	1991	1992	1993
Korea, Rep. of	1.9	0.4	0.5	1.3	1.0	0.5	0.4
Taiwan Province of China	1.4	1.2	1.5	3.5	3.0	2.4	2.4
Malaysia	15.2	11.9	10.8	10.5	24.0	26.0	23.7
Thailand	3.0	1.5	3.2	5.9	5.6	4.9	3.6
Indonesia	4.6	2.4	1.0	2.0	3.6	5.1	4.8

Source: UNCTAD, World Investment Report, 1993, 1994, 1995.

The Republic of Korea has relied on foreign capital mainly as a way to complement the productive capacities of local firms. Through selective intervention, the authorities have utilized foreign capital to enhance the productive capacity of their domestic enterprises. Technological knowledge has been acquired through licensing arrangements, but otherwise the direct participation of transnational corporations (TNCs) in the domestic economy has been limited. Such direct participation of FDI as there has been in the Republic of Korea was largely confined to labour-intensive assembly operations. On the other hand, the government of Taiwan Province of China has allowed foreign firms to participate directly in a number of industries. The technological spillovers from these investments have strengthened the growth of local firms, which has been the government's long-term objective in the economic sector. In addition, the government is currently offering generous joint-venture incentives to foreign capital in strategic industries such as aircraft manufacturing.

By comparison, the role of FDI in the growth and exports of Malaysia, Thailand and Indonesia has been considerably greater than in the cases of the Republic of Korea and of Taiwan Province of China. The share of FDI in gross domestic investment and exports has been particularly high in Malaysia. Indeed, in Malaysia's manufacturing sector in 1991, FDI-controlled enterprises accounted for 40 per cent of fixed assets, 62 per cent of overall manufactured exports, 47 per cent of total manufacturing output and 44 per cent of employment in 1991 (Rasiah 1995: 81). However, the multiplier effects, e.g. subcontracting arrangements, of FDI have generally been limited (Rasiah 1992).

Beginning in the late 1980s, much of the inflow of FDI to the second-tier NIEs has come from several East Asian economies. The increase in FDI from Japan and first-tier NIEs has been prompted by a number of events: the Plaza Accord of 1985 which led to currency appreciations in those countries; the withdrawal from the first-tier NIEs in 1988 of privileges under the Generalized System of Preferences (GSP); and rising production costs in Japan and the first-tier NIEs.

FDI flows to some second-tier NIES, however, may be entering a period of uncertainty. Due to labour shortages and rising wages, some labour-intensive firms are considering moving from Malaysia and Thailand to countries with lower wages, including Indonesia (Snodgrass and Rasiah 1995). Moreover, Malaysia and, to a lesser degree, Thailand are likely to lose much of their textile and garment industries as a result of the Multifibre Arrangement (MFA) quotas being scheduled for elimination. To the extent that fiscal inducements such as preferred tax and tariff exemptions, or export credit refinancing, are rolled back, Malaysia, Thailand and Indonesia may become less attractive to FDI than before. Indeed, there could come a time in the case particularly of Malaysia when profit repatriation outflows might exceed new inflows of FDI, which in a worst-case scenario could precipitate a balance of payments crisis. Finally, as FDI regulations become more liberal across the world, there will be fewer opportunities for South East Asian governments to integrate FDI more effectively into the domestic economy and, through industrial policy initiatives, thereby strengthen domestic capacity.

International trade

Trade policies have been critical to the success of the industrialization drives of the East and South East Asian economies under review. Except for Indonesia, the exports of these economies grew at double digit figures annually over the period 1980-92 (see Table 10.4).

Table 10.4: Trade Growth and Export Share of GDP, 1970-93 (%)

	Average annual import growth		Average annual export growth		Exports/GDP	
	1970-80	1980-92	1970-80	1980-92	1970	1993
Korea, Rep. of	11.6	11.2	23.5	11.9	14	29
Taiwan Province of China	12.2	10.6	15.6	11.0	na	na
Malaysia	3.7	7.9	4.8	11.3	42	80
Thailand	5.0	11.5	10.3	14.7	15	37
Indonesia	13.0	4.0	7.2	5.6	13	28

Note: na - not available. *Source:* World Bank (1994 and 1995).

As a proportion of total exports, primary exports from the Republic of Korea, Malaysia, Thailand and Indonesia fell sharply, whereas manufacturing expanded rapidly in the cases of Thailand and Indonesia, as did machinery and transport equipment in the cases of the Republic of Korea and Malaysia (see Table 10.5).

Table 10.5: Export structure, 1970 and 1993 (%)

	Primary		Machinery and transport equip.		Other manufac-tures		Total	
	1970	1993	1970	1993	1970	1993	1970	1993
Korea, Rep. of	24	7	7	43	69	51	100	100
Taiwan Province of China	na	na	na	na	na	na	na	na
Malaysia	93	35	2	41	6	24	100	100
Thailand	92	28	0	28	8	45	100	100
Indonesia	98	47	0	5	1	48	100	100

Note: na - not available. *Source:* World Bank (1995: 190-1).

The Republic of Korea and Taiwan Province of China, developed their comparative advantages in global trade by first protecting import-substituting industries which subsequently in many cases became export-oriented as well. The average level of protection in these economies was high until the late 1980s. For instance, the effective rate of protection (ERP) in the Republic of Korea was 78.5 per cent in 1988. In the case of Taiwan Province of China, the nominal rate of protection for 40 per cent of that economy's imports exceeded 31 per cent in 1985 (Wade 1990). The industrial structures of these economies are now mature enough to cope with the liberalization required by the World Trade Organization (WTO) framework. Domestic enterprises are currently close to or already at the technology frontier. Samsung for example, is one of the two most efficient and dynamic producers of DRAM chips in the world (West 1995). With high corporate saving rates and substantial external capital reserves, both economies are well-placed to undertake technological expansion. Tariff walls and subsidies are therefore no longer essential for these economies to catch up technologically, whether it be in memory chips, computers, televisions or steel.

In a sense, the trade liberalization policies of the Republic of Korea and of Taiwan Province of China, underline the success of their industrial policies in developing internationally competitive industrial capabilities. This success means that further protection and support are no longer necessary, nor even desirable; indeed, the graduation of national firms in these economies to competitive maturity has exemplified and proven the merit of the rationale for infant industry protection. In so far as selective industrial policy has depended on time-bound disciplinary mechanisms - e.g. temporary effective protection while developing a globally competitive industrial capacity - it therefore follows as a matter of course that the sub-sectors involved should eventually be subjected to the discipline of the international market place. Under these circumstances, any short-term consumer welfare loss is more than likely to be rewarded by the acquisition of new comparative advantages leading to increased labour skilling and remuneration.

Malaysia, Thailand and Indonesia continue to maintain highly differentiated tariff schedules (Rasiah 1995, Jomo and Edwards 1995, Onchan 1995 and Roemer 1994). Where tariff reforms threaten to affect the livelihoods of people or adversely affect the balance of payments, the ASEAN Free Trade Area (AFTA) framework has allowed for products that would be negatively affected by deregulation to be excluded. Thus, Indonesia, for example, is allowed to continue to protect its paddy farmers from potentially crippling competition from Vietnam. On the whole, however, average rates of protection in Malaysia, Thailand and Indonesia have declined in recent years as a result of the adoption of import liberalization policies. Lower tariffs in particular could create competitive pressures particularly for certain heavy industry sectors which, by world standards, are relatively inefficient. Examples include automobiles, steel and cement production in Malaysia, as well as aircraft production in Indonesia.

2 Income inequality and poverty

Rapid and sustained economic growth has been the major force behind the sharp reductions in poverty achieved in East and South East Asia (see Tables 10.6 and 10.7). Most of these economies, moreover, have managed to grow rapidly, at least until the past ten years, without aggravating their income distribution (see Tables 10.6 and 10.8).

Table 10.6: Poverty Incidence and Income Distribution, 1970-1993

	Poverty incidence (%)						Gini coefficient for household incomes					
	1970	1976	1980	1985	1990	1993	1970	1976	1980	1985	1990	1993
Korea, Rep. of	23.4	14.8	9.8	na	4.5	na	0.33	0.39	0.39	0.36[d]	0.40[d]	na
Taiwan Province of China	na	5.0	na	na	na	na	0.29	0.28	0.28	0.29	0.31	0.31
Malaysia	52.4	42.4	29.0	20.7[a]	17.1[b]	13.4	0.51	0.53	0.49[e]	0.47[a]	0.45	0.46
Thailand	39.0	30.0	23.0	29.5	17.9	na	na	0.45	0.47[c]	0.50[f]	0.50	na
Indonesia	57.1	50.1	39.8	21.6[a]	15.8	na	0.35	0.34	0.34	0.33[e]	0.32	0.34

Notes: While inter-country comparison of changes is possible, cross-comparisons of particular year rates are not possible due to classification differences; [a] - 1984; [b] - 1989; [c] - 1981; [d] - 1982; [e] - 1979; [f] - 1989; na - not available. *Sources:* Taiwan Province of China's Gini coefficients are from Yu (1994: 6); Chowdhury and Islam (1993).

In fact, unlike the cross-sectional data which led Kuznets (1955) to formulate the inverted "U" curve relationship between economic growth and income inequality, the Asian NIEs have until recently defied such a trend. An extensive redistribution of government expenditure made possible the sustained reduction of inequality over a long period in the cases of Malaysia and Indonesia (Rasiah and Ishak 1994 and Rasiah 1994). Reductions of income inequality probably provided an impetus to economic growth in the

Republic of Korea and in Taiwan Province of China. Thailand is the only one of the five economies where inequality has increased steadily over a long period.

Table 10.7: Rural-Urban Poverty Incidence, 1970-93[*)]

		1970	1976	1980	1985	1990	1993
Korea, Rep. of	*rural*	27.9	11.7	9.0	4.4[a]	na	na
	urban	16.2	18.1	10.4	4.6[a]	na	na
Malaysia	*rural*	58.5	50.9	37.4	27.3[a]	22.4	18.6
	urban	21.3	18.7	12.6	8.5[a]	8.3	5.3
Thailand	*rural*	43.0	36.2	25.8	35.8	33.9	na
	urban	16.0	12.5	7.5	5.9	6.7	na
Indonesia	*rural*	58.5	na	44.6	na	18.5	na
	urban	50.7	na	19.7	na	8.3	na

Notes: [*)] data for Taiwan Province of China not available [a] - 1984; na - not available. *Sources:* Ragayah and Mohamad (1995: Table 4); Chowdhury and Islam (1993).

Table 10.8: Rural-Urban Gini Coefficient Trends, 1970-93[*)]

		1970	1976	1980	1985	1990	1993
Korea, Rep. of	*rural*	0.33	0.39	0.39	0.36[b]	na	na
	urban	0.35	0.41	0.41	0.37[b]	na	na
Taiwan Province	*rural*	0.32	0.32[a]	na	na	na	na
of China	*urban*	0.31	0.30[a]	na	na	na	na
Malaysia	*rural*	0.47	0.50	0.48	0.44	0.41	na
	urban	0.50	0.53	0.50	0.47	0.45	na
Indonesia	*rural*	0.34	0.31	0.31	0.28	0.26	0.26
	urban	0.33	0.36	0.38	0.32	0.32	0.33

Notes: [*)] data for Thailand not available [a] - 1972; [b] - 1982. *Source:* Krongkaew (1994); Kim (1986: 75); cited in Chowdhury and Islam, 1993); Poot, Kuyrenhoven and Jensen (1991: Table 3.17); Ishak (1996: Table 3).

With increasing liberalization, however, income inequalities in the Republic of Korea and Taiwan Province of China show recent signs of widening. A similar trend is also observable in the case of Malaysia, following the liberalization trend of the 1990s.

The fact that income inequality in Taiwan Province of China and the Republic of Korea declined in the initial stages but may be growing as the two economies became mature turns the Kuznets hypothesis on its head. However, the unique circumstances of post-conflict reforms, in particular agrarian reforms, suggest that the initially egalitarian conditions created by these reforms rather than the subsequent growth process itself have been the determining variables. Because of their implications for income distribution and poverty, land reforms and rural development are discussed below.

Land reforms and rural development

In the cases of the Republic of Korea and Taiwan Province of China the initial boost for poverty alleviation and more equitable distribution occurred long before liberalization policies were adopted. This boost consisted of land reforms adopted as far back as the late 1940s (Hamilton 1983). Land reform in the Republic of Korea was undertaken in two stages: immediately after World War II and following the Korean War (Amsden 1989). In Taiwan Province of China land reforms were combined with government measures to encourage rapid rural industrialization through the establishment of manufacturing activities alongside farming. Both the governments of the Republic of Korea and Taiwan Province of China controlled grain marketing and the distribution of inputs, thereby protecting farmers and consumers from volatile price fluctuations.

Starting with the 1970s, the Republic of Korea and Taiwan Province of China introduced hybrid grain varieties and took steps to modernize farming practices, which expanded the food supply but displaced many farm workers who migrated to the cities to take up the plentiful work opportunities in manufacturing firms. As a result of the land reforms in the rural areas and the growing segmentation of incomes in urban areas, income distribution has been less skewed in the rural areas of the Republic of Korea than in the urban areas (Table 10.8). Likewise, the combination of agrarian reform and migration of large numbers of rural workers to the urban areas contributed to a rapid and substantial decline in poverty in the rural areas.

As land reforms go, the experiences of Malaysia, Indonesia and Thailand have been quite different than those of the Republic of Korea and Taiwan Province of China. Starting in 1971, Malaysia pursued deliberate distributional policies to reduce poverty and achieve greater ethnic parity by the year 1990. As part of government interventions to increase *Bumiputera*[1] participation in the economy, undeveloped rural land in Malaysia was distributed through land development schemes managed by government agencies such as the Federal Land Development Authority (FELDA), Federal Land Consolidation and Rehabilitation Authority (FELCRA) and Rubber Industry Smallholders Development Authority (RISDA). Quasi-government bodies were established to market the cash crops produced by smallholders. Because of institutional shortcomings, these land development schemes had only a limited impact in terms of reducing poverty and inequality in Malaysia (Halim 1991 and Jomo 1986). Beginning with the late 1980s, moreover, the significance of agricultural and rural development schemes declined in importance as emphasis shifted to manufacturing in connection with the launching of the Industrial Master Plan (IMP). The success of this industrialization drive is reflected by the massive migration of rural workers to urban and industrial areas, and by the need to bring in foreign labour to replace Malay workers in the agricultural sector of Malaysia (Mehmet 1986).

Land reforms were formally introduced in Thailand in 1975, following the Agricultural Land Reform Act. However, little progress has been achieved to date in terms of redistributing land to the rural poor (Onchan 1995). Instead, rural poverty has been reduced as a consequence of migration to the cities where labour demand has been rapidly growing. Moreover, the government has helped raise rural household incomes through the promotion of off-farm work opportunities. Largely as a result, the proportion of rural household incomes generated from off-farm activities rose from 46 per cent in 1971/72 to 63 per cent in 1986/87 (Onchan 1995: 32).

The Indonesian experience has in some ways paralleled the Malaysian experience. In an effort to reduce population density in the rural areas of Java, transmigration policies have been in effect during the past two decades to facilitate the relocation of rural households to underpopulated islands of Indonesia. The settlers have been given tools and credits, and the settlements have been equipped with infrastructure and basic services. These resettlement programmes have helped reduce land pressures, and hence poverty, in Java.

---

[1] *Bumiputeras* literally translated means sons of the soil, but is generally used to refer to the indigenous peoples of Malaysia.

Human resources development

Education has been a major factor contributing to the economic growth and industrialization of the Republic of Korea and Taiwan Province of China. Not only has primary education been universal in these economies, but there have also been high attendance rates at the secondary and tertiary levels (see Table 10.9), in particular in the technical and engineering disciplines. Over the years, this expansion of education has not only helped generate technical and professional labour for industrial modernization, but has also enhanced the opportunities for upward social as well as economic mobility (Deyo 1989).

Table 10.9: Educational Enrolment, 1970-92

| | % of age group enrolled in educational institutions | | | | | |
| | Primary | | Secondary | | Tertiary | |
	1970	1992	1970	1992	1970	1992
Korea, Rep. of	103	105	42	90	16	42
Taiwan Province of China	na	na	na	na	na	na
Malaysia	87	93	34	58	4	7
Thailand	83	97	17	33	13	19
Indonesia	80	115	16	38	4	10
United Kingdom	104	104	73	86	20	28
France	117	106	74	101	26	46
Japan	99	102	86	na	31	32

Notes: na - not available. *Source:* World Bank, (1995: 217).

Rising educational levels, combined with rapid economic growth and declining unemployment, have substantially driven up real wages in these economies. Real wages in the Republic of Korea grew at an average annual rate of 10.0 per cent between 1970 and 1980, and by 8.2 per cent between 1980 and 1992 (World Bank 1995: 175). In the case of Taiwan Province of China, real wages grew by 6.0 per cent annually between 1970 and 1980 (Computed from Deyo 1989: 93).

Human resources development has been less successful in the cases of the second-tier NIEs. Partly because of this, real wages grew by 4.3, 2.3 and 2.8 per cent in Indonesia, Malaysia and Thailand respectively between 1980 and

1992 (World Bank 1995: 174-75 and Rasiah 1994: 210); i.e., at rates below those in particular of the Republic of Korea. With achievements in secondary and especially tertiary education below those of the first-tier NIEs, there were only 400 technologists and scientists per million persons in Malaysia, Thailand and Indonesia, compared with 2,200 for the Republic of Korea and 2,100 for Taiwan Province of China. As a result, Thailand and Malaysia in particular are confronted with severe shortages of skilled, professional labour.

Government expenditures on social services other than education have also been important in alleviating poverty, reducing inequality and fostering economic growth. Government participation has been vital from the standpoint of externalities involving the provision of public goods. However, the experience of the economies under review does not support the hypothesis that there is a positive association between higher public expenditure per capita on education and health and improved human capital. For instance, the governments of Malaysia and Thailand spent more per head on education and health care between 1972 and 1993 than did the Republic of Korea (see Table 10.10).

Table 10.10: Central Government Expenditure, 1972-93[*]

	Education			Health			Housing, social security and welfare			Central government expenditure % of GNP		
	1972	1980	1993	1972	1980	1993	1972	1980	1993	1972	1980	1993
Korea, Rep. of	15.9	17.1	16.8	1.2	1.2	1.0	5.8	7.5	11.2	18.1	17.6	17.1
Malaysia	23.4	18.3	20.3	6.8	5.1	5.7	4.4	7.0	11.4	27.7	29.6	26.7
Thailand	19.9	19.8	21.1	3.7	4.1	8.2	7.0	5.1	6.7	17.2	19.0	16.3
Indonesia	7.5	8.3	10.0	1.3	2.5	2.7	0.9	1.8	1.6	16.2	23.1	18.9

Notes:[*] data for Taiwan Province of China not available na - not available. *Source:* World Bank (1995).

Employment and labour markets in the second-tier NIEs

Export-oriented manufacturing has played a major role in augmenting the demand for low-skill labour in the second-tier NIEs. Largely as a result, the demand for wage labour between 1970 and 1990 grew by 8.8 per cent and 6.6 per cent per annum in Malaysia and Indonesia, respectively (see Table 10.11). In particular, female participation in export-oriented manufacturing grew strongly in these economies and in Thailand from the early 1980s on (Kamal and Young 1985, McGee 1986, Onchan 1995 and World Bank 1993). By reducing disguised unemployment and raising household incomes, this growth in low-wage employment has made a major contribution to reducing absolute poverty in the countries concerned.

**Table 10.11: Wage Employment Growth and
Unemployment Rate, 1970-94 (%)**

	Wage employment	Unemployment rate		
	Average growth (1970-90)	1970	1983	1992
Korea, Rep. of	6.6	na	4.1	2.4
Taiwan Province of China	na	1.7	2.7	1.5
Malaysia	8.2	8.0	6.0	4.1
Thailand	6.6	na	2.9	2.2[a]
Indonesia	na	na	2.0	1.4[b]

Notes: [a] - 1990; [b] - 1991; na - not available. *Source:* World Bank (1995); Taiwan Province of China's figures from Yu (1994: 6).

However, wage differentials have grown as the demand for skilled labour outpaces the demand for unskilled workers (World Bank 1995, Rasiah and Osman-Rani 1995). Wage differentials between skilled and unskilled labour have been further exacerbated in the case of Malaysia by the importation of unskilled workers from Indonesia and Bangladesh who, by 1995, accounted for about 15 per cent of the total labour force. Because Indonesia is still at the labour-intensive industrialization stage, there has been less labour market segmentation and, hence, less differences in wages.

3 Conclusions

The rapid economic growth of the Republic of Korea and Taiwan Province of China, was made possible by a number of factors, in particular the adoption of industrial policies and the availability of a well-educated labour force. The industrial policies enabled initially infant industries to mature and develop the capacity to compete successfully in export markets and against foreign imports. As a result, the adoption of trade and investment liberalization policies in connection with the globalization process poses relatively few problems for the industrial structure of these economies. As for income distribution and poverty, the agrarian reforms that were adopted helped initially to reduce inequality and were instrumental in enabling economic growth to take place without making the income distribution more skewed. In fact, because rapid economic growth has taken place in a context of moderate income inequality, absolute poverty has declined in the Republic of Korea and Taiwan Province of China to the point that, after four decades, it has nearly been eliminated. Concern is mounting, however, over the possibly adverse effects that liberalization policies may be having on income distribution.

Malaysia, Thailand and Indonesia have also enjoyed rapid economic growth. Industrial policies have been less pivotal in the growth of these countries than in the Republic of Korea and Taiwan Province of China. Instead, foreign direct investment has played a major role in developing the industrial export capacity of these countries. By generating low-skill jobs and economic growth, foreign direct investment has helped reduce poverty substantially. The adoption of outward-oriented liberalization policies by these countries should therefore pose little problem, given the openness to trade and foreign direct investment already exhibited by these countries. Future progress, however, will also be conditional on there being additional investment of public resources in human capital formation. Thus, enhanced liberalization policies in the economic realm will have to be complemented by increased public and private sector attention to human resources development through higher education and technological training.

References

Akyuz, Y. and C. Gore. 1996. The Investment-Profit Nexus in East Asian Industrialization. Forthcoming in *World Development* 24(3).

Amsden, A.O. 1989. *Asia's Next Giant.* New York: Oxford University Press.

Chang, H.J. 1994. *Political Economy of Industrial Policy.* London: Macmillan.

Chowdhury, A. and I. Islam. 1993. *The Newly Industrializing Economies of East Asia,* London: Routledge.

Deyo, F. 1989. *Beneath the Miracle: Labor Subordination in East Asia.* Ithaca: Cornell University Press.

Halim, S. 1991. State Capitalism in Malaysian Agriculture. *Journal of Contemporary Asia,* 21(3): 327-43.

Hamilton, C. 1983. Capitalist Industrialization in East Asia's Four Little Tigers. *Journal of Contemporary Asia* 13(1): 35-73.

Ishak, S. 1996. Ekonomi dan Implikasinya Terhadap Usaha Pembasmian Kemiskinan di Malaysia. Paper presented at Rancangan Malaysia Ketujuh: Penerusan Usaha Membasmi Liberalisasi Kemiskinan, Kota Kinabalu, 7-8 May.

Jomo, K.S. 1986. *A Question of Class.* Kuala Lumpur: Oxford University Press.

_____. (ed). 1994. *Privatizing Malaysia: Rents, Rhetoric and Realities.* Boulder: Westview.

Jomo, K.S. and C.B. Edwards. 1995. Malaysian Industrialization: Policy, Prospects and Performance. Paper presented at the seminar Governance Mechanisms and Technical Change in Malaysian Industrialization, Bangi 15-16 July 1995.

Kamal, S. and M.L. Young. 1985 Penang's Industrialization: where do we go from here? Paper presented at the Future of Penang conference, Penang, 6-8 May.

Kuznets, S. 1955. Economic growth and Income Inequality. *American Economic Review* 45(1): 1-28.

Landau, D.F, G.J. Schinasi, M. Cassard, V.K. Ng, C.M. Reinhart and M.G. Spencer. 1995. Effect of Capital Flows on the Domestic Financial Sectors. in APEC Developing Countries. In Khan M.S. and Reinhart C.M. (eds), Capital Flows in the APEC Region. Occasional paper 122, Washington D.C: International Monetary Fund.

Lee, J.S. 1994. The Role of the State in Economic Restructuring and Development: The Case of Taiwan. Occasional paper series No. 9403, Chung-Hua Institution for Economic Research. Taipei.

McGee, T.G. (eds) 1986. *Industrialization and Labour Force Processes: A Case Study of Peninsular Malaysia*. Canberra: Australian National University.

Mehmet, O. 1986. *Development in Malaysia: Poverty, Wealth and Trusteeship*, London: Croom Helm.

Nam, S.W. 1993. Korea's Financial Markets and Policies. *mimeo*. Seoul: Korea Development Institute.

Nayyar, D. 1978. Transnational Corporations and Manufactured Exports from Poor Countries. *Economic Journal* 88: 59-84.

Onchan, T. 1995. Economic Growth, Income Distribution and Poverty in Thailand. Paper presented at the Fifth tun Abdul Razak Conference, April 21-13, Athens, Ohio.

Poot, H, A. Kuyvenhoven and J. Jansen. 1991. *Industrialization and Trade in Indonesia*. Yogyakarta: Gadjah Mada University Press.

Ragayah, M.Z. and A. Mohamad. 1995. The Effect of Price Liberalization and Market Reforms on the Poverty Situation of Farm Communities and Rural Families. Report prepared for the Economic and Social Commission for Asia Pacific (ESCAP), Bangkok.

Rasiah, R. 1992. Foreign Manufacturing Investment in Malaysia. *Economic Bulletin for Asia and Pacific* 63(1): 63-77.

_____. 1994. Capitalist Industrialization in ASEAN. *Journal of Contemporary Asia* 24(3).

_____. 1995. *Foreign Capital and Industrialization in Malaysia*. London and New York: Macmillan and St. Martins.

_____. 1995a. Macroeconomic Management and Economic Growth in Developing Economies. In W.M. Wan Manan and Sundramurthy (eds), Penang: Malaysian Social Science Association (forthcoming).

_____. 1996. State Intervention, Rents and Malaysian Industrialization. In J. Borrego J, A.B. Alvarez and K.S. Jomo (eds). *Capital, the State and Late Industrialization: Comparative Perspectives on the Pacific Rim*, Boulder: Westview.

Rasiah, R. and S. Ishak. 1994. Malaysia's New Economic Policy in Retrospect. *mimeo*.

Rasiah, R. and H. Osman-Rani. 1995. Enterprise Training and Productivity in

Malaysian Manufacturing. Paper presented at the World Bank Conference on Enterprise Training and Productivity, Washington D.C., June 12-13.

Rodrick, D. 1994. Getting Interventions Right: How South Korea and Taiwan Grew Rich. NBER Working Paper No. 4964.

Roemer, M. 1994. Industrial Strategies: Outward Bound. In D.L. Lindauer and M. Roemer (eds). *Asia and Africa: Legacies and Opportunities in Development* 233-68. San Francisco: ICS Press.

Singh, A. 1994. Openness and the market-friendly approach to development: learning the right lessons from development experience. *World Development* 22(12).

Snodgrass, D. and R. Rasiah. 1995. Promotion of Manufactured Exports in Malaysia: Lessons for Indonesia. *mimeo.*

UNCTAD. 1993. *World Investment Report.* Geneva: UNCTAD.

_____. 1994. *World Investment Report.* Geneva: UNCTAD.

_____. 1995. *World Investment Report.* Geneva: UNCTAD.

Wade, R. 1990. *Governing the Market.* Princeton: Princeton University Press.

West, J. 1995. Two Strategies for Technology Innovation Under Complexity and Uncertainty: Source of Knowledge Integration Capability in Advanced Semiconductor Development. *Journal of Industry Studies* (forthcoming).

World Bank. 1993. *The East Asian Miracle.* Oxford: Oxford University Press.

_____. 1995. *World Development Report 1995: Workers in an Integrating World.* New York: Oxford University Press.

You, J.I. 1995. A Reflection on the Korean Miracle: Toward a New Concept of Development. *Ritsumeikan Journal of International Relations and Area Studies* 8.

_____. 1995a. Income Distribution and Growth in East Asia. Paper presented at the UNCTAD conference on Income Distribution and Development, Geneva, December.

Yu, T.S. 1994. Does Taiwan's Industrialization Have Its Own Paradigm. Occasional paper series No. 9404. Chung-Hua Institution for Economic Research, Taipei.

11

The importance of foreign direct investment for exports, economic growth and poverty reduction in China

Padma Mallampally*

The People's Republic of China is the latest and largest in/a series of East and South East Asian countries that have grown rapidly and sustainably in the past two decades or more (see Mr. Rasiah's paper in this volume for a review of the experiences of the Republic of Korea, Taiwan Province of China, Malaysia, Thailand and Indonesia). In terms of size, China has a population of over 1.2 billion, of which 70 per cent live in the countryside. Despite China's rapid growth rate, as of 1993, 31 per cent or 372 million of the population continued to live below the $1/day absolute poverty line (see table 1 of Mr. Husain's paper in this volume). Indeed, China continues to be poorer than the other rapidly industrializing countries of Asia.

   In terms of saving rates and the government's share of GDP, China is not unlike the other Asian NIEs. At 40 per cent of GDP, China's gross domestic savings rate is even higher than that of the Republic of Korea, Thailand or Taiwan Province of China. Likewise, the government's share of GDP is less than 12 per cent, which places it below the roughly 20 per cent level of the other rapidly industrializing countries of the region. It should be noted, however, that part of China's savings helps support over 100,000 state-run enterprises that employ two-thirds of the urban workforce. Because this support passes through a financial system which is not yet fully market-oriented, government spending figures understate the extent of implicit government subsidies to the state-owned enterprise sector.

---

* TNC Affairs Officer, Research and Policy Analysis Branch, Division on Transnational Corporations and Investment, UNCTAD

Like the other rapidly growing economies of Asia, China has been able to capitalize on the benefits of growing foreign investment and trade in the world. Whereas in 1978 China's exports totalled US$ 9.8 billion, by 1994 they amounted to $121 billion, which makes China the eighth largest exporter of manufactured goods in the world.

Foreign direct investment (FDI) has accounted for about 30 per cent of China's exports (though merely 2 per cent of total manufactured output). In terms of FDI inflows, China received US$ 34 billion in 1994, which places it second only to the United States in inward investment flows obtained. It should be noted, however, that these figures are somewhat inflated because of (a) overvaluation at times given to in-kind FDI and (b) round-tripping of investment originating in some domestic firms that is rerouted through foreign affiliates in Hong Kong back to China in order to take advantage of the fiscal incentives awarded to foreign investors.

The initial inflows of FDI began once China began to liberalize its FDI regime in 1979. Substantial volumes of FDI flowed in particularly after 1990. About two thirds of this FDI has been from other Asian NIEs, in particular Hong Kong, Taiwan Province of China, and countries of South East Asia having an economically important overseas Chinese population. The remainder of FDI has been from Japan, the United States and other OECD countries.

Initially, FDI was concentrated in the coastal regions and special economic zones of East and Southern China, but subsequently expanded to the Northern and Central Provinces of the country. Sectorally, labour intensive manufacturing (textiles and clothing, footwear, food processing, electrical and electronic goods) has accounted for the main share of FDI in China, but other mainly domestic-oriented industries have been important as well (energy, automobiles, tourism). More recently, raw materials, telecommunications and transport have also begun to attract FDI.

China's economic dynamism and rapid growth can partly be attributed to the country's success in obtaining and utilizing FDI. In fact, FDI has represented a package of valued resources – external finance, technology, organizational knowhow, and export channels and contacts – that has been crucial to China's development. The demonstration effect of FDI is potentially important for the modernization and restructuring of the state-owned enterprises sector. The dynamism of the export sector has also spearheaded the rapid growth of China's private sector.

The absorption of FDI has contributed to the country's economic perform-ance in additional ways as well:

- It has provided an important supplement to the domestic supply of capital. The ratio of FDI to gross domestic investment rose from 3 per cent in the second half of the 1980s to 20 per cent in 1993.
- It has helped mobilize domestic capital by opening up investment opportun-ities in joint ventures.
- Foreign affiliates have contributed substantially to fiscal revenues. For example, in Shanghai, the country's largest industrial city, tax contributions by foreign affiliates accounted for over 10 per cent of tax revenues in 1993.

As for its social impact, FDI has contributed significantly to low-skill employment generation and, as a consequence, to the reduction of poverty. According to official estimates, in 1992 there were over 6 million Chinese employed by more than 45,000 foreign affiliates in the country. As a result, more than 4 per cent of workers in the urban areas of China were directly employed in foreign affiliates, in addition to those employed in economic activities generated by associated forward and backward linkages (perhaps an additional 4 per cent). In the process, however, FDI has contributed to the augmentation of income disparities between the better-off coastal areas and poorer inland provinces. Rural outmigration has grown as a consequence. It should also be noted that, because of the enormous size of the country's labour force, it will be a long time before China experiences an upward pressure on low-skill wages as a result of labour shortages. In this respect, China's ability to reduce poverty through a secular rise in wages does not compare with the experience of Malaysia and most of the other rapidly growing Asian economies (see Mr. Rasiah's paper in this volume).

What are the lessons to be learned from foreign investment in China? China's case is, of course, unique in the sense that a good deal of the FDI has come from overseas Chinese stakeholders. However, there are also circum-stances that make China a prototypical recipient of FDI: a liberalized FDI regime, political stability, a large domestic market and, what is most important in terms of low-skill exports, a low-cost, hard-working labour force.

12

What prospects does India have of benefitting from globalization?

Sumit Roy*

South Asia is the key to how much globalization and liberalization are likely to reduce poverty in the coming decades. There are two reasons for this. First, the region accounts for about 45 per cent of the incidence of absolute poverty in the world. Secondly, while the region as a whole has not yet benefitted much from globalization, there are reasons to believe that it has the potential and capacity to do so. To date, the adaptation of the region to the globalization process has been slow, in particular if compared with East Asia, South East Asia, and China. Sri Lanka adopted liberalization measures in the 1970s and is now one of the low-income countries of Asia that supplies labour-intensive manufactured products to world markets. Bangladesh has benefitted from the MFA, and has thereby managed to insert itself in international trade as a significant exporter of textiles. India and Pakistan, on the other hand, are newcomers but have the potential to become major participants in the globalization process during the decades ahead. Because it alone accounts for about a third of the world's absolute poverty, what happens with regard to India's insertion in the global economy is particularly important with respect to the prospects of globalization and liberalization eventually reducing absolute poverty in a major way in the world. India is hence the focus of the present paper.

India is a relatively large, hitherto generally closed economy with a significant industrial base. It has a low per capita income and an important agrarian sector. Trade and foreign investment have played only a limited role

---

* Senior visiting fellow, Department of Economics, City University, London.

in India's development. Compared with Asia's other giant, China, India
exports much less, receives relatively little investment from abroad, has an
economic growth rate that has been half that of China's over the past decade,
has an income per capita that is currently less than two-thirds of China's, and
has infant mortality and illiteracy rates that are twice China's. The reasons for
this unfavourable comparison are complex, but may be partly related to
China's "strategic globalization" in which, given coexistance between the state
sector and the market, there has been in China rapid and far-reaching success
in liberalizing selected sectors of the economy and becoming a major exporter
of manufactured goods. While India's political economy has made the pace
of its outward orientation slower than has been the case of the Asian NIEs
and China, progress in this area could become firmly rooted and sustainable
over the long term. An indicator to whatch closely will be the way in which
India's current government implements the liberalization policies which were
adopted in 1991 as part of an effort to become more market- and outward-
oriented.

    In contrast to many developing countries, liberalization policies have been
adopted in India out of a desire to stimulate growth and outward-oriented
development, and have been driven by the recognition that the State is limited
in what it can accomplish to accelerate economic growth. Although there were
earlier experiments in the early 1980s, India initiated its principal liberalization measures in 1991, after it became apparent that the economy was
overextended and overborrowed, and that fiscal pressures meant that the State
must rely more on market forces. To deal with the shortage of foreign
exchange reserves, a soaring budget deficit and rising inflation, the government devalued the rupee, slashed import tariffs from 300 per cent in 1991 to
50 per cent, abolished much import-licensing, ended the public sector's
monopoly in areas such as power and telecommunications, liberalized foreign-
investment rules, and in general took steps to integrate India more closely into
the world economy. The trade and exchange-rate regimes were liberalized
immediately while other liberalization measures have been phased-in more
gradually, in accordance with what government leaders have thought that the
Indian electorate would tolerate. For instance, labour laws have not been
liberalized and the privatization of public-sector companies – where labour
unions are especially strong – has proceeded at a slow pace, with only about
US$ 3 billion raised by state sell-offs since 1991. Such gradualism has made
political sense. With a shock therapy approach to liberalization likely to create

immediate losers among the population and only over the medium-term gainers from the reforms, a more gradual approach has made it possible to defer some of the pain of adjustment until the benefits became more apparent. What is important to note, however, is that the externally-oriented liberalization measures were adopted at once, which means that India could become more rapidly integrated into the global economy than if the government had slowly phased-in the entire liberalization package.

Although economic growth slumped in 1992, it has since rebounded to between 5 and 6 per cent. This rate, however, is little different from the growth rates experienced before the 1991 liberalization measures were introduced. Moreover, higher food prices resulting from the reforms have negatively affected food-deficit households. Largely because of these price hikes in both the market and public distribution system, the real wages of unskilled agricultural labour declined by an estimated 2.5 per cent during the first half of the 1990s. With respect to changes in the trade regime, despite substantial devaluations and other outward-oriented liberalization policies, trends in exports, imports and the trade balance remain largely unchanged since the 1980s. Furthermore, relatively little foreign direct investment has entered the country for the purpose of manufacturing goods for export. The key question, therefore, is how long will it take for the liberalization policies to make a difference and enable India to enjoy the fruits of globalization, including growth rates of 7-8 per cent a year, i.e. the level needed to create the eight million jobs or more a year necessary to keep pace with population growth and reduce the backlog of accumulated underemployment and poverty. However unsuccessful they have been so far at rapidly turning the economy around, it should nonetheless be pointed out that India's liberalization policies have not resulted in a "lost development decade", as happenned to much of Latin America and Africa during the 1980s.

Anti-poverty strategies in India have largely looked to economic growth as a major instrument for reducing poverty. The importance attached to economic growth as a way of reducing poverty has, if anything, grown under liberalization. However, structural barriers, such as the skewed distribution of land ownership, and institutional factors affecting the operation of markets have, through their interaction with each other and growth, continued to limit the benefits of "trickle-down" growth for the poor. In fact, the nature of the growth and pattern of productivity that may result from globalization and liberalization can be expected to be as important as the rate of growth in terms of reducing poverty. The spread effects of growth are likely to be more substantial if accompanied by public investment in infrastructure and human resources development.

The fiscal crisis at the start of the 1990s not only forced the central government to turn to market mechanisms in the search for new means to generate growth; it also had devastating effects on the role of government in fostering social progress. In particular, there were fewer budgetary resources to invest in education, health and nutrition. Apart from the social costs involved, such cutbacks, unless reversed, could foil India's long-term prospects to benefit from the globalization process. Without expanded education, for instance, India cannot broaden the participation of the population in the globalization process by creating a more productive and internationally competitive labour force. The benefits of globalization might, as a consequence, go to only 10 to 15 per cent of the population, thus contributing to growing income inequality and a widening divergence in wages.

The liberalization measures of the 1990s in India have tended to treat social expenditure as a residual. Such expenditure has been only minimally protected in the central budget. While the states are responsible for the bulk of social spending, on their own or as agents of centrally sponsored programmes, little attempt has been made to devise a national policy for social expenditure. Central government allocations to education and health care declined since 1990-91, with a slight corrective upward rebound in 1994-95. The sharpest cuts have occurred with respect to preventative disease control programmes, such as malaria, tuberculosis and leprosy, which affect particularly the poor. Cuts in central grants have particularly negatively affected the poorest states, where disbursements on medical and health expenditures have fallen in real per capita terms since 1991. In the aggregate, human development expenditure has declined in the country's state budgets from 16 per cent to 12.4 per cent during the 1990s. The decline has been even larger for infrastructure, where the share fell from 15.9 per cent before liberalization to 5.7 per cent of total expenditure after liberalization.

Among the only social measures specifically included in the liberalization policies of the 1990s has been a compensatory scheme designed to mitigate the hardships created by liberalization measures on workers in the organized sectors of the economy. The programme created to cope with such groups is called the National Renewal Fund (NRF), which was established in February

1992 with support from the World Bank and bilateral donors. The NRF is administered by India's Ministry of Industry. One of its programmes consists of the National Renewal Grant Fund (NRGF), which compensates workers made redundant in the closing of enterprises in the public and private sectors. The second programme, called the Employment Generation Fund (EGF), seeks to facilitate the redeployment and retraining of affected workers, as well as to fund specific employment generation initiatives for sectors affected by industrial restructuring and technology upgrading. Until now, however, only public sector workers have been covered by the NRF, and they only in terms of the provision of compensation for retrenched workers.

National poverty reduction goals, however, cannot be met through compensatory schemes alone. Significant public investment is also required in basic needs programmes targeted at the poor; in investment in agriculture to stimulate the sector's growth and the market for industrial goods; in redistributive measures such as land reform and strengthened property rights for the poor; in the public distribution of food grains; and in emergency employment schemes. Compared with many developing countries, India has had a long and relatively successful history in terms of employment schemes to alleviate poverty, such as the Integrated Rural Development Programme (IRDP) and National Rural Employment programme (NREP) that were launched in 1980, as well as the Rural Landless Employment Guarantee Programme (RLEGP) that was initiated in 1983. The NREP and the RLEGP were combined in 1989 to form the Jawahar Rojgar Yojana (JRY). While some of the programmes have not been entirely free of problems, e.g. benefit leakages and improper targeting, others have been successful. Rural youth training programmes, such as the Training of Rural Youth for Self Employment (TRYSEM), have also been important, although the quality of the training and other forms of support have not always been as high as desired. With regard to nutrition schemes, several can be cited: the Public Distribution System (PDS), the Mid Day Meals Programme of Tamil Nadu, and the Rice for the Poor Programme of Andra Pradesh. Such interventions have focused on overcoming shortages in the food intake of poor households, on remedying seasonal or drought-induced malnutrition, and on satisfying the fundamental needs of special groups, in particular children. Generally speaking, these programmes have been untargeted and therefore have tended to bypass many of the less accessible absolute poor, benefitting instead mainly those social groups who are not at nutritional risk. Some smaller schemes, however, were introduced in the 1980s that featured innovative, targeted interventions directed at women and children in vulnerable households.

A major challenge for India, therefore, remains one of obtaining resources to carry out infrastructure and social programmes which only government can do, while at the same time pursuing a strategy of increased economic opening and integration in the global economy. If it is to attain these two objectives, India may need to consider promulgating more flexible labour laws, as well as privatizing, making more efficient, or closing down ailing public and private enterprises, and speeding up corporate bankruptcy procedures, where applicable. Subsidies to the public and private sectors and a policy of not making redundant public and private employees continue to consume a sizeable proportion of the budget, which represents foregone resources that could be invested in, among other sectors, agriculture, infrastructure, and basic education, health and nutrition. Implicit and explicit subsidies at the central and state levels in India account for around 15 per cent of India's GNP, of which relatively little reaches or benefits the absolute poor. Moreover, making taxation policy more progressive and efficient would also help generate additional government revenues.

Labour market liberalization would no doubt have severe implications for surplus workers made redundant by labour law reforms and the inter-enterprise competition resulting from globalization and liberalization. However, these workers tend to be better educated than the absolute poor, can be compensated and retrained under schemes such as the NRGF and EGF discussed above, and have skills and connections that make it easier for them to be re-employed elsewhere in a growing economy. While labour law reforms and reduced subsidies to the parastatal and private sectors in no way assure that a more outward-oriented and labour-intensive strategy will be crowned with success, such policies would enable India to compete more successfully internationally. The policies could release public resources to help fulfill development objectives such as investment in the human capital of the poor.

13

Globalization and liberalization in Latin America: implications for growth, inequality and poverty

André Urani[*]

Latin America's *lost decade* is not expected to be repeated or extended into the 1990s. According to the Economic Commission for Latin America and the Caribbean (ECLAC), the region's GDP cumulative growth rate for the first half of the 1990s (14.9 per cent) was higher than for the entire period of the 1980s (13 per cent). Meanwhile, the average rate of inflation, which attained 1,200 per cent in 1990, averaged 25 per cent in 1995. Poverty has declined during the 1990s, although not sufficiently to compensate for the increased incidence during the 1980s.

Heterodox stabilization measures and, to a lesser degree, liberalization policies have played a fundamental role in bringing about this metamorphosis. However, the progress in implementing macroeconomic stability and liberalization measures has varied from country to country in terms of the depth and swiftness with which the reforms have been carried out.

The eruption of the foreign debt crisis at the start of the 1980s coincided with the declining role of import substitution as Latin America's engine of growth and development. The adoption of structural adjustment programmes, initially typically at the behest of the IMF and World Bank, further contributed to the demise of the import substitution paradigm. The examples of the East and South East Asian newly industrialized economics (see Rasiah's paper in this volume) and, more recently, of Chile have through their demonstration effects provided an additional impetus to adopting an outward-inclusive

* Associate Researcher, Instituto de Pesquisa Aplicada (IPEA) and Adjunct Professor, Faculty of Economics and Administration, Federal University of Rio de Janeiro.

growth strategy.

It is important to bear in mind, however, that the import-substitution strategy of past decades had generated sustained high growth rates and enabled Latin America to industrialize rapidly during those years. This phase of development was largely completed by the time of the debt crisis. The aim of the stabilization and structural adjustment reforms that have been adopted, therefore, has been not only to restore growth but also to enable the countries concerned to become more outward-oriented and thereby benefit from the globalization process. An important question in this connection is what have been the likely effects of stabilization and outward-oriented liberalization policies on the employment prospects, income distribution and incidence of poverty in Latin American countries. In examining this question, the present paper focuses in particular on Argentina, Brazil, Chile and Mexico.

1 From import substitution to outward liberalization

Initial conditions

The import substitution strategies followed by most Latin American countries after World War II were successful in achieving high GDP growth rates, and hence in reducing poverty. However, the extreme degree of income inequality that prevailed in many of the countries concerned meant that poverty declined less than would have been the case if income distribution had been less skewed.

One of the factors that contributed to income inequality during the import substitution phase of development was the capital-intensive nature of this process. A related factor was the highly dualistic nature of employment conditions (Cortazar, 1993). A minority of workers benefitted from formal contracts that included rights to a minimum wage, paid vacations, a fixed number of working hours per week, and social insurance, while the remainder of the labour force worked as informal sector employees, or were self-employed. However, because of the virtual absence of unemployment insurance schemes and the supply-driven, absorptive role of the informal sector, open unemployment was generally small in Latin America, the same as in other developing regions.

The import substitution model of development ceased to be dynamic in the

1970s, when inertial inflation became a growing problem. In an effort to restructure their economies and resume a sustainable growth path, Chile and Argentina in the late 1970s liberalized their foreign trade and capital accounts and sought to stabilize their economies and bring down inflation through a policy of exchange rate overvaluation. This liberalization drive, combined with massive external borrowing, ended disastrously with the debt crisis of the 1980s. Although the indebtedness had been incurred mainly by the private sector, the burden of debt repayment fell predominantly on the public sector. As is well known, orthodox stabilization and adjustment policies were adopted throughout Latin America in the 1980s in order to cope with the debt crisis.

Trade and financial liberalization

A fundamental characteristic of import substitution consisted of the high tariff and non-tariff barriers that were erected to protect domestic manufacturers. Most Latin American countries in the early 1980s continued for a while to maintain protectionist policies in response to the foreign debt crisis (Barros et al 1996, with respect to the Brazilian experience). However, many governments of the region subsequently liberalized their foreign trade regimes. Argentina and Mexico reduced their average import tariffs by half or more between the mid-1980s and 1993, while Brazil and Chile reduced their's by over two thirds during that period (ECLAC 1995).

   Financial liberalization policies were generally adopted at a later date than trade liberalization policies, and usually with greater trepidation. Partly due to its accession to NAFTA, Mexico was the first Latin American country to liberalize radically its capital account (Gurria Treviño 1995). Argentina has gone even further in this respect by adopting a policy of perfect capital mobility based on the parity of the US dollar and the Argentine peso (Fanelli and Machinera 1995). Brazil has been a more recent convert to financial liberalization. Mindful of its disastrous experience with financial liberalization in the 1970s, Chile adopted a "crawling-peg" exchange rate and prudent restrictions on short-term capital inflows (Agosin et al 1995). Mexico's recent financial crisis – largely the result of liberalizing its trade and financial policies concurrently – is examined in the paper by Ms. Correa in this book.

Foreign direct investment and privatization

By 1994, the stock of foreign direct investment (FDI) in Latin America and the Caribbean had reached US$ 186 billion. Inflows exceeded $20 billion in 1994. Taken together, Argentina, Brazil, Chile, Colombia, Mexico and Venezuela accounted for 71 per cent of the region's FDI inflows between 1988 and 1994 (UNCTAD 1995, p. 69).

Privatization programmes have played an important role in attracting FDI to the region. During 1989-1993, privatization-related foreign investment accounted for 17 per cent of total FDI flows to the major Latin American economies (Argentina, Brazil, Chile, Colombia, Mexico, Peru and Venezuela). Privatization has been resorted to not only with the intent of stimulating capital inflows, but also of reducing public debt and improving the performance of the infrastructure and basic goods sectors. Chile privatized on a large scale in the 1980s, followed by Argentina and Mexico during the 1990s. In Chile, fiscal receipts from privatizations were equivalent to 6.5 per cent of GDP during 1985-1990, and were equivalent to 6.0 and 8.5 per cent of GDP in Argentina and Mexico, respectively, during 1991-1993 (ECLAC 1995).

Macroeconomic performance

The adoption of heterodox stabilization policies sharply reduced inflation and had an expansionary effect in Argentina and Brazil during the first half of the 1990s. Argentina brought inflation under control through a combination of instruments that included nominal exchange rate fixation. Brazil later adopted a basically similar package of policies. However, to the extent that they were driven partly by an expansion in aggregate demand induced by exchange rate overvaluation, such economic recoveries risk being short-lived and eventually followed by the reimposition of orthodox stabilization measures. In fact, this phenomenon combined with the contagion effects of Mexico's financial crisis were largely responsible for bringing about Argentina's current economic recession. Moreover, an appreciation of the currency is antithetical to long-term investment and job-creation in exports production. As explained in Ms. Correa's paper in this volume, a benefit of the recent financial crisis in Mexico has been the creation of export-related jobs in connection with the devaluation of the peso.

2 Employment, income inequality and poverty

Employment

Liberalization and heterodox stabilization policies have had an ambiguous effect on formal sector employment in Latin America. On the negative side, import liberalization has been responsible for a decline in the level of employment in import-competing sectors (Cox Edwards and Edwards 1994). This phenomenon has in some cases been compounded by an overvalued exchange rate due to heterodox stabilization policies, which has led to increased imports of consumer goods and reduced export competitiveness, thus hurting jobs in both the import-competing and export sectors. Public sector cutbacks and privatizations have further contributed to employee retrenchment in some countries. On the other hand, the inflation-abating effects of heterogeneous stabilization policies have helped spark economic growth during the 1990s, which in some countries has more than offset the negative effects of currency appreciation, import liberalization, privatization and public-sector retrenchment policies. Among the benefits of this economic revival has been the fact that most laid-off workers have been able to find new formal sector jobs. Some of these have been in own-account employment, as in the case of former modern sector workers who, once retrenched, have started up small businesses with their severance pay and in many cases have obtained contracts with firms seeking to make their operations more flexible. As usual, moreover, the informal sector has functioned as a buffer that has absorbed redundant workers without formal-sector alternatives.

Trends in real wages and working conditions in the 1990s have also been subjected to contradictory pressures. Labour market liberalization policies, on the one hand, have eroded real wages and job security. On the other hand, renewed economic growth, currency appreciation, macroeconomic stability and low inflation have contributed to a growth in real incomes. On balance, the trend in wages has been positive. Real wages grew in the 1990s in Chile and, until its financial crisis, in Mexico as well. Currency appreciation and the taming of inflation in Brazil have enabled real wages to grow in recent years. On the other hand, reduced labour union bargaining power and significant unemployment levels have offset in Argentina the benefits accruing to it from macroeconomic stability and low inflation, with the result that real wages have stagnated during the 1990s.

The evolution of real earnings has not been the same for different segments of the labour market. In Chile, wage increases were more significant in the formal economy – where decentralized collective bargaining and productivity gains have contributed to bring about higher wages – than in the informal sector. In Brazil, on the other hand, because relative prices in non-tradeable sectors (where informal workers are concentrated) rose as a consequence of the overvaluation of the exchange rate, the income differentials between the formal and informal sectors narrowed (Camargo and Ramos 1988, Urani and Winograd 1994, and Urani 1995).

Income inequality and poverty

The trend of the 1980s when income losses were inversely proportional to educational levels was reversed in the first half of the 1990s. Indeed, household income and expenditure data show that Argentina and Brazil experienced growing inequality throughout the 1980s, followed in the 1990s by decreasing inequality as inflation subsided. In Mexico, income distribution became more skewed in the 1980s and less divergent in the early 1990s, while in Chile income inequality has remained roughly constant since 1987. Orthodox stabilization and adjustment policies contributed to the growth of inequality in the 1980s (Urani 1993 and van der Hoeven 1995). In particular, fiscal and monetary austerity combined with currency devaluations resulted in higher inflation and the loss of jobs in non-tradeable sectors. Conversely, because of their effect on inflation and relative prices, the heterodox stabilization policies of the 1990s reduced income inequality.

A parallel trend can be detected with respect to the incidence of poverty. The proportion of people living in poverty changed in Chile from 38 per cent in 1987 to 28 per cent in 1992; in Argentina from 9 per cent in 1986 to 16 per cent in 1990 and back to 9 per cent in 1992; and in Mexico from 34 per cent in 1984 to 39 per cent in 1989 and to 36 per cent in 1992. The increase of poverty in Latin America during the 1980s was due to stagnant growth, increased income inequality, high inflation and a decline in real wages. In the first half of the 1990s, lower inflation and renewed economic growth combined to reduce poverty during the first half of the 1990s. Heterodox adjustment policies played an important role in bringing about this reversal in poverty trends.

3 Conclusions

The import-substitution paradigm of development has largely run its course in Latin America. Hope for renewed sustainable growth lies in economic liberalization and greater participation in the globalization process. Heterodox stabilization policies have spurred short-term economic growth and have provided elements of a macroeconomic foundation on which further growth can be built on a sustainable basis. Negative effets resulting from the introduction of liberalization policies – which in the short term have contributed to a loss of jobs and wages in import-competing and privatized enterprises – have been offset by the effects of heterodox stabilization policies in spurring growth and reducing income inequality and overall poverty. However, if Latin American countries are to benefit from the export opportunities that have been made possible by the globalization process, they will have to rely more than they presently do on budget-deficit containment, and less on exchange rate overvaluation, as a way of containing inflationary pressures and maintaining economic stability.

References

Agosin, M., R. French-Davis and A. Uthoff. 1995. Movimientos de capitales, estrategia exportadora y estabilidad macroeconómica en Chile. In R. French-Davis and S. Griffith-Jones (eds.): *Las nuevas corrientes financieras hacia America Latina – fuentes, efectos y políticas*. Lecturas CEPAL/El Trimestre Económico No. 81. Mexico: Fondo de Cultura Económica.

Barros, R., M. Foguel, R. Mendonça and L. Miranda Cruz. 1996. Os impactos da abertura comercial sobre o mercado de trabalho brasileiro. Mimeo. Rio de Janeiro: DIPES-IPEA.

Camargo, J. M. and C. A. Ramos. 1988. *A revolução indesejada*. Rio de Janeiro: Campus.

Cortázar, R. 1993. *Politica laboral en el Chile democratico: avances y desafios en los noventa*. Santiago: Ediciones Dolmen.

Cox Edwards, A. and S. Edwards. 1994. Labour market distortions and structural adjustment in developing countries. In S. Horton, R. Kanbur and D. Mazumbar (eds.): *Labour markets in an era of adjustment.* EDI Development Studies. Washington, D.C.: World Bank.

ECLAC. 1995. *Balance preliminar de la economia de América Latina y el Caribe 1995,* Santiago: United Nations.

Fanelli, J. M. and J. L. Machinera. 1995. El movimiento de capitales en la Argentina. In French-Davis, R. and S. Griffith-Jones (eds.): *Las nuevas corrientes financieras hacia America Latina – fuentes, efectos y políticas.* Lecturas CEPAL/El Trimestre Económico No. 81. Mexico: Fondo de Cultura Económica.

Hoeven, R. van der. 1995. Structural adjustment, poverty and macroeconomic policy. In Rodgers, G. and R. van der Hoeven (eds.): *The poverty agenda: trends and policy options.* Geneva: International Institute for Labour Studies.

Gurria Treviño, J. A. 1995. Corrientes de capital: el caso de Mexico. In R. French-Davis and S. Griffith-Jones (eds.): *Las nuevas corrientes financieras hacia America Latina – fuentes, efectos y políticas.* Lecturas CEPAL/El Trimestre Económico No. 81. Mexico: Fondo de Cultura Económica.

UNCTAD. 1995. *World Investment Report 1995: Transnational Corporations and Competitiveness.* New York and Geneva: United Nations.

Urani, A. 1993. Políticas de estabilização e eqüidade no Brasil: 1981-1983. *Pesquisa e Planejamento Econômico* 23(1). Rio de Janeiro.

_____. 1995. External adjustment, stabilization attempts and the lobber market in Brazil: 1981-1992. *FOCAL-CIS Discussion Papers* 95/2. Toronto.

Urani, A. and C. Winograd. 1994. Distributional effects of stabilization policies in a dual economy: the case of Brazil; 1981-1988. *Revista Brasileira de Economia* 48(1). Rio de Janeiro.

14

Mexico's financial crisis and its effects on income distribution and poverty

Eugenia Correa[*]

The financial crisis

Beginning in 1986, Mexico devalued its currency and its slashed import barriers. Liberalization accelerated under the presidency of Carlos Salinas when, in 1989, restrictions on interest rates and compulsory deposits were removed, and money market funds and other foreign investment capital were allowed into the country. A privatization programme was also initiated in 1989, which included the telecommunications and banking sectors. As a result of these reforms, the average tariff on consumer goods fell from 60 per cent in 1985 to less than 20 per cent by 1992; exports (not including maquiladora assembly plants) grew by 8 per cent between 1988 and 1994; portfolio inflows grew from US$ 351 million in 1989 to $28.9 billion by 1994; and inflation fell from 159 per cent in 1987 to 7 per cent in 1994.

On the other hand, even with the debt rescheduling and inflows of foreign money, Mexico during the Salinas years grew on average at only 3.1 per cent per year and real per capita income remained lower than in 1980. Moreover, imports rose by 19 per cent annually between 1988 and 1994, i.e. by 11 per cent more than exports. Because of the imbalance between imports and exports, the trade deficit increased to $56.5 billion between 1990 and 1994. This amount plus foreign debt interest payments created a current account deficit of $98.7 billion over the same period.

---

[*] Professor, Faculty of Economics, National Autonomous University of Mexico.

Portfolio investment inflows totalling $71.2 billion between 1990 and 1994 financed 72 per cent of this current account deficit, which reached nearly $30 billion, or 7.6 per cent of GDP, by 1994. Foreign investors in the equity market profited by 50 per cent annually between 1990 and 1993, while investors in government bonds earned in dollars 15 or more points over equivalent US bonds. Dependence on portfolio inflows to finance the current account deficit resulted in high financial costs in local currency relative to productivity and output. Because of the large current account deficit and the risk of portfolio flows drying up or flowing back out of the country, Mexico in 1994 was highly vulnerable to any shocks that might cause capital to seek safer havens. Officials, however, counted on growing foreign direct investment and increased exports associated with the opening up of the North American market as ways to ease the current-account problem.

Rather than being channelled into productive investment, much of the foreign money filled the gap created by a steep decline in domestic savings, which fell from 22 per cent of national income in 1988 to 16 per cent in 1994. With Mexico living beyond its means, stores were full of goods and consumer credit was offered on a generous scale. These factors led to over-indebtedness on the part of many households and banks, as well as enterprises and the government.

Mexico's vulnerability to shocks was put to the test in 1993. First, there was a peasant uprising in the impoverished state of Chiapas. This crisis was followed by the assassination of the presidential nominee, Luis Donaldo Colosio. During that year, moreover, United States interest rates rose, which attracted money out of emerging markets in general, and Mexico in particular. As a result, the country's foreign reserves dwindled in 1993 from $25 billion to $6 billion. In response to the events, the government issued $29 billion worth of dollar-indexed bonds called "tesobonos". However, despite the over-valuation of the peso, the government shunned a devaluation out of concern that such a move would rekindle inflation and damage Mexico's credibility as respects its commitment to a sound currency. Moreover, because 1994 was an election year, fiscal and monetary policies were eased instead of tightened.

When Mexico's liquidity crisis became evident to the world, the United States arranged a $50 billion rescue package and, in March 1995, the Zedillo government announced a credible economic plan. The need for a credible plan had become urgent as the exchange rate, which in December 1994 had amounted to 3.5 pesos to the dollar, fell to a low of 7.5 pesos by March 1995.

Likewise, the stock market lost nearly half of its value in those months. Because the NAFTA agreement precludes the adoption of import controls, the Zedillo government was compelled to impose tight fiscal and monetary policies. As a consequence, interest rates reached as much as 80 per cent, value-added taxes were raised from 10 to 15 per cent and public spending was reduced by 10 per cent. As a result of these changes, the economy shrank by over 5 per cent in 1995, which was the sharpest recession experienced by Mexico since the 1930s. In 1995, moreover, investment in gross fixed capital formation was 19 per cent lower in real terms than in 1990.

Mexico remains to this day highly vulnerable to possible future shocks. The interest due in 1996 on the public foreign debt of $117 billion is equivalent to 1.3 years of oil exports, or 2.3 per cent of estimated GDP for 1996, while interest payable on the total foreign debt of $170 billion represents 5.5 per cent of the estimated GDP for 1996. Furthermore, the banking sector is in crisis because of its foreign-exchange exposure and large number of non-performing loans which, on some estimates, amount to 10 per cent of GDP. The fiscal cost of bank-rescue operations in 1995 was equivalent to 7.2 per cent of GDP.

On the other hand, there are some grounds for comfort. The macroeconomic stabilization plan adopted by the Zedillo government has produced swift and positive results. The trade balance, not counting the maquiladora industry, is in balance and finances have been restored to health. The peso has steadied, the stock market has rallied, the tesobonos have been mostly redeemed, inflation has come back down, exports rose by 40 per cent in 1995 compared with 1994, and trade is back in the black. In particular, encouragement can be taken from the fact that exports now account for nearly 30 per cent of GDP. However, it should be cautioned that with most exports still relying heavily on imported inputs, export success will eventually depend not only on a realistic exchange rate and access to the North American market, but also on the ability of Mexican companies to compete on quality and service.

The social costs of the financial crisis

The aftermath of the financial crisis has particularly negatively affected the middle-class and poor of Mexico. Income inequality, already substantial with the wealthiest 10 per cent of Mexicans obtaining over 40 per cent of total income and the bottom four deciles getting a mere 13 per cent, has probably grown. The rich, with their savings invested in dollars, have hardly suffered at all. On the other hand, it is estimated that the poor have seen their share of national income decline by as much as 20 per cent. According to UNDP calculations, the incidence of poverty rose from 64 per cent in 1989 to 70 per cent in 1995. The daily consumption of Mexico's basic staple, maize, was 22 per cent lower in 1994 than 1989, with undernourishment affecting 30 per cent of children.

Open unemployment, which more than doubled in 1995 alone, currently stands at 6.3, as compared with 2.1 per cent in 1990. With 3 million unemployed workers in 1996, many of those who continue to be employed have had to contend with falling real wages. In this connection, real wages in manufacturing were 40 per cent lower in 1995 than in 1990. In the construction sector, employment in 1995 was 41 per cent lower and average wages 17 per cent below their levels in 1990. The only bright spot has been on the export side, where the number of jobs has grown as a result of increased foreign direct investment and exports production. The expanding maquiladora industry currently employs more than 600,000 people in Mexico. However, the multiplier of this sector is only about two in supplier industries and local services, rather than the four or five jobs for each direct export-oriented job that is typically the case for national exporting firms in developing and industrialized countries.

Growing unemployment and lower real wages have affected not only the poor but also the middle-classes. In addition, indebted middle-class households have been faced with ruinously high interest charges. They have thus been squeezed on both the income and expenditure sides.

Mexico is attempting to tackle head-on some of the hardships that have been affecting the poor as a result of the crisis. Emergency employment programmes and other temporary-jobs and retraining schemes are being designed along the lines of some of the successful programmes that exist in rural India (see Mr. Roy's paper in this volume). An innovative credit card system has been launched which targets and benefits only the absolute poor and directly links for them food subsidies with basic health care attention. Extra subsidies are also being contemplated to encourage poor parents to keep their children in school. Additional schooling makes sense not only as a social welfare measure but also as investment in human capital formation. For example, it is worth noting that only 55 per cent of young Mexicans enrol for secondary-school education, versus 90 per cent in the case of the Republic of Korea. The challenge, of course, lies in financing these programmes. Domestic resources under the macroeconomic stabilization plan are constrained whereas assistance from multilateral institutions such as the World Bank and the Inter-American Development Bank imply the assumption of additional external debt.

Lessons learned

The principal lesson to be learned from Mexico's experience is that the adoption of external financial liberalization policies and import liberalization policies should be carefully phased-in and sequenced. The temptation to finance persistently low domestic savings rates and large current-account deficits through highly volatile portfolio inflows should be resisted. Instead, any persistent growth in imports should be matched by equivalent sustained growth in exports. A realistic exchange rate, rather than the over-appreciation that may result from large-scale financial inflows, can help maintain the desired current account balance.

The other main lesson is that far-reaching liberalization policies are less likely to succeed if the macroeconomy is not soundly established (see also Mr. Heller's paper on this subject). The combination of financial and import liberalization, when undertaken in the context of loosened fiscal and monetary policies (as can happen in an election year), may lead to a boom-and-bust cycle. Such an outcome is likely to be aggravated when too much reliance is placed on speculative flows of capital to finance the boom, since such flows tend be pro-cyclical and hence flow back out of the country when conditions deteriorate and they are most needed. With respect to the impact of boom-and-bust cycles on poverty, the poor are more likely to participate in the underconsumption of the bust phase than the overconsumption of the boom phase. That is because the poor normally do not have access to the consumer credit and imported luxury goods consumption that the non-poor enjoy during the boom phase, but are equally or more affected by the loss of jobs, falling real wages, high inflation, increases in regressive consumption taxes, and reduced public expenditure that form part of macroeconomic stabilization measures adopted during the bust phase of the cycle. In such circumstances, it is likely that inequality and poverty will be greater after boom-and-bust cycles than they were before.

15

Globalization and liberalization in Sub-Saharan Africa: implications for growth and poverty

Paul Mosley*

Relations between the developed and developing countries can in principle produce either "backwash effects" (favouring the developed countries) or "spread effects" (favouring the developing countries). There is increasing evidence of "backwash effects" amongst the least developed countries (LDCs), which over the last 15 years have experienced a decline in real per capita income of 0.8 per cent per annum (World Bank 1994a). The majority of countries in this group, of course, are concentrated in Sub-Saharan Africa.

It is beyond the scope of this paper to give an explanation of why the backwash effects of interaction between developed and developing countries have become concentrated in the African continent. A range of explanations is available, focusing on human capital shortages (Dowrick and Gemmell 1992); a combination of external shocks and bad luck (Easterly et al. 1993); and faulty governance and policy (World Bank 1994). The present paper focuses on some of the policy-related aspects and implications of this backwash phenomenon.

1 Globalization, adjustment and policy

During the 1980s and early 1990s commercial capital flows to developing countries virtually dried up due to a fear of default and the desire of commercial lenders to limit their exposure to developing countries. Whereas

---

* Professor or Economics and Director, University Development Centre, University of Reading

this retreat proved to be only temporary in the case of Latin America and East and South East Asia, it has been long-term in the case of Sub-Saharan Africa. Thus, whereas private capital flows to developing countries in the aggregate totalled US$ 47.7 billion during 1985-90 and $108.0 billion during 1991-93, the flows to Sub-Saharan Africa during 1985-90 amounted to $1.0 billion, and during 1991-93 totalled only $0.3 billion. On the other hand, the ratio of aid to GNP, which elsewhere in the developing world was stagnating or declining, trebled between the late 1970s and the early 1990s and became very large in relation to the economies of the region (see Table 15.1). In fact, aid flows – and the associated imports of capital goods – have been far-and-away the principal channel through which foreign investment and technological change have entered the African economies.

Table 15.1: Aid/GNP ratios

	1969-76 average (%)	1993 (%)
Africa	3.1	11.5
South Asia	2.6	1.5
East Asia	0.8	0.8
Latin America & Caribbean	0.7	0.3

Source: World Bank (1995).

Sub-Saharan Africa's increased dependence on aid partly accounts for the continent's adoption of liberalization policies in the 1980s and 1990s. In fact, aid flows increasingly took the form of programme aid that was conditional on assorted policy measures being adopted that would reduce government intervention in particular sectors of the economy. The rationale underlying these desired policy changes was, in the short term, to increase the effectiveness of donor projects and, more ambitiously, the aim of moving the recipient economy supply curve outwards through the removal of politically-imposed inefficiencies.

In a majority of Sub-Saharan countries the formal linkage between aid and liberalization was mediated through policy-based loans offered by the World Bank and bilateral and multilateral agencies willing to co-finance adjustment operations. Although pressure to liberalize was universal for recipient countries, the form it took depended on the structure of the recipient economy, and varied as well according to the reforms which the World Bank and other donors believed to be politically achievable.

As is now well known, the response of African governments to the liberalization proposals of the international community was usually patchy and erratic. Enormous though the share of overseas aid in recipient country budgets had become, donors were in general not able to convert massive assistance into an effective voice over policy matters, with the consequence that many of the proposed reforms were not implemented and, among those implemented, some were subsequently reversed. The reasons for these events have been examined elsewhere in the literature (World Bank 1990a, 1992; Mosley, Harrigan and Toye 1995). The point to be emphasised is that, despite the appearance of donors having a dominant role, economic liberalization in Africa was – except in a handful of countries such as Uganda, Ghana and Togo – an incomplete, halting and often reversed process. Some movements towards a freer economy did in fact occur, particularly in the field of agricultural marketing and exchange rates; but, as shown in Table 15.2, these shifts were almost as far-reaching amongst countries which rejected a formal adjustment-lending relationship with the World Bank as amongst countries which accepted one, which suggests that much of the economic liberalization that took place in the 1980s was freely chosen rather than imposed by donors.

Table 15.2: Adjustment indicators for African countries as a group, 1980-92

	all African countries		Reform programmes	
			Strong [*]	None or weak
	1980	1992	1992	1992
Real effective exchange rate (index 1978 = 100)	104	81	72	82
Public sector deficit as share of GDP	10.2	8.2	6.3	8.0
Real interest rates	-7.9	0.2	8.6	-6.5
Agricultural export prices (index 1980-2 = 100)	96	125	146	108

Note: [*] A 'strong reform programme' is defined by the existence of a World Bank policy-based lending programme in that country. *Source:* World Bank (1994).

The effectiveness of liberalization policies has been a moot issue. In this connection, there exist various methods by which the effectiveness of these and other policy changes can be assessed. In principle, the simplest approach is to compare the performance of liberalizing countries with non-liberalising countries. The problem with this counterfactual approach is that liberalization policies have been attempted virtually everywhere in Sub-Saharan Africa, though with varying degrees of commitment and success. As a consequence, in instances where the "with and without" approach have been attempted (World Bank 1990a, Table 2.6; World Bank 1992, Table A1), the results have generally been inconclusive, apart from the almost tautological conclusion that liberalization tends to open the economy up and improve the balance of payments (for further comments on the counterfactual approach, see Mr. Woodward's paper in this volume).

Other possible methodologies include regression analysis and simulation exercises for individual countries. Both of these approaches have the advantage of providing an estimate of the effectiveness of individual policies, rather than providing a generalized judgement concerning whether adjustment "worked" or "did not work". However, even these approaches may produce opposite conclusions. For instance, regression results from a study undertaken by the World Bank support the publication's conclusion that:

"Better macroeconomic policies have already turned growth around in Africa. Avoiding overvalued exchange rates and keeping inflation and budget deficits low might sound like a boring recipe, but it works. It has worked in East Asia and it will work in Africa." [World Bank 1994: 184]

Other regression findings (Mosley, Sabasat and Weeks 1995) produce a less optimistic interpretation: certain components of liberalization policies, notably devaluation of the real exchange rate and liberalization of agricultural prices, are seen as having positive effects on growth; however, other components, notably tariff liberalization and the removal of agricultural input subsidies, are considered to have negative effects.

It can be argued, therefore, that economic growth in Sub-Saharan Africa may have been little affected regardless of whether countries resisted or surrendered to the orthodox liberalization pressures of aid donors. More fundamentally, liberalization policies have not helped the countries of the region come to grip with the adverse initial conditions which differentiate Sub-Saharan Africa from other developing regions, in particular East Asia and

Latin America: inadequate and run-down infrastructure, lower levels of education and training, and a more adverse external trading environment. An augmentation of aid and domestic public investment levels is necessary at least with respect to infrastructure and educational needs.

Investments in infrastructure and education in Sub-Saharan Africa have been hampered not so much by inadequate aid transfers as by the general ineffectiveness of those flows. The problem of aid ineffectiveness is especially acute in Sub-Saharan Africa. Circumstances have varied, however, for different modalities of aid; technical assistance, in the agricultural sector in particular, has had positive results, whereas non-emergency food aid has had a very low pay-off (Mosley and Hudson 1995: Table 3b). However, there are some signs, as yet still fragile, of a marginal improvement in aid effectiveness in Sub-Saharan Africa as a result of policy dialogue and the reduced scope for fungibility.

2 The macroeconomy and poverty

As Sub-Saharan Africa's growth performance has faltered in relation to that of other parts of the developing world, so has its share of global poverty risen. Sub-Saharan Africa currently accounts for some 300 million of the world's approximately 1 billion persons below the poverty line, which is an increase of 70 million on the early 1980s (World Bank 1990). Without doubt this increase is largely due to the region's poor growth performance in relation to other regions of the world, and in particular the poor performance of the agricultural sector which provides a livelihood, directly or in directly, for some two-thirds of the African population.

When sustained growth is restored to Africa, the best chance of maximising the poverty-reducing impact of such growth will most likely be through the choice of labour-intensive technologies, since labour is the main asset which the poor have to sell. For many years, unfortunately, the ability of any growth to reduce poverty has been held back by policies which tend to cheapen physical capital in terms of labour, and hence to minimize the employment-creating potential of economic growth. Among these policies have been (a) tariff policies biased in favour of imported capital goods and against other kinds of input; (b) tax holidays and import duty exceptions on imported equipment granted to transnational corporations; (c) the continuing harassment, by regulation and sometimes by physical force, of informal-sector production; and (d) the policies of the aid donors themselves who provide capital equipment, often to their own bilateral advantage, at zero or concessional cost, and who in general do not pay for local costs, in particular unskilled labour. The bias imparted by these forms of globalization have been almost directly antithetical to the goal of poverty reduction.

One aspect of this bias deserves particular attention. This is the influence of policies on technical modernization in agriculture, particularly food-crop agriculture. As is well known, the green revolution has spread less far in Sub-Saharan Africa than elsewhere in the developing world, with yields per acre of grain crops in Africa during the early 1990s less than half the level that prevails in Asia. Hence one of the most powerful instrument for poverty-reduction known in the developing world has scarcely made any headway in Sub-Saharan Africa, except in parts of South Africa, Zimbabwe, Northern Nigeria and Western Kenya. Certain causes of this neglect are domestic, in particular low population densities and inadequate infrastructure and research systems, but an important contributing factor to agricultural underdevelopment has been the role of donors in indiscriminately promoting market liberalization policies, as in the reduction of subsidies on fertilisers and other agricultural inputs, and in inadequately supporting agricultural research and extension systems.

3 Conclusions

Sub-Saharan Africa represents the most stark and important example of the phenomenon of limited convergence: the tendency of poorer developing countries to experience deteriorating relative income levels, in spite of having access, in principle, to higher rates of return on capital and improved possibilities for technological catch-up. The policies followed by aid donors and by the governments of the countries concerned partly account for this dismal record. For one thing, there is empirical and theoretical evidence which argues against continuing with certain forms of liberalization in the Sub-Saharan African context, in particular with regard to tariff reduction and the removal of agricultural subsidies. Long-standing policies that discriminate against cheapening capital as a ratio of the cost of labour also need to be revised and replaced with policies that recognize one of the main comparative advantages of Sub-Saharan Africa: its low-cost labour.

To date, aid donors have been the main agents of globalization in Sub-Saharan Africa. Unfortunately, increased aid flows to the region have failed to improve economic performance in the aggregate in spite of very elaborate attempts by donors to enhance the outcomes of their assistance. Important lessons to be drawn from donors' experiences are that (a) aid needs to be given after, not before, policy reform is adopted; (b) aid should compensate the losers from policy reform, in order to prevent them from blocking it; (c) policy conditions attached to aid need to be empirically credible, in the sense of demonstrably leading to an improvement in performance; and (d) policy conditions tied to aid should be persisted with only if their implementation produces the desired results (Mosley and Hudson 1995).

References

Dowrick, S. and N. Gemmell. 1992. Industrialisation, catching up and economic growth: a comparative study across the world's capitalist economies. *Economic Journal* 101:263-75.

Easterly, W., M. Kremer, L. Pritchett and L. H. Summers. 1993. Good policy or good luck? Country growth performance and temporary shocks. *Journal of Monetary Economics* 32:459-483.

Mosley, P., J. Harrigan and J. Toye. 1995. *Aid and power: the World Bank and policy-based lending*. London: Routledge.

Mosley, P., T. Sabasat and J. Weeks. 1995. Assessing Adjustment in Africa. *World Development* 23(9): 1459-73.

Mosley, P. and J. Hudson. 1995. Aid, conditionality and moral hazard. *University of Reading Discussion Papers in Development Economics 26.*

World Bank. 1990. *World Development Report 1990*. Washington D.C.

_____. 1990a. *Report on Adjustment Lending II.* Washington D.C.: World Bank Country Economics Department.

_____. 1992. *Report on Adjustment Lending II.* Washington, D.C.: World Bank Country Economics Department.

————. 1993. *The east Asian miracle.* New York and Oxford: Oxford University Press.

————. 1994. *Adjustment in Africa: Reforms, results and the road ahead.* New York and Oxford: Oxford University Press.

————. 1994a. *World Development Report 1994.* Washington D.C.

————. 1995. *World Development Report 1995.* Washington D.C.

16

Is the Asian NIEs approach relevant for Sub-Saharan Africa?

Fantu Cheru*

To what extent can Sub-Saharan Africa learn and benefit from the experience of the Asian newly industrialized economies (NIEs)? The countries concerned in both regions have relatively outward-oriented economies. Moreover, they started at similar income per head levels in the 1950s. Apart from their income disparities, a main difference between the two groups is that the Asian first-tier NIEs are endowed primarily with human capital, and the Sub-Saharan countries with natural resources. This raises the question of whether African countries possessing a rich endowment in natural resources should focus only on their primary sector or should they also consider diversifying into manufactures for export.

The dichotomy between countries endowed with natural resources versus human capital is, of course, only one factor that distinguishes the Asian NIEs from Sub-Saharan countries. In the cases particularly of the Republic of Korea and Taiwan Province of China rapid economic growth and poverty reduction were made possible by political stability, land reform, infrastructure upgrading, incentives to infant industries to help them carve out a competitive niche in world markets, and the aid and easy access to initially markets provided by the United States (see Mr. Rasiah's paper in this volume). In Sub-Saharan Africa, on the other hand, the countries of the region have suffered not only from misguided national policies and mismanagement, but also in recent years from depressed commodity prices, declining official development assistance, and unsustainable levels of debt.

---

* Professor, Department of Development Studies, The American University, Washington D.C.

With the support of the IMF and the World Bank, stabilization and adjustment policies have been pursued throughout Sub-Saharan Africa. Supply-side measures have emphasized greater reliance on market forces. However, there has been no substantial, sustained economic turnabout in the region. Instead, living standards for the majority of Africans have declined in relation to the 1970s, the same as investment in the productive and social sectors of the economy. Non-economic problems such as civil strife have added to the litany of economic ills from which the region is suffering.

Sub-Saharan Africa has made efforts to incorporate itself into the globalization and liberalization process. Besides the implementation of structural adjustment programmes, the region has moved away from economic nationalism policies, such as indigenization decrees and requirements for incorporation of foreign capital, and toward policies that welcome the inflow of foreign capital. However, experience to date suggests that there are limits to the effectiveness of trade liberalization and export promotion policies under conditions of static comparative advantage. Unlike the Asian NIEs, where countries have been able to move up the trade hierarchy and export more sophisticated products, in Sub-Saharan Africa initial conditions have been lacking for diversifying out of commodity exports. As is well known, commodity prices have experienced a secular decline since the start of the 1980s as a result, among other things, of increased competition among African, Asian and Latin American producers for global market share in commodities for which demand elasticity is low. This trend pattern suggests that such primary exports can only be one ingredient of a balanced national strategy to attain economic growth and poverty reduction over the long term.

For Sub-Saharan economies that cannot be pulled along by export-led growth, concentration should also be placed on domestic development concerns. The sector to begin with is farming. Agriculture provides the main economic livelihood for most rural households, is a major earner of foreign exchange, and is becoming increasingly indispensable as the main supplier of food for rapidly growing urban populations. Paradoxically, under structural adjustment and liberalization policies, the material needs of the sector have been neglected even as relative price reforms and market incentives have been encouraged. The reduction of subsidies on fertilizers and other agricultural inputs, and the cutting back of agricultural research and extension systems have had a disastrous impact on smallholders' capacity to produce for domestic and foreign markets (see also Mr. Mosley's paper in this volume).

Raising the productivity of farmers also requires investment in upgrading the infrastructure in rural areas – from irrigation and roads to credit and marketing channels. Programmes to increase food security and preserve the natural resource base must begin with rural women, since they are responsible for most of the food production, processing and domestic marketing in Sub-Saharan Africa.

As for exports, rather than seeking to emulate the experience of the first-tier NIEs, Sub-Saharan countries would be better advised to pay close attention to the experiences of second-tier NIEs such as Indonesia, Malaysia and Thailand that have concentrated their export efforts on both their primary and manufacturing sectors. As a first order of priority, more support should be given to traditional agricultural exports – as indicated above – in order to increase Sub-Saharan Africa's ability to compete with Latin American and South East Asian producers. In addition, diversification into the processing of primary products would add value to Sub-Saharan Africa's traditional exports. There is also scope in some of the countries concerned to diversify into non-traditional agro-exports, in partnership with the foreign capital, know-how and export-marketing connections of transnational corporations. Beyond that, each country should examine its potential comparative advantage to see if there could be scope to compete with second-tier Asian NIEs and other exporting countries with respect to the production of simple, labour-intensive manufactures for export.

Annexes

Annex 1

Background paper for the seminar[*]

1 Introduction

International economic relations and their effects on growth and poverty in developing countries have long been at the centre of the development debate. Traditional issues such as the theory of comparative advantage in trade, capital and technology transfer through official development assistance (ODA), and the roles of trickle-down growth and targeted services in reducing poverty have been expanded in recent years to include the accelerating and intensifying effects of globalization and liberalization on development. These twin forces have provided an impetus to market forces and further economic opening on the part of a growing number of developing countries that are attempting to take advantage of the opportunities presented by globalization and liberalization, minimize the associated risks and compensate for market failure and asymmetries that, among other things, could widen the gap between the rich and poor. The focus of the seminar will be on these relatively new dimensions of international economic relations and their new implications for poverty in the developing countries.

An attempt is made below to map the main globalization and liberalization issues that could be discussed at the seminar. However, the present note should be viewed as a starting point to stimulate thinking and discussion on the issues, not as a rough draft statement of the conclusions and recommendations expected of the meeting. Moreover, the format of this note does not denote how the seminar discussions will be undertaken; e.g., the issues will also be decomposed by regional groups of countries and countries at different stages of development. The issues will be discussed in an exploratory,

---

[*] By Mr. Anthony Woodfield, UNCTAD secretariat. March 1996.

"brainstorming" manner in order to gain a better understanding of the effects on poverty and possible policies to consider. As there could be a pluralism of views among the seminar participants, the conclusions of the seminar could reflect and individually incorporate diverging perceptions. In the present note, a balance is sought between the aspects of globalization and liberalization that inspire optimism and those that create pessimism as to their likely effects on poverty. The note concludes with a number of policy considerations.

2 Globalization and liberalization defined

Globalization can be described in terms of the growing economic interdependence and cross-border linkages that increasingly connect countries worldwide. Rapid advances in transport, communication and information technologies have facilitated this globalization process. Shifts in economic thinking, policy and the behaviour of economic agents have also contributed to increased opening and globalization. Both trade liberalization and the role of transnational corporations and financial institutions in augmenting the pace of capital mobility have provided a further impetus to the globalization process. By removing administrative barriers to the international movement of goods and capital, domestic and international liberalization policies alike have been essential to globalization.

3 Trade and poverty

The international division of labour has changed in that each nation or region now depends more and more on others for its supplies of goods and for markets for its products. Lower barriers, both natural (transport and communications costs) and artificial (tariffs, quotas and other policy obstacles), have facilitated manufactured exports from developing countries and the inflow of such inputs as components, machinery, finance and information, thus making possible the fuller participation of a growing number of developing countries in the international division of labour. As concerns import liberalization, its value to poverty reduction depends on the mix between consumption and investment imports, with the latter offering the long-term prospect of reducing poverty through a shift of resources to more efficient uses which boost productivity, and hence general living standards. In the short and medium term, however, conjunctural poverty may grow as a result of labourers being laid off who work in import-competing domestic industries. Furthermore, developing countries that have drastically reduced their import tariffs and quantitative restrictions have risked experiencing surges of imports that can produce unsustainable trade deficits resulting in devaluations and tight macroeconomic policies. In addition, reducing import tariffs represents a loss of government revenue, in many cases at a time when public finances are weak. Finally, for some countries, Uruguay Round-induced price rises on proprietary drugs and temperate agricultural imports could have negative implications for certain consumer groups (although higher food prices could induce domestic producers eventually to meet more of their country's domestic food needs).

Because developing country exports are more labour-intensive than their imports, any increases in poverty due to import liberalization could eventually be more than offset by the creation of new earning opportunities and export-oriented jobs employing poor, unskilled workers. Balanced trade can therefore be considered on net beneficial to poverty reduction. In this connection, it is estimated that there could be a one-off net reduction of absolute poverty of 1.4 per cent as a consequence of the implementation of the Uruguay Round agreements. However, it is mainly a handful of relatively industrialized Asian countries that are likely to gain significantly from improved access to developed country markets. In fact, for many low-income countries, the new trade system could result in rent losses due to the erosion of trade preferences. Moreover, it should also be cautioned that low demand elasticiticity could eventually leave developing countries specializing in low-skill manufacturing production vulnerable to declining terms of trade, as has happened with commodity-producing countries. Indeed, compared with the industrialized countries, goods in which developing countries have a comparative advantage are more susceptible to the fallacy of composition problem because the categories of goods concerned are fewer and less differentiated, and a number of them involve competition between a large number of countries.

4 Foreign direct investment and poverty

Intra-firm foreign direct investment (FDI) accounts for a growing share of trade. Moreover, FDI has helped finance productive investment, create instant export markets, transfer business know-how and technology, provide foreign exchange for purchasing crucial capital goods imports, and enable recipient countries to capture economies of scale that are otherwise not possible in most closed markets. Spurred in part by a positive shift in the attitudes of developing countries toward FDI, flows to developing countries surged from $31 billion in 1990 to $80 billion in 1993. The unskilled, low-paid employment opportunities created by FDI have especially benefitted poor women who, in the case of export processing zones (EPZs) in particular, have typically constituted more than three-quarters of EPZ labour. Around 80 per cent of FDI, however, has gone to only ten developing countries. Moreover, because of "rules of origin" provisions, the backward linkages and multiplier effects have generally been limited, especially in the cases of EPZs. Furthermore, while creating some 12 million jobs in developing countries, which amount to 2 per cent of their total labour force, it should be noted that many of the newly-created jobs may have displaced workers in competing domestic industries. Likewise, much of the FDI flows to Latin America have been associated with privatization efforts which have cut rather than increased employment.

5 Finance and poverty

With the lowering of many barriers to financial transactions, the globalization of financial markets has proceeded at a rapid pace in developing as well as developed countries. Coming on the heels of the debt crisis, developing country governments have tended to view portfolio investment as a way of attracting non-debt-creating financial capital that can help ease the foreign exchange constraint and mitigate the severity of stabilization and adjustment policies. Such finance, however, has tended to flow to only a small number of middle-income countries. Moreover, to compensate investors for relatively high levels of risk, portfolio investment can be quite expensive. Furthermore, the volatility and pro-cyclical nature of international capital flows have increased the likelihood of extreme demand compression policies being applied in the event of external and/or domestic negative shocks. Even on their own, such flows can engender a boom-and-bust cycle of unsustainability in which first the exchange rate appreciates, luxury-import consumption grows and the trade account gets out of hand, followed by absorption-cutting and renewed inflation. Because the poor are likely to participate more in the underconsumption of the bust phase than the overconsumption of the boom period, the net intertemporal effect on poverty can be negative. Bust-period factors that hurt the poor include the loss of jobs, reduced purchasing power of wages, higher inflation and a fall in the tax revenues necessary to sustain public expenditure. Macroeconomic instability resulting from the volatility of global financial flows may also have the effect of discouraging productive investment that is ultimately necessary to reduce poverty over the long term. Finally, financial opening can become a source of increased external private debt, since it facilitates direct access to sources of external financing in foreign exchange.

6 Overall poverty effects

For a variety of reasons, the overall impact of globalization and liberalization on poverty is likely to be ambiguous, particularly during the short and medium term, and to vary considerably between subgroups of countries. First of all, since globalization means not only integration but also competition among countries, a pattern of increasingly uneven development could result in which developing countries that are already well-integrated into the global economy stand to gain more than countries that lack the ability to compete. Second, while the hope is that globalization and liberalization will produce economic growth that will reduce poverty, if the growth thereby generated is slow and income inequality at the same time grows, the net result could be an increase in poverty. In this respect, it appears that income disparities have widened between unskilled workers, whose role in the competition for FDI and increased export-market share is to provide the cheapest labour possible, and owners of capital who have profited most from globalization and liberalization. Third (and more positively), to the extent that countries' efforts to participate in globalization and liberalization commit them to achieving and maintaining macroeconomic fundamentals, the resulting reduction in inflation will be beneficial to poor and non-poor alike. Fourth, within developing countries certain categories of the poor could be positively affected and others not. For instance, workers in tradeable sectors could benefit as export-oriented jobs multiply, while workers in import-competing domestic industries and privatized enterprises might lose out as a result of import liberalization and FDI competition for local market share. In view of the greater choice of consumer goods made possible by imports liberalization, another distributional effect could be an income shift in favour of rural households, in which rural consumers would benefit more than urban households who as a group would be made worse off as a result of the loss of industrial sector protection and, in many cases, exchange rate overvaluation. Fifth, while fears have been expressed that moves by agricultural smallholders from staple food to export production could impact negatively on nutrition, available evidence suggests that food production per capita normally does not decline and, in fact, may rise for the poorest of households because of the income effects of an increased hiring of rural labour. Sixth, to the extent that substantial currency devaluations prove initially necessary in order to (a) avoid declines in foreign exchange reserves in the face of imports liberalization, (b) attract or retain footloose FDI in search of cheap labour and (c) maintain or increase export share and competitiveness in global markets, purchasing power would be reduced and inflation (a form of tax on storeless poor) could grow on a one-off basis. When combined with domestic and global financial liberalization, currency devaluations could also lead to higher interest rates – as part of efforts to dissuade domestic and private foreign capital outflows – that would be passed on to the poor in the form of higher curb borrowing costs and higher unemployment. Seventh, tariff reductions and a loss to governments of policy autonomy as a consequence of global financial liberalization could lead to cutbacks in public expenditure, including for programmes that alleviate poverty.

While conjunctural poverty could increase or show little departure from trend during the short and medium term, overall poverty may eventually decline in countries that successfully orient their economies and grow at a considerably more rapid pace as a result. The long term thus provides hope of reducing poverty through the fruits of increased trade, efficiency, incentives and productivity. The mix of factors that would reduce poverty could range from direct objective factors, such as the creation of additional jobs, to indirect, spillover effects such as the demonstration impact of EPZs that mainly employ women in strengthening the incentive for poor families to send their daughters, in addition to their sons, to school. For poverty reduction to occur, however, incentives are not likely to be sufficient to overcome long-standing structural weaknesses and market failure; the public sector and international community will also have a critical role to play.

7 Policy considerations

Barring the autarkic option of de-linking from the world economy, the forces of globalization and liberalization suggest the need for developing countries to adopt suitable policies that, rather than being reactive or defensive, reflect a decision to adapt to the influences of the globalization process in ways that reinforce overall national development goals and aspirations. The pace and extent of adjustment to the new international economic environment, however, could vary from country to country. In countries with macro-economic imbalances, for instance, domestic liberalization policies may either have to be deferred or sequenced and phased gradually, as discussed further on below. Many least developed countries (LDCs) in particular may not be in a condition to dismantle protective measures rapidly if they are in the infant stage of industrialization, and if they are to avoid placing too much of a burden on the exchange rate as an instrument to dampen demand for consumer good imports in the face of a severe foreign exchange constraint. It should be noted in this connection that a number of Asian countries structurally transformed themselves and became highly competitive in global markets as a result of growth strategies that did not initially stress liberaliz-ation policies. Whatever the nature and timing of the measures adopted, an essential policy concern should be that better economic performance resulting from globalization and liberalization ought not be at the expense of poor and vulnerable members of society.

Governments can assist the poor by facilitating their participation in the benefits of globalization, in particular low-skill production for export, and – to the extent that economic liberalization strategies are adopted – by mitigating the hardships to those poor who are likely to be negatively affected by liberalization in the short and medium term. Effective targeting of constrained resources to alleviate and reduce poverty through the provision of basic-need services must thus remain high on the development agenda. In particular, long-term human development opportunities in education and skills-acquisition should be provided. A caveat, however, is that relative skills accumulation is not easily or quickly achieved, not least because of the increasing returns (the more skills one has, the easier it is to acquire new ones) and externalities (the more skilled the people around one, the more one learns) that make the catch-up process for lagging countries and social groups so difficult.

To the extent that liberalization policies are adopted or reinforced, they should add up to a coherent development strategy for the country concerned. For instance, a prudent approach to the sequencing and phasing of liberalization policies is important when macroeconomic imbalances exist in fiscal, inflation and balance-of-payments positions. The liberalization of imports, for instance, ought to go together with, rather than before, improved access for and production of goods for export. Likewise, financial liberalization that precedes the successful implementation of monetary policies risks producing knock-on effects that could intensify the social hardships of macroeconomic stabilization programmes.

It should be noted that capital inflows resulting from financial liberalization may represent an additional source of vulneralibity, especially in the cases of countries that are already burdened by heavy debt service obligations from the debt crisis of the 1980s. Such flows also risk contributing to an overvaluation and high interest rate trap. The establishment of efficient supervisory mechanisms may be necessary to help reduce to prudent levels the volatility of capital flows and minimize the risk of boom-and-bust economic cycles that may augment poverty. More fundamentally, efforts should be redoubled by many countries to increase their savings rate in order to reduce their dependence on outside capital. Privatizing the pension fund contributions of middle- and upper-income households could provide a step in this direction in some countries.

While beggar-thy-neighbour devaluations should be avoided, the maintenance of realistic exchange rates is important for eliminating the biases that can occur against exporters when currencies are overvalued. Steps taken to phase out implicit and explicit taxes on exports are important for the same reasons (although it should be pointed out that reduced revenue from these relatively easily collected border taxes may have significant implications on the fiscal side).

Given the reduced revenue from export taxes and lower tariffs, together with the increased difficulty (on account of evasive tactics that domestic and global financial liberalization have facilitated) of direct tax collection from the rich, other approaches such as a strengthened system of cadaster-based property taxes may need to be considered if overreliance on regressive indirect taxes to fund government expenditure is to be avoided. Moreover, financial resources previously going to public enterprises that have been privatized could be reallocated to the funding of social programmes of benefit to the poor.

An important question is whether the adoption of conventional liberalization policies represents a coherent development strategy for least developed countries (LDCs) if they are not likely to benefit very much from the forces of globalization. A system based on competition implies that not all countries will benefit equally, and that those that are likely to fare less well consist primarily of LDCs where poverty is widespread and less tractable. Since around half of their population is below the (international) absolute poverty line, these countries must first and foremost achieve higher economic growth over the medium and long term if they are to reduce their incidence of poverty. Many of these countries, however, are locked in a vicious circle in which low commodity prices produce inadequate export earnings and external resource inflows, which in turn make export diversification strategies dependent on imported inputs more difficult to undertake. Their capacity for real capital formation is limited due to their low domestic saving capacity. FDI can help by enabling these countries to produce commodities on a more competitive basis, add value and diversify beyond their existing static comparative advantage. To attract or retain FDI, LDCs supported by ODA could consider giving priority to replacing rudimentary or dilapidated communication and transport networks by modern systems (although there is the risk that a considerable amount of public investment might be required to attract a relatively small amount of additional FDI), as well as improving the skills of their labour force. Economic and political stability will also be important in determining which LDCs prove successful in attracting foreign as well as encouraging domestic private investment.

There is also the important question of how the transfer of capital, in the form of technology, is absorbed and fed into overall changes in productivity and output, and the consequences thereof for employment in terms of skills composition and remuneration. It should be noted that a high degree of dependence on imported inputs, machinery and technology may lead to a consumption of foreign currency that exceeds the amounts gained or saved by the sector itself, and which thus must largely be met from primary exports if not from new debt creation or through FDI. In import-competing as well as exporting sectors, therefore, it makes sense to rely more on the comparative advantage of low-cost labour than on labour-displacing technologies intended for industrialized countries with high labour costs. On the other hand, to be competitive, developing countries should adopt certain technologies and, when possible, adapt them to their own conditions. In particular, technologies that increase information, skills and methods of work so as to improve output quality are essential for modernization and increased competitiveness. Greater utilization of subcontracting practices could help large firms satisfy many of their low-skill labour requirements at the same time that they concentrate on modernizing their equipment and upgrading the skills of their core staff.

Through the flexibility that they provide in absorbing fluctuations and shifts in demand, small-scale enterprises can augment the competitiveness of large firms by lowering their fixed costs. At the same time, small enterprises tend to be more low-skill and labour-intensive than large firms, and therefore more suitable to creating jobs that directly reduce poverty and, in many instances, augment the participation of women in productive activities. The small-scale sector also functions as a bridge to help integrate the informal sector with the formal sector, thus enhancing the poverty-reducing role and economic potential of the informal sector in the national economy. However, the development of this sector will in many instances need to be supported by active intervention on the part of the State in countries where competitive entrepreneurship is not deeply embedded. Governments can help strengthen the small-scale, tradeables-producing part of the economy through the provision of technical assistance and credits (through efficient financial intermediaries backed by suitable guarantee schemes) aimed at promoting and expanding the supplier role of small enterprises to large firms. Contracting firms also have an interest and responsibility to train small entrepreneurs to meet quality specifications and delivery schedules. Donor governments and NGOs can also play an important role, as in helping provide direct access to global markets for clusters of small-scale enterprises.

Like employment and public expenditure, nutrition (and its relation to human capital) is an intermediate variable that links globalization and poverty. Reduced surplus food aid stocks and higher and less stable international prices for food (as a result of agricultural reforms in the developed countries) could have significant poverty repercussions for food-insecure LDCs, given the high share of income spent on food by food-deficit households. On the producer side, supply response could be relatively limited, even in the long term, unless complementary public investment is made in roads, irrigation, research and extension. Official development assistance (ODA) will be essential for such undertakings in countries where public investment in agriculture has fallen over the years as a result of fiscal retrenchment. In order to bring benefits to the maximum number of the poor, the policies of donors and governments with respect to research, extension and the provision of public investment should pay special attention to small farmers. Specific conservation measures could be required in cases where agricultural production becomes so intensive that the natural resource base risks being degraded. As for food-deficit poor households, well-targeted consumer food subsidy programmes could prove useful as transitory and emergency safety-nets until domestic supply responses manifest themselves.

ODA is as essential as ever to developing countries, in particular the LDCs. In this context, it is important to reiterate that relatively few developing countries receive significant amounts of private capital inflows, and that such flows are profit-oriented and pro-cyclical in nature, thus of limited help in reducing poverty, particularly in times of economic crisis. Besides playing a part in ODA, multilateral institutions also have an important role to perform in safeguarding the internationally agreed-upon rights and interests of developing countries in international trade, investment and finance. Consensus on norms and measures that strike a balance between the respective roles of multilateral cooperation, the free market and the State are necessary in managing not only local economies but also international economic relations.

Annex 2

List of participants

Agency participants

Mr. Yogesh Atal
Director, Sector of Social and Human Sciences, United Nations Educational, Scientific and Cultural Organization (UNESCO), Paris

Ms. Nadia Auriat
United Nations Educational, Scientific and Cultural Organization (UNESCO), Paris

Mr. Sjaak Bavelaar
United Nations Population Fund (UNFPA), European Liaison Office, Geneva

Mr. Guido Carrin
Division of Intensified Cooperation with Countries, World Health Organization (WHO), Geneva

Mr. Hubert Dixon
Chief, Health Situation Analysis and Projection, Division of Health Situation and Trend Assessment, World Health Organization (WHO), Geneva

Mr. Hans D'Orville
Director, Technology Task Force, Bureau for Policy and Programme Support, United Nations Development Programme (UNDP), New York

Mr. Zdenek Drabek
Counsellor, Economic Research and Analysis Division, World Trade Organization (WTO), Geneva

Mr. Neville Edirisinghe	Policy Affairs Service, World Food Programme (WFP), Rome
Mr. Lulio Fersurelli	United Nations Population Fund (UNFPA), European Liaison Office, Geneva
Mr. Dharam Ghai	Director, United Nations Research Institute for Social Development (UNRISD), Geneva
Mr. Peter Heller	Senior Adviser, Fiscal Affairs Department, International Monetary Fund (IMF), Washington, D.C.
Mr. Rolph van der Hoeven	Head, Employment Planning and Policies, International Labour Office (ILO), Geneva
Mr. Ishrat Husain	Director, Poverty and Social Policy Department, World Bank, Washington D.C.
Ms. Antonella Ingrassia	Environment and Trade Unit, United Nations Environment Programme (UNEP), Geneva
Ms. Colette Kinnon	WHO Task Force on Health Economics, World Health Organization (WHO), Geneva
Mr. Peter Koenz	Representative, European Office, United Nations University (UNU), Paris
Mr. Ferdinand Z. Littaua	Division of Interagency Affairs, World Health Organization (WHO), Geneva
Mr. Lars P. Ludvigsen	European Office, United Nations Centre for Human Settlements (Habitat), Geneva
Mr. Alphonse MacDonald	Chief, European Liaison Office, United Nations Population Fund (UNFPA), Geneva

Ms. Padma Mallampally	Division for Transnational Corporations and Investment, UNCTAD, Geneva
Mr. Santosh Mehrotra	Office of Social Policy and Economic Analysis, United Nations Children's Fund (UNICEF), New York
Mr. Michael Sakbani	Officer-in-Charge, Division for Economic Cooperation among Developing Countries and Special Programmes, UNCTAD, Geneva
Mr. Rogerio Studart	Global Interdependence Division, UNCTAD, Geneva
Mr. Alan A. Tait	Director, Special Trade Representative, International Monetary Fund (IMF) Office in Geneva
Mr. Grant Taplin	Assistant Director, International Monetary Fund (IMF) Office in Geneva
Mr. Mohamed Toure	United Nations Industrial Development Organization (UNIDO), Geneva Liaison Office, Geneva
Mr. Anthony Woodfield	(Chairman) Chief, Poverty Alleviation Unit, Division for Economic Cooperation among Developing Countries and Special Programmes, UNCTAD, Geneva
Mr. Sergei Zelenev	Microeconomic and Social Analysis Division, Department for Economic and Social Information and Policy Analysis (DESIPA), United Nations, New York

Independent experts

Mr. Fantu Cheru

Department of Development Studies, The American University, Washington D.C.

Ms. Eugenia Correa

Faculty of Economics, National University of Mexico

Ms. Carol Graham

Brookings Institution, Washington D.C.

Mr. Paul Mosley

Department of Economics, University of Reading, Reading

Mr. Rajah Rasiah

Institute for Malaysian and International Studies, National University of Malaysia, Bangi Selangor

Mr. Sumit Roy

Department of Economics, City University, London

Mr. André Urani

Institute of Applied Economic Research and Federal University of Rio de Janeiro.

Mr. David Woodward

Independent consultant, London

Other participants

Ms. Anne-Marie Bonner

Senior Director/Advisor on Social Policy, Office of the Prime Minister of Jamaica, Kingston